Mannock, VC

Major Edward Mannock, VC, DSO, MC – the highest-scoring Allied fighter pilot of the 1914-18 conflict.

FORTUNES OF WAR

Mannock, VC

ACE WITH ONE EYE

BY FREDERICK OUGHTON
&
COMMANDER VERNON SMYTH

CERBERUS

First published by Frederik Muller Ltd in 1956

This edition published in 2004
PUBLISHED IN THE UNITED KINGDOM BY;
Cerberus Publishing Limited
Penn House
Leigh Woods
Bristol BS8 3PF, United Kingdom
Tel: ++44 (0) 117 974 7175
Fax: ++44 (0) 117 973 0890
e-mail: cerberusbooks@aol.com
www.cerberbus-publishing.com

British Library Cataloguing in Publication Data.
A catalogue record for this book is available from the British Library.

ISBN 1 84145 029 4

PRINTED AND BOUND IN MALTA.

Contents

This book is dedicated to those gallant men who formed the
Royal Flying Corps, and later the Royal Air Force, in the First World War,
and especially to those members of the three Squadrons in which
Major 'Mick' Mannock served:

No. 40 Squadron, No. 74 Squadron, No. 85 Squadron

'There shall be wings. If the accomplishment is not for me,
'tis for some other.'

LEONARDO DA VINCI

Acknowledgements

Research for this book continued over a period of four and a half years, necessitating correspondence and personal meetings with many of those who knew Major Mannock during his lifetime. For this reason, we believe that all the conversations are as close as it is possible to get to the original, while the impressions of Mannock's moods and general outlook are equally accurate. The following is a complete list of the large number of people who did, in fact, assist us in the creation of the book, and to them we now desire to extend not only our sincere thanks for their patience, tolerance and trouble, but also the hope that what they have done is to help create a lasting and worthy monument to the man himself:

R. Andrews; Colin J Ashford; C G Beeby; W Bovett; Norman Brear; Sybil Brown; Captain J E Buchanan; Air Commodore Keith L 'Grid' Caldwell, RNZA; L Chidlaw-Roberts; S Collier; Captain W E W Cushing; Herbert W Daw; Christine Day; D V Fuller; Frederick Gilbert; W B Giles; Captain D S Glover; A. G. Graves; Miss J Hammond; R G Henry; G R Hews, MC, TD; Colonel S B Horn; Henry Jaffe; J T Johnson; Ira 'Taffy' Jones, DSO, MC, DFC, MM; R S Knight; Major David K Morrison; Margaret Navin; Archibald G Ogden; W G Palmer; Thomas Pettit; Chief of Air Staff, Air Chief Marshal Sir Thomas Pike, GCB, CBE, DFC; George C Pilgrim; S J Powell; Lilian R Sippett; Robert M Smart; C H Stephens; Frank S Stone; Eric F Tomkins; Squadron Leader C Usher; Mrs. A M Vivian; Myles S Waller; James White; H T Wolff; W E Young; Ronald Adam.

We also wish to tender our special thanks to the following: George Newnes Ltd., for permission to reproduce quotations from Fighter Pilot, and Nicholson and Watson Ltd., for quotations from King of Air Fighters.

Dorothy Mannock, who went to incredible pains and trouble to supply not only information but also other relevant material and documents having a direct personal association with her late brother-in-law. Without her help it would have been practically impossible to complete a picture of Major Mannock's life prior to his enlistment.

Nora Mannock, who was kind enough to provide many of the personal touches which helped to bring the portrait to life for the authors and, it is hoped, the reader.

John G Sinclair, who spent a great deal of time in research. Mrs E W Woolford, a friend of Major Mannock, for the loan of his personal diary, formerly the property of Mr A E Eyles of Wellingborough and which was passed to Mrs Woolford on his death, this being his wish.

E Murray Witham, MA, of Wellingborough School, who supplied some of the information concerning Major Mannock's early life in Wellingborough with Mr and Mrs. Eyles.

The Air Historical Branch of the Air Ministry, where certain documents relating to operations and individuals between 1914 and 1918 were made available to us, and advice and assistance rendered by members of the staff.

Miss Joyce McKinnell, who injected the morale and the willpower at times when progress appeared to be slow and frustration grew frequent. Her cheerful and intelligent counsel during the writing of this book was of inestimable value.

Foreword

It seems possible that we are about to see an end to basic human courage, unless we choose to call fortitude and resilience by that name. In our estimation fortitude and resilience can endure setbacks and doubts. Courage, on the other hand, is the prime mover of calculated action and when it shows itself it shines brightly, like a new star.

When all is said and done, it takes very little courage to sit in a concrete blockhouse some thousands of miles away from a target city and press a button which will send a flight of computer-controlled missiles on their way. Contrast this with the fortitude and resilience which will be needed to watch your town dissolving in a gigantic heave of grey and black smoke.

If one man should set out in a primitive aircraft to try and destroy the blockhouse, then he has courage.

It is important to differentiate between the two.

If we accept that the struggles between nations must inevitably culminate in physical conflict, employing nuclear weapons, then it is obvious that the Army must take on a new role. It is exactly the same with the Navy. The most significant fact of all is that the air forces of the world have already been re-cast to carry nuclear weapons, not to fight as fighting was understood throughout two world wars.

During the last fifteen years little more than an indrawn breath in the long life of the earth the so-called science of war has changed. Man is now conditioned by new techniques and he tends to go out to fight in a white coat instead of a drab battledress. In this era it seems that there is little which can stand in any relationship to that of half a century ago, and a number of questions now demand an answer. For instance, do all those men who press the buttons to launch the missiles have in their own outlook or way of thinking any link with their fighting ancestors? Can the new militarist claim any true kinship with the men who fought at Crecy, those who sailed against the Armada or even the young men who took their 'crates' into the 1914 sky against the Germans? If the answer is yes, then we must define the quality of courage in order to understand our own history.

Courage shows many different faces. Cartoonists lampoon it, depicting it as a stiff upper lip which is too paralysed even to quiver. Writers in the genre of our time create the recurring figure of a Don Quixote in a lounge suit who makes an idiot of himself while trying to pursue entirely laudable ends.

There is another face of courage, the popular one which so many magazine writers coat with a sort of machine-turned sentiment to try and raise tears in our eyes. Sentiment is poured out for millions of readers, who mistakenly believe that stories about people who face terrible odds are about human courage. The majority are nothing of the kind, they are about commendable individuals who have done their best, that is all. Courage happens to be something else.

Yet another face of courage is the one which has been turned away now that the sixties have moved us with great speed towards what is often dubiously called a 'new phase of civilization'. It used to be exemplified in men like Lawrence of Arabia. Later assessments have interpreted their lives in a variety of different ways, but it now appears that they lived their span and attempted to blend belief and physical action, the one interacting on the other.

Lawrence of Arabia was symbolic of another, far more striking, generation of young men and among them was Edward Mannock, an Irishman who created a strong and remarkably enduring characteristic among those who now fly in the service of their country.

The debt to Edward Mannock has never been very amply repaid, primarily because there still exists a large amount of ignorance and erroneous supposition concerning his life and character. He cannot be classified as easily as the others. If you attempt to relate his brand of flying and behaviour with the careers of men like McCudden, Guynemer, Fonck, Lufberry, Ball, Bishop and Richthofen, you will probably fail. He was unlike any of them because he was unique. His background and qualities were completely different, both as a man and as an innovator of aerial combat. He sometimes set his own precedents, which brought censure down upon his head, but there is no doubt that he did impress many people and his name still lives on, more than forty years after his death.

Like Lawrence of Arabia, Mannock was in part a mystic. He was granted an often painful insight into himself and he expended a large part of his mentality in trying to help younger men. He was a searcher after new values. He was never consciously courageous, but his frequently painful quest for perfection, both as a young boy and later as a pilot, seared him until he was close to breaking point.

Up to the present time the story of Mannock's life has not been told in any great depth. We have been interested to discover bow he was motivated, or what made him 'tick'. In carrying out extensive research over a period of more than four years, and meeting many of the people who actually knew him, we have discovered innumerable new factors which have now come together to make what we consider to be the only honest and objective picture of a First World War pilot who appears to be entitled to greater recognition in the light of modern military aviation. In our eyes, at least, courage has taken on a new form and it is finally personified in Edward Mannock. That is the reason for this book.

Swansea and London, 1963.

CHAPTER ONE

The pay wasn't all that bad even if some of the men were forever complaining, but what they forgot about was the security. You had to take security into consideration and if you got your stripes you could be god a'mighty provided you kept your nose clean and your gun barrel polished. It was all a matter of how you weighed things up. The strange and happy thing was that when civvies knew you were in the Second Inniskilling Dragoons – *ah, the Irish*! they'd gasp – they always wanted to come up to you and stick out those pigeon chests of theirs and pick a free fight. The bloody nose was a badge to show you had defended the honour of the regiment. If your nose matched your tunic you were in, Murphy, you were in! Some civvies might turn up next day, shouting the odds, reckoning you had clonked them first and all that sort of stuff, but any sar'major worth two pennorth o' copper knew from the look in their eyes it wasn't true, not by the longest chalk a man could find.

What a peaceful world it was for a soldier boy – better than being a sailor or one of them explorers, for instance. Just look at those fellers on that Yankee naval boat – the *Jeanette* she was called – who had gone to the North Polar ice and had their ship crushed like an eggshell. It was better to be a soldier here in cosy old Ballincolig where you could have a good time with your pay.

The perfume of spring was everywhere and just up the road was Cork city with a pub on every corner and a few more in between. There was old Edmund Spenser's 'spreading Lee that like an island fayre encloseth Cork with his divided flood'. And there was all that fine stateliness created by the shops and the buildings, and everybody had to agree there was nothing to compare with Cork, that dear old city. It was better than Dublin, better than dirty old Belfast, but all the same how long would a soldier be left in peace to enjoy it when they were forever saying, 'Let's shift the Inniskillings' about every few months; 'Let's give those lads something to think about'. Did the authorities know what they were doing?

Corporal…

Sah?

Parade the platoon …
Sah!

A great clicking of polished heels, then off at a brisk march, watching out that the men were as smart as you were, doubling them' up, forming fours, bringing them to a sharp HALT!

Number the men, Corporal …
PER-LAT-TOON-numbah!

One… two… three… fourfivesixeveneight… nine… Smart as new paint, their arms down stiff by their seams; every man perhaps a general.

But then as a man got older and felt his weight he needed a woman about him, a good kindly woman. There were plenty for the picking in Cork city, young and widowed and most of them falling instantly in love with a scarlet tunic and a man who had his moustaches well waxed, sharp as needlepoints. Bevvies of country colleens came into Cork of a weekend to get away from their prisons of unmortared stone-walled farms, and the look in their eyes was not all for the shop windows, where they could see such pretty things as ribbons and trinkets, 'twas for a broad-chested soldier. Those farm-labouring little weasels, they could not get anywhere in the love stakes. It was the soldiers who flocked to Cork who were the special men, the laughing men, the joking men, the men who had a bit of life in them. And all with money and a gusty capacity for doing their courting outside the city on the rough road to Kinsale, sometimes as far afield as Kinsale Head where nobody watched them except the birds and the voles.

Life was not all love. There were bits in the paper to be read and studied. Not many of those Inniskilling lads bothered following the news and the Corporal would not have worried either except that reading seemed to be in his blood and it was this very thing that made him read anything he could get hold of. The Cork papers were nothing but solemn old blather sheets, full of farm news and fatstock prices, gossip about the filthy state of the Lee, the new taxes, the price of spuds. But now and then the London papers came in and – 'Ha, here's the paper my daddo edits-he runs it, he's a big man in that Fleet Street in London, and there's not a man who doesn't say he's not a good Irishman. And what a linguist! He's showing the English a thing or two…' The Mannocks never lacked a bit of culture.

Those girls over there on that corner, watching and waiting, taking a man's attention!

Give me a minute, will you, to read all the London news in my daddo's newspaper!

Corporal Mannock, NCO, Second Inniskilling Dragoons, known as Corporal Corringhame (he first enlisted under his mother's name, then later re-enlisted as Mannock) leans against a rough-faced wall and devours the columns of print, one after another. Corporal Mannock, surprisingly the son of a Fleet Street newspaper editor, is supposed to be a cut above the average dragoon NCO.

And the girls are still watching him, for he is made to be looked at and admired, fully a fine figure of a man.

There was Julia O'Sullivan, soon to be Mrs Mannock even if she did not know it when first she clapped eyes on the Corporal, and she could not know that she would have to be ready to follow her husband out of feelings of loyalty and out of the fact that she had chosen him. For all the restless and the maddening gleam which came into his eye when he told her how hard it would be for him to settle down because he was a professional soldier and a good one at that, she put up with him. At times he was like a noisy dog on a leash with the end held between her own thin fingers. In the heat of their courtship – and an Irish courtship is something to see! – neither knew what the other really felt, but it was not very long before the Corporal's wild flyings about in Cork city were halted by her with all her quiet but very powerful ways of persuading him to be quiet and behave himself. The strong man became the child.

Move here and move there! The orders came, dictated by somebody unseen way up there in the top layers of the Army. The Mannocks went together, he and she. He felt more complete now that he had his Julia around, looking after him, and there was always the married man's allowance on top of everything else. Married men received the favours. Officers thought you were more responsible if you got yourself hitched up.

Both were good Catholics, she more than he which is not unusual in the religion, and the children came along. The eldest was Jess, and she was followed by Patrick and, on May 24th, 1887, Edward, looking no different from any other baby, just a snub nose and a pair of blank blue eyes. Apart from Jess there were two other sisters. Edward was born at Preston Cavalry Barracks, Brighton, but the children grew up in India. The Inniskillings were ideal men for duty out there, the sort to withstand a long chore in the debilitating days of colonial duty.

Edward was quiet 'reserved' they called him because it seemed the only word for it – but those who knew about children said that he would grow out of it by the time he reached the hard discipline of the Army school where education was provided. He said very little, just sat pale-faced and still, listening and looking intelligent. One day followed the next.

'Why doesn't the laddo play with the others now?' His father, seam-faced but still very much the smart NCO, watched his son through the bungalow window. 'Anybody'd think he didn't belong.'

'And what would you mean by that?' Julia was used to these moods. There were times when she could not look at her husband for fear of hitting out at him because he was so damn ignorant! She knew everything about Edward's little ways better than she knew the Corporal. It was a dreadful thing to have a husband against whom the heart was beginning to harden, and it was made no better when she could not understand why she should start disliking her own husband. Whatever came, though, she was going to put up with him. That was marriage, for better or worse, but pray to God it was not going to be for worse.

'That boy now – is he what you'd call a normal boy or is he half a girl?' The Corporal was restless, looking first from one side of the window, then the other, as though an answer would come up and hit him in his big face. He flung out his arm. 'Just watch him now, just you watch, Julia Mannock, and you'll see!'

She craned forward to see Edward walking unnoticed away from the rowdiness of the playing children, his eyes fixed on a black bustard as it flapped about like a small devilish banner near the silky-brown trunk of the banyan tree, trying to entice a smaller bird towards it.

'I've seen him do that before. He's got quite the liking for these Indian birds.'

The Corporal sniffed. 'Birds!' What could a boy get of any useful value out of forever looking at birds?

'Is there anything wrong with that? He's a small boy. It's a kind of a whim of his. Ah, come on now, take no notice.' She knew that no amount of reproving would shift the Corporal, standing there in his braces as though he was lord of all creation. He might be on the drill square with fifty men lumbering about when he cracked his whip, but it was different in the home. That little mustard seed of not being able to understand his own son was starting to grow, anybody could see it.

All the aggravation over Edward's mute and steady refusal to stand and watch morning parades and play soldiers with the sons of the troopers flared up now. 'Birds! Books! And now he's taking up with animals, I hear.' His voice mounted to a roar. '*Animals!*'

Edward, very still in the shade of the great tree, watched the bustard wheeling clumsily in its death dance. He could hear the wing feathers clicking dryly together, it was so close; and it looked imperfect and dusty, a bird made of funereal rags. It dropped in a swoop towards the smaller bird and for one gulping moment it did look as though carnage would be over and done with in less than a second if the curved yellow beak reached its prey. But for Edward's warning shout it would have happened, but then the bustard wheeled, chickering angrily in his face while he stood his ground prepared to reach up and beat it off if it went for him. In the end it fled upwards into the bronze disc of the sun.

He sat down against the banyan bole, trying to remember exactly how the bustard had moved. It was the first time he had seen one so close to.

The Corporal washed incidents like this away with a wide sweep of disinterest while still trying to understand him, trying to talk to him. He was as clumsy as only an Irish father can be, half the time longing to be able to lift his hand and cuff the kid into sensibility. You could talk by the hour, you could rave in his face, but all he did was turn away, pale and disinterested. The Corporal had started early, as soon as Edward could understand what was being said to him. Nothing the father had to say meant anything to the child.

The Corporal's temper bubbled in its emotional cauldron. It was Julia who put the lid on and kept it clamped down. She would never have admitted it, but Edward was her favourite child, different from Patrick, the elder one. She told herself that Edward would need protecting.

In the evenings the boy sat close to the lamp, reading and writing out his notes on birds and beasts. Julia often leaned gently over his shoulder, wanting to understand what he was trying to do, but it really meant nothing to her. He had his own secret way of going about things. She had to pretend that the Corporal's ugly grunts of dissatisfaction over Edward's behaviour were just an ordinary clearing of the throat, but deep down she knew that the bitter truth was he did not care any longer about his youngest son. It galled her. She could never resign her spirit to accepting it.

Edward did not like to say so, but the lamp seemed so dim for this sort of work. It cast a sort of soft haze over the page and his pencil kept wandering. There ought to be a direct shaft of light here, but it was all yellow and indistinct. He moved quietly to one side, blinking, thinking he was tired, but he had to get his notes done before they packed him off to bed. There was never any chance to read between the blankets. Dad was a great one for coming round on what he shouted were his 'last inspections', and you had to be sharp and pretend to be asleep when he threw open the door. Rushing through a sentence, Edward tried turning himself right around, hoping the lamp would be better, but it wasn't, and he almost gave up. Why did it feel as though somebody had thrown a dark cloth over your face?

'What're you movin' about for, eh?' The Corporal's rough voice sliced meaningly through the domestic peace.

Julia looked up from her sewing, hoping he was not spoiling for one of his long stupid arguments.

Frightened and unable to conceal a mixture of fear and dislike of his father, Edward tried to explain that there must be something wrong with the lamp. Cursing at the interruption to his thoughts, the Corporal clumped across to examine it, looking at it first from one angle and then the other. So what was wrong with the damn thing? A good old flame, it was, burning clear as a bell. Look at the glass! He put his flattened hand underneath Edward's chin, forcing him to look straight into the flame. The boy winced and wriggled free, swallowing a growing anger.

'Don't be daft, boy!'

As soon as the Corporal had clattered out of the room, making a divil of a din about it, Julia slipped across to look into Edward's face. She knew his fears, she tried to dispel them with words, but it was no good, because Edward was always wanting to avoid trouble and rather than admit to anxiety he would say nothing. In the next few years she would have to try and be more strict with him and show him that he would do better if he stood up for himself. Nuances of thought passed across her features. It was hard to do as so many did and let the future look after itself when you had a creature like the Corporal for a husband. Sometimes she thought that a good knock on the head with one of his empty beer bottles might do more good than all the words in the world, but if she took to violence he would only retaliate and Edward would suffer in the end.

What was happening to this house? After the marriage – a gay affair that had been to be sure! – the Corporal got into the habit of wearing his slippers about the house as though he enjoyed married life. He hadn't been altogether his old self while they were at Preston, but those barracks were so depressing they would change any man, especially one who had to carry all the responsibilities of an NCO The officers were an uppity lot; Julia had no patience with them and all their fancy ways. They wanted, she thought, a good shaking up. But it was not the barracks, nor was it the officers; it was something else, a sort of uneasiness which crept over the Corporal like some sickness. He had tried to shake it off on the boat coming to India, then in the end had given in to the drink. She wanted to forget all the unpleasantness of those weeks as the weather grew hotter and he became more aggressive. If only there had been some good dry land about she was sure she would have gone to it and let that old boat carry him away, provided she could have the children with her. At times she felt just like a mother hen with her chicks. One look at Edward made her sure that she must find strength to go on living, Corporal or no Corporal!

'Take no notice of him now, love. He doesn't mean half of what he says. Now, you tell me what's wrong.' She slipped an arm about Edward's shoulders, drawing him against her breast, pouring out all the comfort he needed.

He tried to make her see the difference between left and right. If you sat to the left of the lamp, it went dim, it really did l He made her try it. She kept shaking her head. The Corporal need not have gone on so about it, but he had been right and there was nothing wrong with the lamp. Edward, the darling, must be tired. Off to bed with him!

The next night it became unbearable and for them all the atmosphere grew into a pustule of unspoken suspense. While Julia tried to get on with her work the, Corporal was hunched in his chair, glaring at his son, his great fists clenched in his lap, his eyes narrowed as though he was about to spring across the room and knock everything spinning in his violent temper. This was something he could not understand. Physical disability was almost a disgrace, especially in his own son.

Edward went on moving round and round the lamp, trying to find a new angle, sure that everything would suddenly come right. He kept on rubbing his left eye, screwing his bunched fist deep into the socket as though a big speck of dust had become lodged underneath the eyelid. He did not like to tell them, but it had been the same all day, alternately burning and watering. From where Julia was sitting, polishing forks and spoons, she could see the growing anger of a patch of red inflammation which was now beginning to spread down his cheek.

Mother and father went into the kitchen. The Corporal tried to bottle up a mixture of trepidation and anger.

'Well, so what are we going to do?' she asked quietly. The door was thin. They did not want Edward to hear too much.

He swallowed hard, trying to find the proper words. 'It's bad, isn't it, Julia?'

'Bad you say? It is that! I'll tell you now, you've got to arrange for him to see the Army doctor.'

'There's a civvy in the town, a good man,' he offered eagerly.

She spun round on him. 'Mannock, we're all in the Army, right? If we're along with you, we've got a right to use the Army welfare, haven't we?'

He had to acknowledge that she was right. When he made the suggestion about the civilian doctor he did it out of a feeling that no Army surgeon would want to be bothered with kids. All the women went to this civilian fellow.

She was waiting for his decision, leaning against the cupboard with a determined look on her face.

'I'll try and make arrangements,' he faltered.

'Try? You *will*. And quick, too. Tomorrow!'

'That'd be hard enough, Julia. There's an early parade.'

'Parade?' Her voice was shaking. 'What do I care for your rotten parades? What's a parade against Edward's eye? Tell me that, Mannock, Go on, you tell me!'

An Army surgeon examined the boy while he sat there, good as gold, his mother's pride. The medical man peered into his eye, touched the puffiness of the check, asked a few questions, and then went into conference with himself, humming and hawing under his breath. Edward answered all his questions timidly, afraid of saying the wrong thing, and it took some time before the surgeon could find the seat of the trouble or what seemed to be causing the pain. Straddle-legged, in his shirt sleeves, he made one more examination and then asked Julia to take Edward outside while he had a word with the Corporal, who was already very ill at ease in the presence of an officer who smelt strongly of ether. He had never reported sick in his life and did not know the surgeon except by sight. He was right out of his depth in such an atmosphere.

The surgeon started tapping the top of the wooden desk with a pencil. His eyes were on the white ceiling as he assembled words of explanation understandable to this man. He realized that the Corporal would probably take it without changing his expression, he was that type of fellow, but all the same one must not be too brutal. 'There's something wrong with that eye all right,' he admitted at last.

Conditioned by years of discipline, the Corporal stood perfectly straight, nodding his agreement. Why didn't the damn man speak out? He knew everything there was to know, yet here he was blathering like an old woman.

'It's a weakness. Had it since he was a baby, I expect.' The surgeon rose and rolled down his shirt sleeves, then wriggled into his uniform jacket, looking thoughtful. 'You say it's been going on these few nights, Corporal?'

'Sir.'

'Hm – well, it might be purely temporary, you know. Now, if we were in the old country we could shoot him round to see a specialist. Wretched place, India! I'm not a specialist myself. Just here to keep an eye on you fellows, that's all.'

The Corporal could not contain himself any longer. Kicking discipline aside, he said insistently: 'It can be cured, sir. It'll have to be cured!'

The surgeon finished buttoning up his tunic and gave him a sidelong look. '*Have to*? Oh, I know how you feel. Surgeons know… hm. Well, it's not up to us really, y'know, it's up to the condition itself. If it's too far advanced…'

'Sorry I spoke out, sir.'

Some days later, after examining Edward's left eye again, the surgeon gesticulated helplessly. 'No, I'm sorry, Corporal, but he's just about blind in the left eye. It might get worse, but I don't think it will ever get any better. You wanted the truth and that's it. He's still got the right eye. It will get strong, do the job of both…'

Corporal Mannock stood there, thunderstruck. He wanted to get down on his knees and pray for a miracle, calling for instant help from God. He could now see that the surgeon was no good, he couldn't do anything for the boy. There was still Julia, he could turn to her. Weakness and indecision practically paralysed him for the first time in his life.

Heartbreak moved into the house and it stayed for a fortnight. Every time Edward turned to look at you, wavering unsteadily on his feet because of his bad eye, you felt your heart being pulled this way and that way, and it was worse whenever he smiled as though trying to tell you that he was all right.

The Corporal sat there, punching with imaginary fists at imaginary enemies. This was not happening to him, it was somebody else's worry. He could have cried the day they came back to the bungalow through the midday heat, Julia with a silk scarf over her head and Edward kicking up puffs of road dust. The entire journey had been in complete silence. The Corporal did not want to go through anything like that again.

Sealed inside behind Edward's pale face, the pain thudded about and settled for the thousandth time behind his left eye. For fourteen days he was almost totally blind, because his right eye developed reciprocal action. If he coughed or made a sudden movement it brought on a splitting headache. When his right eye started working again he kept quite still and tried to encourage it to take in the words in the book he was reading. The parental silence was no mystery to him; he knew what the surgeon had said, and it was something he had to put up with. All he wanted was for the pain to die away. He would not mind having only one sound eye.

He put the book down and went quietly outside into the dying light of the evening, pretending to examine the soft red outline of the sandstone barracks and the occasional movement of colour as a soldier hurried across the square. Colour now worried and puzzled him. In the last week blue had become green, and he could not make out yellow at all. He was trying to make his right eye do the work of both, just as the surgeon predicted, but it was harder than anybody imagined because of the presence of the black macula which rested across his left eye. In the mornings it was always at its worst, especially first thing after waking, but he had so far managed to keep this a secret from Julia.

To a boy who is at one with the flight of the bird, the quick scurryings of small animals and the loping gait of dogs, even partial blindness can be a sickening disaster. He can do only two things, and both depend on his basic character, the variable mental intertwinings which make him what he is: he can start sulking in dark corners, reviling his personal fates for what has gone wrong, or else be can start trying to compensate for his loss by turning his mind elsewhere, away from all movement and lively action, away from the exuberance of running fast across the sun-crusted Indian ground towards the corpulent pet pig, the flutter of rising birds. He throws into the recess of memory the day when he outpaced an agile pi-dog. Having put all these thoughts away, he must now start finding other things to fill the void. It takes the strength of youth.

Edward's mind gently turned him towards the cadences of poetry and verse, and he fell in love with the sounds which passed through his head as his blurred eyes moved across the lines. Poets painted his visions. Ideas fashioned by metre shimmered, fascinating him when they grew into mind's eye pictures. He sensed new worlds.

There must be more to it than this. There must be other things that don't need eyes. Music? But he could not play any instrument. There was nothing but a Jew's harp, two pieces of metal with a springy piece stretched across the middle. If you sucked and blew and kept twanging away at it with one hand, a sort of humming noise started up. At first the flexible metal clattered painfully against his teeth.

His mother paused, listening. 'For pity's sake...'

The Corporal's face fell into a crinkled human map. 'It's like the screeching of some crazy thing. What's he up to now?' He rose, preparing to investigate. He looked as though he intended blasting the side out of a quarry. Every emotion gushed out of him like beer from a spigot.

'Now, you leave him... let him try whatever it is he's doing.' Julia was firm about it. She knew all about the harrowing experience through which Edward was slowly passing; she knew about his gropings for new senses and satisfactions. She had to try to save him and provide mercy.

The blowings and the suckings fell into a tune, just one simple tune, then Edward put the Jew's harp back in the drawer where he had found it. A few days later he discovered an old kettle-drum in the house. Tapping it, he felt the hairs on the back of his neck start bristling with excitement. What a sound it could make! Just by tip-tapping that dry yellowed pigskin drumhead you felt like going marching over mountains. His fingers moving up and down, he imagined regiments of men crossing the crags, held together by the drum, this very drum with all the cords torn off its sides and most of its scarlet and blue paint gone. He tried again. Excitement welled up in him as he heard the underlay wires give back a militant rustling. Invigorated, he suddenly started to thump with his fist and then with a short stick.

'*Great God Almighty in heaven above!*' The Corporal put his hands to his agonized ears.

'Stop blaspheming, will you!' Julia started up, not knowing whether to lose her temper with Edward or go for the Corporal first. While the tattoo resounded upstairs she contained herself. She had married a man who could not accept any sort of misfortune or bad luck, and that was the truth of it. She could have kicked him from here to kingdom come. 'If you don't like it, you go right out of this house and take a walk – and don't you come back till your mouth's cleaner than it is now, Mannock.'

He glared at her. 'A walk? A walk? Isn't that what I'm doing all day long, walkin' round and round with all them stupid rookies, keeping them in step, then when I come home out of that terrible heat all my wife can tell me is take a walk, Mannock, she says, while that lad goes on bashing a damned old drum. I've had enough of it, Julia ... ENOUGH!'

The reason for the argument in the downstairs room suddenly pierced Edward's new enjoyment. He stopped drumming and carefully laid the kettle-drum back on the shelf where he had found it. Blinking quickly to clear his vision for the next few moments, he went down, smiling to himself, not a bit afraid of the old man and all his arguments. The raised voice was common enough in this house, and while there had been plenty of times when he felt like a good blubber, he always held himself in. Ten years old and him crying, his father would exclaim. That would bring Mum running and fluttering ...

He walked in, saying nothing, and sat down, noticing how quickly they stopped their rowing when they saw him. He didn't want them to be so sorry for him. He could not find the words to tell them.

'Supper time, eh?' his father said in an artificially agreeable tone.

'So it is!' His mother called for the old Indian woman to come in and lay the table. More often than not she did it herself but somehow it seemed that she wanted to be with Edward at every opportunity, and she tried never to leave him alone with the Corporal for long.

'How're you, Edward?' The Corporal was trying to be kind, but it was against his nature because he had spent a lifetime on barrack squares, rapping out harsh commands. His softer voice was rarely heard, but the sight of Edward's composure when he was supposed to be half blind was enough to stop any man in his tracks. The Corporal knew that if he had been in his son's state he would have been a rampaging bull for sure. 'I asked you, how're you?' he almost pleaded.

Edward put on a make-believe smile good enough to deceive the brassy nature of the Corporal. 'Getting on all right,' he said formally, as though meeting his father for the first time.

Nodding, the Corporal retired. What a dignity the boyo had! But was he trying to seem better than he was, maybe having a quiet laugh up his jersey sleeve at his own dad? Was that it, was it his idea of a good old joke or something? Mulling it over, watching Edward out of the corner of his eye, he was about to speak when he knew that he must check himself or lose the situation. There was enough trouble with Julia and the way she led off. It'd only lead to some damn arguing, and it was more than he could stomach tonight.

'How'd you like that drum?' he said suddenly.

'Fine, it's a good drum.' Edward remembered the thrill he got out of the ratatatating.

'Makes a divil of a row in the house.' The Corporal wondered whether to give permission for Edward to use it outside, then remembered the neighbours. He was waiting for Julia to say something.

'He must have a proper musical instrument,' she suggested primly, quite unlike her usual cast-iron self.

The silence closed in.

Then the Corporal uttered a harsh barking laugh. 'How about a fine old church organ for a start then? That's a musical instrument.' He could not disguise his sarcasm. To hear Julia talking anybody would think an NCO could go out and buy an orchestra full of instruments. And even if the money were available (if she had her way he would have to save it and spend less on beer) it wasn't easy to find such things in the middle of India.

Julia frowned. 'I meant it, you know.'

'I know you did, me darlin' ...' He deliberately put on a braying accent.

She turned to the boy. 'You'd like an instrument, wouldn't you, Edward?' Then quickly to the Corporal: 'Of course he would.'

'Did I hear him say so? Not at all. Not one word did he say about it.'

Her whole being pleaded with Edward until he volunteered 'I'd like one.'

'There you are – you satisfied now?' she asked the Corporal.

'For the sake of some vocal peace from you I'll see what can be done.'

The Corporal had some dubious qualities which were ruled out in Julia's eyes by his sudden dependability. In the last year he'd done nothing but rant and rave, but now there was a definite demand for his function as a husband and parent he veered round a little, his vanity tickled because he was wanted, even if it was only out of mercenary motives. A few days later he strode into the house with a long black case which he slammed down on the kitchen table without saying so much as a word and then walked out, on his way to a ceremonial parade. Looking at it, Julia knew how short of time he was, but bless him, he'd thought to run home with this whatever it was. It made up for a lot of things. She settled down to look at the case, noticing that it was not new because there were scratches all down one side, as though a rough tomcat had been having a go at it. But it was here and that was what really mattered.

Edward did not know what was going on. He was sitting in the next room, trying to read a book until his eyes grew watery again. The short lines of verse worried him, he could not seem to focus on them at all unless he shut his left eye and made the right one work, but that, too, soon started going out of focus and he was now on the point of giving up. Another visit had been paid to the Army surgeon. More questions were asked and again he had been asked to wait outside while the surgeon had a word with dad. It was all a mysterious business and he could not understand it.

'Hey, Edward, you come in here and see what the Corporal's brought in this minute.'

He found the bookmark, laid it in the page and closed the volume, then went into the kitchen where Julia was standing, all smiles while she cradled a queer-looking black box in her arms. She put it down, inviting him to open it and see what was inside. He forced back the two rusty catches and pushed back the lid.

The instrument lay on a bed of black velvet, most of it threadbare, the nap worn down with long usage. But that did not matter. From the way it shone you would think it was made of some precious metal.

'It's a violin,' he said unemotionally.

Unable to hold back her feelings, she danced him round the kitchen. 'It certainly is! It's a lovely old violin for you, for my own Eddie!' She stopped suddenly, puckering her brow. 'I Wonder where the old fraud got it from?'

'Pinched it?'

She cuffed him lightly, laughing. 'Him pinch', Not him. I'll bet he played a hand or two of crib for it, that'd be so like him, wouldn't it? Now, you'd better thank him. He's doing a parade, but he'll be home soon, then you can tell him how nice it is and how good he is.' She hesitated, then said in a gentler tone: 'Go on, aren't you going to lift it out and try it?'

Running her fingers through his strong dark hair, she urged him on until at last he carefully pulled the violin out of its case and waited, not quite knowing what to do next with it.

She supplied the answer. 'There's the bow for it.' She picked it out of its clip and thrust it in his other hand. 'That's for playing it. They're grand instruments. We'll send you off to lessons…'

Oh, the birds in flight, the scurrying of animals, the air and the sun, lost, lost.

'That will be very nice,' he said convincingly. 'I'll like that, mother.'

Then there was the business of knowing how to hold the violin. This was very difficult because it was a full-size instrument made for a grown man. He was only ten years old with short arms and when his left arm was out to its fullest extent he could not get a good grip on the shiny neck with any ease at all.

'Keep on trying,' Julia breathed.

'I am,' he retorted grimly.

'Stretch out a bit.'

'I am stretched – look!'

The birds and the scurrying animals, gone, gone...

He spent a long time looking closely at all the polished woods which had gone into the making of the violin, then he moved up to the graceful carved neck and the black hardwood pegs. This one must have been well played by somebody (the Corporal never said where he got it and nobody ever asked him), but there was quite a bit of dust on it, in all the crannies. Edward went and found a cloth and cleaned it. As the duster went to and fro the soft gold of the patina on the edges began to show through and gleam in the sunlight.

The playing, that was quite another thing. But for Julia, Edward would have been glad to be the custodian of the violin, not the learner, but she nagged on at him until he made a start on his own. They would find a teacher, she said, then he could start properly, but until that day dawned he would have to get on with it by himself.

The violin is among the most difficult instruments to learn. The notes go askew if you don't pin them down with your finger tips, and the belly of the instrument gets in the way of seeing what is happening up there on the neck. The bow is always too long, it has no great flexibility, and if you scrape one way at an angle and then come back on it, it never sounds exactly the same as it did the first time. After ten minutes both your wrists start burning and you have to stop for a minute not only to rest but also to promise yourself that you *will* play it in the end.

Edward kept on with it because there was nothing else he could do. He could not go out very much, being unable to keep up with the fast games of tag played by other European children, he could not read for more than half an hour without developing a headache which felt like hot acid in the brain. And he could not just stand about round the house after school every day, hoping something might happen to keep him entertained. It always came back to that violin.

Some tunes could be played all on one string. You could glide up and down just so far and even if you played part of it out of tune a bit it didn't really matter so much because nobody really noticed. One day he discovered that it was easy to transfer some of the difficult tunes from one string to another one if you were nippy enough and could think ahead. In getting to know the instrument he saw that when you were passing the bow across the strings they vibrated quickly, and the tighter the string the faster the quivering string moved. It was a new wonderful world locked up in a piece of polished wood and some catgut.

Now for a tune. The 'Londonderry Air' was easiest. After a few weeks he always started off with it, hopping about from one string to another, fumbling for the notes.

'It's a rare old sound, it is,' his father muttered.

'It is that,' Julia agreed.

'Like a cat in its dying,' the Corporal added maliciously. 'How can you say such a thing?' Julia smiled to herself, turning away so that be should not see and knowing all the time that he could hardly complain seeing that he himself had brought the violin into the place. 'It keeps the boy quiet –' she started to explain in hopes of soothing him.

'*Quiet?*' He clasped his head. 'You know what I heard say today? I'll tell you! There's a trooper and his missus in the bungalow but one down this road. This trooper he came up to me and he said as calm as you like, 'Corporal Mannock, what sort of wild animal is that in your house?"

'So you told him off, I suppose.'

'Told him off? What could I say? I pulled m'self up straight and I looked this bloody trooper in the eye and I told him, 'That's me son, and he's learnin' the violin so you go and get on with your duties, trooper, otherwise you'll be off for a week with a busted nose!' '

The 'Londonderry Air' again, wailing, sounded from upstairs.

'That's if me own son doesn't bust me brain before I bust that trooper's nose.' The Corporal went back to his newspaper, crumpling it noisily in retaliation.

A change of topic was what he wanted. Julia said: "I heard a rumour today we're going back to England soon. Is that right?"'

'Heard it myself. I'll let you know.'

But the truth came in separation, because the regiment went to South Africa to fight the Boers, and families stayed where they were until orders carne to reunite them at Shorncliffe, then back to Canterbury.

When regiments moved, the wives of NCOs were generally better off than the wives of ordinary soldiers. There was that extra bit of comfort, a few small concessions, sometimes better-cooked food, and it made it worthwhile being the wife of the Corporal. Julia knew before they started back to England that no amount of better treatment could compensate having a sickly child like Edward on your hands. The others were all right; Patrick and his sisters could look after themselves, but it was Edward with that eye of his and his unnatural quietness that troubled her. Examining the state of the two-funnelled troopship, she knew that the decks, so solid now, would soon become rolling wet monsters when they hit the westerlies, torturing the stomach day after day until you wished you were dead and in heaven before your time. As this was the only way of getting back to England she had to make the best of it, but it was a poor look out and there was a surgeon on board who knew nothing at all about children, only seamen and passengers. So what could you do about it? Although the Army was supposed to look after the wives and dependants of serving men, if you were caught up in this situation you could not very well protest about it. She knew from experience that it was hard lines on anybody who said a word out of place and she made up her mind to endure it. A good Army wife was expected to be able to rough it at times.

Three or four days out and it was still calm. She began to laugh at her own fears as she took the children on deck to look at the sea while she settled herself in a deckchair.

The boy came wandering down the deck, tottering slightly when the ship took a slow roll and taking everything in his stride but still worrying about his violin. If you called to him he turned and had a look on his face as though to say, 'Ah, there you are!'

'See the dolphins, Eddie?'

No, he had not noticed them. They were too quick for his one good eye, but he could make out the flecking of white against the blue sky as she pointed out the kite-like flight of the gulls. They were fragments of poetry, feathered and fleeting.

'See the sea, love?'

His head tilted. 'Yes, the sea. It's getting rough, isn't it?'

His sight must be improving, Julia thought.

Aboard any home-going trooper discipline was relaxed, and apart from a routine muster or two on the forrard well-deck the soldiers had very little to do except sit in the sun, chatting and joking among themselves, betting on each hand of cards while their women, wisely muffled up and barely showing their faces to the skin-roughening sea breezes, kept midships. It was steadier midships, with very little pitch and toss and roll to shift your stomach, and there they sat, the older ones occasionally glancing towards the men in habitual disapproval. Round them loitered the children aimless and restive, Edward among them, always flexing his fingers round the neck of that imaginary violin. He knew he could play it now and a queer sort of satisfaction caught at him because he could do something none of the others could do. He wanted to keep it a secret from them all.

Sitting in a tight tribal circle on a tarpaulined hatch cover, the soldiers stuck their cards in their fists and fags in their mouths, going through the daily ritual of gambling.

'Aces high…'

'It would be.'

'Ach, come on now, let's get the bloody game going!'

Half-listening to all the talk, Edward wandered about, sniffing at the wind and taking it down into his lungs as though about to go bunting. The waves went slap slap against the keel, mocking him in his vague dissatisfaction over everything. There wasn't much to be done on a ship once you had looked around, but maybe an ocean was better than a barracks. It was always moving you, taking you somewhere. The restless feeling that flooded your flesh and your bones was a cruel unremitting thing, tamed and held in check only by knowing you were off to somewhere. Edward would need some looking after, blind in one eye, always shrinking back or seeming to.

'Mam.'

The boy stood there, knee high, looking up with his pale forehead wrinkled against the strength of the weather. She lifted him and sat him down on a bollard, chucking him under the chin. 'How's our violinist, eh? Can you manage a reel yet?'

'No.'

'And not a tune out of you since we set sail, that's a shame for sure, Edward.'

'Mam.'

'Whyn't you get down off there and go to the cabin and practise a bit? Look at that sea, blue and green, all shifting about. There's plenty of water, isn't there? There's a million fishes down there, swimming about, big and little, a million or more. And what's on the bottom, on the seabed? Guess!'

Edward caught hold of the tendril of excitement in his mother's voice. 'A city?' he gasped.

'A city it is! A big, tall city with a cathedral and a statue of our St Patrick down there, all drowned with the fishes circling round his head, bless him. Streets full of fishes, houses full of fishes. The city of fishes, Edward.'

Edward moved so that he could look down into the sea. He watched the waves as they were cut in half by the ship's prow, saw the lathered foam spraying backwards with a steady hissing sound. He could even make out the deeper cutting sound as the ship broke through the water. He was twelve. It was all new.

'Don't you go telling anybody yet but we're off to Canterbury in England. That's after we've been to Shorncliffe. How d'you like that? I heard it today.'

'I like it fine. Canterbury.'

'There's a cathedral there, not as good as anything in Ireland but they say it's a very fine place. Maybe we could go and have a look at it after we land?'

Canterbury came as surely as India had gone and Edward quickly accepted the change. He had his part to play, the same as his mother and brother and sisters, working hard to get them all settled. At the end of the street, close to the barracks, was a sign, 'Military Road', and in it the houses stood one after the other, the same as parading troopers, each one identical with the rest and just enough to house a soldier's family. The Corporal was at the barracks most of the time, on guard duty or drilling, but waiting only for demobilization. It was just about the same as India except that it rained more during the winter and there were no servants. Julia did not mind that so much because mothering was her life, regardless of her husband's carefree attitude towards domestic responsibility. All those long nights when he left her alone with the children did not matter to her as much as they did to some wives. She had her basic loyalties.

Queen Victoria died.

In the peace of Canterbury the muffled bells of St Paul's, tolling out for the royal death, went unheard, but there were services in the cathedral, a great showing of black crepe, extra ceremonial duties for the Inniskillings.

The Corporal thought of the sea, not the departed Victoria. He'd had enough of India and in South Africa a bellyful of the Boers. The Army had begun to irk him like a new boot on a swollen foot. Things were going on everywhere which suggested excitement. There was the building of the Panama Canal, everybody was talking about it, because it was rumoured that hundreds, thousands maybe, of men would be needed out there and the money would be good. There was this Italian, Marconi, and his method of sending messages through the air; it could lead to something. Special ships were setting out to lay down submarine cables between places like America and Manila. There was money and freedom in everything that went on, and the Army seemed drab in comparison. The scent of opportunity wafted across oceans until the Corporal felt like 'tearing off' his uniform.

Britain slumbered like a dog in midsummer, ignoring all the fleas, not even wagging a peaceful tail as the rumblings echoed across the world from Liao-yang where the Russians and the Japanese fought for nine bloody days. Britain's fur was still unruffled when other nations started sympathizing with the downtrodden Boers in South Africa. Britain was an island.

Out of this mass of tempting currents the Corporal secretly determined his direction and took it, wading forth, searching, crying out for something more than family loyalties and the decencies. Julia would be all right, she would look after the kids, he kept reassuring himself, but sometimes, when he thought about Edward's face, he could have sobbed. The currents were stronger and they were carrying him away, day after day.

But when all the juice had been sucked out of the sour orange of his freedom, the Corporal began to ache again for a woman. He wanted a woman not for physical reasons but for the sake of a few words of comfort now and then, so he married bigamously. Julia would never have divorced him, she was too proud for that, and besides they were both Roman Catholics.

There were children by the Corporal's bigamous marriage. They took his name. Years later their mother refused to adopt another name. In her way she seemed proud of the Corporal.

Julia became known as Mother Mannock. More than forty years later she was described by Dorothy, wife of Patrick, Edward's elder brother by one year, as being 'a lovely homely lady, but she frightened me with what she had to say about her husband who'd run off and left her with all the children to bring up. She once snatched up a broom and drove the handle straight through his picture.'

Twenty years after deserting Julia and the children the Corporal arrived at Buckingham Palace during an investiture to claim Edward's posthumous Victoria Cross from King George V. It was put in his pocket along with his memories of the excited voice of a small boy, which kept coming back down the years. And now Edward was dead.

In the horror of his new loneliness the Corporal tried to sell the medal, but nobody would buy it. You might be able to sell a chalice cup stolen from a chapel, but you cannot dispose of the Victoria Cross. Was it so worthless? Why did prospective buyers give him such strange and questioning looks as he stood there, his unusual merchandise in his outstretched hand? He could not understand it.

Mother Mannock dissolved into her own mists to die during the Second World War. She used to visit Patrick, her eldest son. Almost her last words to Patrick's wife were: 'Edward was always my favourite,' but then she stopped coming to the house and the rest was silence. She lived out part of the balance of her days in a small cottage at Canterbury, and when she went to live in Edgeley Road, London, with Jess her other daughter, it was pulled down to make way for a block of modern maisonettes. Somebody suggested calling it Mannock House, not in her memory but in that of her son. The nameplate was screwed to the wall.

Edward's Victoria Cross was found by Patrick. A woman who said that she had been the Corporal's 'wife' handed it over, but only after a long argument which was settled with a five-pound note. Patrick remembered what Edward's Canterbury solicitor, Mr C A Gardner, had said: 'Try offering her a fiver – she'll take it.'

In 1961 Patrick entered hospital with his last illness. He was seventy-six and clearly unable to grasp the fact that his memory and faculties were deserting him. In the early days of their marriage Beatrice used to ask him about the Mannock family, but he looked grim, and all he would say was: 'It's too black to talk about, too black.' She once found him destroying some family papers as though trying to destroy history by feeding it to the flames. Some, like the documents taken from his brother Edward's seared body, had, he said, a 'gruesome' quality about them.

'It's too black to talk about...'

The blackness can be pierced.

CHAPTER TWO

That Autumn Julia Mannock tried hard to come to grips with all the difficulties created by not having a man about the house. What she felt most was not having anybody to turn to when the need arose. She had to be so secretive about the Corporal, and it started getting on her nerves more than anything else, but she realized that the degrading truth was better kept under lock and key because most of the neighbours could be harsh when it came to judging others. She could not bear the thought of her children suffering just because of the Corporal's daftness. If ever she saw him again, and she doubted if she would, she would tell him to get his fat head seen to! Oh, it was a common enough story, the sort to set some people laughing, when they chewed over the idea of the fickle roving Irishman who skedaddled so he could enjoy himself, but all the same she never wanted openly to acknowledge that it had happened to her. She was going to make a fresh start Everything must be new! If she needed any friends there were Edward and Patrick and the two girls, all to them still in the gawky stage. Of course, you could not share real confidences with your own children, they would not understand, but they could be talked to and they were sensible enough now they were all growing up. They had, thank God, a good home in the King's Street cottage, poor though it might look from outside. After the Corporal's flight they could not stay on in Military Road where everybody seemed to know what had happened, and by pure luck she managed to get the cottage for a few shillings a week. The move served two purposes: it gave them new surroundings and it gave them neighbours who accepted that she was only a poor widow woman with a horde of children to feed. Under this roof, swarming over one another, a warm solidarity began to grow, keeping them together. When they were out working or at school, she often put her feet up for a few moments and found herself starting to tot up all their individual qualities in her own mind, going over them one by one and thanking her lucky stars that none of them took after the Corporal. Then her train of thought was brought up short. The boys were really too young to take after anybody. You never could tell with boys. Girls were different, you were always sure of them, but boys...

Retracing her mental steps, she could see that Patrick was going to be trustworthy and well disciplined because he was that sort and would never change. It was young Edward who needed watching. After all that trouble with his eye, which had never improved one bit, he might do anything, though thank heaven the malaria he caught in India was wearing off a bit now. She thought she knew enough about children to realize that he would probably go out of his way to prove that he was just as good as the rest, the little terror! It was showing already. He started wanting to join things. They had some awkward discussions about it.

'What's all this about the Church Lads' Brigade thing?' She mixed a cake, creaming pale margarine with white flour, then taking the single step across the cramped kitchen to the battered black oven. She threw open the door, putting her face down to see if it was hot enough. 'What do they do, Eddie?' She was trying hard to gain his confidence.

Standing against the sink, playing with the cold water tap, he said simply: 'Meet. They meet. Somebody told me they –'

'If you say *meet* again I'll give you such a thump!' She tempered her sharpness with a quick smile, wishing he would learn how to express himself in sentences of more than two or three words, because it was getting to be such a habit with him, and a bad one, too, as though he expected you to understand exactly what he was thinking about. After sliding the cake tin into the oven, she washed her hands and dried them on a scrap of an old towel. 'Well? Go on,' she encouraged him.

'There's a Mr Cuthbert Gardner,' he volunteered after a considered pause.

'What about him? Oh, he's that solicitor in the town, isn't he?' The name was suddenly familiar to her, because she had almost put him on to the Corporal but changed her mind at the last minute. 'Yes, I've heard of him all right,' she repeated slowly. 'And he's connected with this Brigade, is he?'

'He's an officer or something. I've met him. He says I can go any time I like. I saw him yesterday. His name's Mr Cuthbert Gardner.'

'Heard you first time! Now is this a Church of England thing?' She was on her guard, newly conscious of the religious obligation to the children. Maybe she should go and have a word with the priest and see what he thought about this Church Lads' Brigade. She could always do that. A priest might not approve of it at all, and it was up to her to see that Eddie and the rest were brought up properly, so if he said no that would be that. 'Which church does it belong to, this Brigade?' After Edward promised to find out and let her know, she nodded, relieved that she would not have to go and speak to the priest about it at once. Meeting him was always an ordeal. She dreaded his asking about her husband, no matter how soft-mouthed he happened to put it. 'Good! When you know you can come and tell me. But what's this Mr Gardner like?'

'He's – oh, he's all right. He's nice. I've seen him.' The illogical Edward starting knotting a length of string, sliding it between his fingers and concentrating. 'They go off to a camp Mr Gardner said, and they have a lot of fun.'

'Well, I can just see you having some fun in camp, you like your bed too much for that !' She stopped herself in time. Why shouldn't he join it and enjoy himself when he would probably have to be working next year? She experienced a sudden meanness at trying to hold him back and asked forgiveness under her breath.

She heard the door latch click in the passage and Patrick walked in. Now he was working he had gone all serious and thought of nothing but earning some money. For the thousandth time in the last few months she reflected how unlike each other the boys were, not really like brothers at all. Patrick had grown up so much more quickly, he was nearly a young man now, but there was Edward, still hanging on to the last of his childhood.

Taking no notice of Edward's obvious discomfort at involving Patrick in her personal affairs, she burst out: 'What's all this about the Church Lads' Brigade, Pat? D'you know anything about it?'

'Oh, it's all right,' he said, grinning at Edward's embarrassed flush. 'So he's been asking you, has he? Thought he would … He wants to join because they go to camp and it's why he wants to get in. He's been talking to old Cuthbert about it.'

'*Mister Gardner* to you!' Edward reminded him fiercely, nibbling a fingernail. 'So why can't I join? Who's stopping me?'

'Never said you couldn't, did I?' Julia decided to let him have his little fling. It could not do him any harm and he was entitled to it. 'Oh, go on and have a good time!' Her eyes went to the oven. The cake! Boys! 'Out of here, all of you. Go on – give me some room now! *This house!*'

In his own quiet way Edward was worried about Patrick. It seemed that up to a few months ago, when Pat left school and started with the National Telephone Company, they had been on an equal footing, but now he was earning a wage he had become more – Edward ransacked his vocabulary for an apt word – more *distant*, and when he did speak it seemed he was talking to somebody else, not his own brother. Oh, he was still part of the home all right, but he would try and give you the impression he was all grown up, especially when he handed his wages over every Friday. It was quite a ceremony with him! Mum hadn't noticed anything, Edward felt sure, and neither had any of the girls. Pat certainly was changing his tune, as though he'd decided to go into a monastery! He noticed the way Pat now used a sort of grown-up voice to tell him off if he did anything wrong, while Mum watched with approval. That was the worst part of it, not being able to say anything about it. He would have liked to pull Pat's dull old leg about it a bit, he was so serious, but it would only make Mum come in on Pat's side and there would be ructions.

So that was why they always thought he was being so odd and queer. It was only because he felt lost, trying to get used to all these changing relationships which were unsettling when you were the youngest.

It started the day Pat went for that interview for the telephone job just before he left school, and came home looking as cocky as the skipper of a winning football team. He sat down to tea in his shirt sleeves and he said: 'Of course, they want a certain standard of education in telephones, you know that?'

'You swallowed the dictionary?' Julia's tone was joking but Pat was quick to take umbrage.

'They're looking for the refined type of lad, the manager said,' he answered.

'What did they ask you about?' Seeing Patrick being given all the attention, Edward felt a little shy. Once he had contributed his question he was glad to get on with his jam and bread.

'Arithmetic and English. They're very keen on both those.' 'No good to me,' Edward could not resist retorting. 'Me, I can't add two and two up.'

'Oh dear, love, why can't you *try*? You won't make anything of yourself. You're good at English but your sums are so bad!' Julia was genuinely concerned as she remembered his last school report. She could not afford to see him slowly decaying in some deadend occupation, and heaven knows there were plenty of them in Canterbury, symbolized by swarms of rough errand lads pushing their delivery trikes round the city, day after day. Edward must not be like that! He'd got a brain if only he would use it, they said at school. Perhaps he could get into a trade of some sort? Of course, you could hardly expect a boy from St Thomas's to become Prime Minister of England overnight. Her Irish loyalties pulled her up. Would any self-respecting Irishman *want* to be Prime Minister?

Pat was talking about his interview, glowing with prospects. What a job they'd had, getting him ready! She had made him polish his own boots but in the end was forced to fix the knot in his necktie to give it some neatness. Just before he went off down the street she called him back and smothered his wiry hair with water, smoothing it down to a cowlick. If only Edward took more notice of things! But he didn't seem any more interested than if his brother had just landed a job looking after the animals in the zoo.

There was another thing, and it was more important to her mind. Now they were all growing up, their appetites were increasing, all except Edward, and he ate enough to keep himself going and that was about all. None of them knew what it was really to go hungry, although they had come close to it now and then. He just had to get a job, it was a question of survival.

Apart from such long-term consideration Julia felt happy enough even if she were not always contented, but what she really liked was the fact that they were all keeping well together. Only the other day she heard a neighbour call them 'those Mannocks' and it gave her a sense of one-ness with her five children.

And what about that Corporal? He was probably sitting there in some pub, snapping his beer, having a crack with his new friends, enjoying himself. Oh, what an injustice it all was!

'Edward, what would you like to be when you get out of school, love?'

'I don't know. Why?'

Was he like his father? Pray God not! I could never stand that, with him being a little reflection of what the Corporal was. And yet he's as undecided as his father used to be when it came to making up his mind.

'You'd best join Patrick. He's getting such a nice safe job.'

'What's a nice safe job?'

Was he deliberately being awkward and mocking her? Her Eddie? No, he would never do it, he wasn't like that at all.

Edward did not want to hurt her.

School still failed to make much sense and he tried hard not to waste any of the knowledge which came hurtling at him from all directions, but he felt drawn more towards English and literature than to things like arithmetic. On Fridays, when the rest of them were gnawing their stained wooden penholders, working out what they should write about, he was always finished before anybody else. Folding his arms – one of the school rules – he had time to look about him, at the old desks. He noticed the iron cross-stays, chipped and scarred, and under them the planked floors, hollowed out by thousands of boots and always grained with dust. St Thomas's school seemed endless in its imprisonment of boys.

Many of them said he was odd, a real queer 'un. To them he was 'that Irish lad who's bin to India and his dad's been and gone and left them ...'

Yah, yah, yah, his dad's gone off with a black wooman.

Yah, yah...

Black wooman...

By the time he was thirteen the cruelty of it no longer hurt, because he was suddenly free to leave St Thomas's and escape the tedium of seeing the grey faces of the teachers as they poured out the unreal facts behind the Industrial Revolution, the reasons for Henry VIII and the Reformation, the rise and fall of the Romans. How much of it was real? He would soon be as free as a bird, free as a lark lifting in the midsummer air, which represented reality.

Edward had an almost angry need to be out and doing. He could never discuss his true feelings with his mother, not so much because he was afraid of her as the fact that she must not be hurt.

He walked out of St Thomas's school for the last time and felt like singing his head off at the waiting world. There was nothing he could not do, nowhere he might not go! His heart sang with his brain in sheer hedonistic satisfaction. The great symphony went on until he heard a sudden discord and knew that his left eye might after all prevent him from making his wild wishes come true. Patrick had already pointed out that having only half normal vision would stop him from getting some jobs. He would not get in the Navy, for instance, and some industries would not take him on. The best way was not to mention that left eye! Say nothing about it! Let them find out for themselves. There were plenty of secret compensations such as poetry and music. They meant something special and put you in a special category. Some people might laugh at it and called it cissyish, but it did mean *something*! Ever since coming back from India it had been the same, and he had been laughed at quite a few times by other boys who got to know that he liked playing the violin. He'd given one of them a black eye, and that shut the rest of them up! He was learning to keep himself under cover, always being polite, but not making the mistake of giving away too much to others. They called him a 'good lad'. In the Church Lads' Brigade he was classed as 'gay and adventurous'. He had these two sides to him and that was how he wanted it.

Hey, no more school, think of that! I can do as I like! What'll Mum say to that? She'll go on about money, it's all she thinks about, but you can't blame her. She's seen Pat bringing in his wages every week and she thinks everybody else ought to do the same. Pat must have an easy time, writing figures down in those ledgers all day. He told me – what was it? – he said, 'Nobody worries Pat Mannock at work, you remember that, Eddie. I've got a good job, that's the reason, and I know how to do it.' And then he softened up and he said, 'Wouldn't you like to come into telephones, Eddie? It's safe, you know… safe.'

Edward walked on, swinging his patched canvas satchel. He went through the park towards the respectable-looking road with the big, red-brick houses on the far side of the cricket pitch where he had a knock or two every Tuesday and Thursday night. A fresh wind came through the trees, battering against him and making him pause for a moment as dry leaves fluttered in his face. Then he walked on, quicker now with the sachel tucked under his arm.

Should I become a ledger clerk, like Pat? You know they'd said it was a nice clean respectable job, Mum would like us all clean and respectable, you can tell that by the way she's always talking about it. Why can't I work on a – a farm? I could help somebody with the cows and pigs. But that would mean travelling out every day. I could get a bike. Pat might help me there.

Watching Pat across the tea table, he quickly abandoned his plan to ask for a loan because he was no longer certain he would get it. Pat had become too polite and grown-up to lend a sympathetic ear. Clerking could not be much of a job if it did that to you. Pat sat there, dolled up in his best suit, swearing he'd got the best end of the stick just because he kept his hands clean.

'There's increments,' he was saying. 'Only a shilling or two a year, but no end to the amount of promotion you can get. By the time you're ready to retire, you can be up there at the top of the tree!' He turned to Edward. 'It's worth thinking! You get a good pension after thirty-five years' service. If you happened to get married pensions are important.'

Thirty-five years?

Edward found it hard to think about without laughing. He was only just turned thirteen and found it difficult to imagine being forty-eight.

He was offered a position by a local greengrocer who needed general help. It was work and it meant money, half-a-crown a week, so he accepted. Because his heart was set on it, Julia and Patrick had to give in even if they did not agree with him. He went at it as though sack-humping, sweeping up and running errands comprised his entire future. Saturdays included, he slogged on through the week until his face was caked with sweat and dust. When the boss was out at the front, he slumped down, trying to get his breath back. After two more weeks of muscle-pulling box lifting, unpacking fruit and shovelling potatoes, he began to doubt if there were a future after all. He felt guilty when he noticed the wear and tear on his clothes, which Julia patiently mended, ready for next morning. Sooner or later he was going to need new ones, and this would be a problem because there was no money to spare and he could not go about in rags. Julia fought terrible inner battles with herself as she worked to preserve his respectability. The slightest tear in a shirt or jacket was enough to send her flying for needle and thread, but she had to admit that most of his clothes were practically beyond repair.

All Edward could think about was his half crown reward every Saturday. It seemed miraculous that the boss would actually ring up the till, scrabble about in the open drawer and then toss the coins over to him. He took his money with pride and raced home, panting as he ran into the house and planked it all down on the table, waiting for Julia's cry of satisfaction. And that would be that for another seven days! Even his small contribution made some difference, because there was an imperceptible increase in the food, a bit more butter appeared on the breakfast table, there was more meat for dinner, and a few fancy bits appeared on the supper table.

Julia's concern for him did not diminish. His pale face and exhaustion when he came home were far from healthy, but it was impossible to say anything for fear of hurting him. Nor could she speak to his boss, because she did not know him and a word out of turn might get him the sack, then there *would* be a row! During the week, as she passed the shop, she could see Edward's slight figure tugging at a hundredweight bag of potatoes and she could have wept for him. He was working so ferociously with nobody to guide him. He thought everybody did the same, and he was doing his best to match up to grown men, that was the pity of it. Whenever she tried to tell him, all he did was nod vigorously and say how much he enjoyed the work.

She was silent for a long time while he went on reading, then she started again, this time speaking with more emphasis. Why didn't he think about getting a job with Pat? She knew how he felt about clerking and maybe she agreed with him, but the wage would be more than he was making now and the telephone company would like to have two brothers working in the same place.

His muscles felt torn, his head ached, but to please her he promised to think about it. He still believed that clerking was useless, although he knew next to nothing about it. What he had to have was plenty of variety, a chance to work with his hands. There was a limit to what you could do with a column of figures and a pen, as Pat admitted. And what was the good of a pension if you hated the job?

After another week of hard work for the greengrocer Edward made up his mind to find something better. It was not capitulation, it was ambition that moved him. There must be more to the world than Canterbury!

He started schooling himself for the experience, and, like the Corporal, read any papers he could lay his hands on, often bringing bundles of old ones home from the shop. He read everything and, like his father, was suitably dazzled by a world in which opportunity waited. In comparison Canterbury was a village.

Then by luck he heard about a barber who needed an assistant. It did not sound much of a job, but spurred by thoughts of making money he walked in and got it, starting at once, all wrapped up in a long white apron supplied by his new boss, who liked the look of him. The pay was five shillings a week, double what he had been getting, and he lost no time rubbing it in when he reported his change in status at home. There was only one snag to it, he had to be at work earlier than when he was in the greengrocery trade, and there were several late nights to be worked. Despite everything, it was worth it, especially when he was able to go home with his wages and make a loud rattling with the coins as he paid out. He was even able to afford a ha'penny for a daily paper, which he carried rolled under his arm.

To a friend he said: 'I'm getting somewhere now!'

There was not enough room for them all in the tiny cottage kitchen, that was the trouble. If you did not get to the table quickly after all the tea things were cleared away, you found yourself hunched up in a corner. Edward generally reached the table first and spread out his papers.

On the other side of the cramped room Patrick solemnly studied a manual of book-keeping, picked up second-hand for sixpence and now carefully glued together. He said that he was 'bettering himself', getting ready for that senior post when it came along. Already he had an air of superiority, but he was always ready to try to get Edward into the department if he wanted a *proper job* to do.

Edward politely thanked him for the offer. After only a few days of lathering chins and trying to remove whiskers, he felt that he was probably on the right track in the barbering business. There were a few drawbacks; some of the rowdy tough-looking customers came in, puffing out clouds of beery breath, and gave him a playful shove, then criticized his work. This sort of thing was hard to stomach, but after trying to put up with it and say nothing he decided that a bit of pugnacity was needed. But all he got for his burst of spirit was a kick up the backside and a good telling off. Secretly they enjoyed his Irish 'lip'. He gauged his success by the tips; some dropped him a ha'penny, but he had received as much as threeha'pence or tuppence.

Throughout the day there was a constant flow of chatter.

'Just look at him dreaming! Three waitin' and Vs got his mind somewhere else. Come on, lad, lather 'em up and then finish your sweepin'!'

A thin man with a croaking voice twisted round, pleading 'Here, you 'urry up, kid; got to get ter t' factory.'

The soap creamed under his whisking brush. Lifting a daub out of the pot, he started rubbing it in, slowly at first then faster until flecks of it flew off in all directions.

'Easy, young Mannock ...' His boss eyed him, holding back a smile.

Grinning, Edward retorted: 'Sorry, gaffer. It's all wet.' Twenty-eight round, pointed or blunted chins were smoothed before eleven-thirty, then he had to slip out and fill the sooty kettle with water from the slopstone tap and settle it on the gas ring for tea. He enjoyed this, the practical side which involved handling the enormous brown teapot and mashing the tea until it went the colour of dark varnish. Then he had to collect the mugs and give them a bit of a swill before pouring out the tea and taking it through to the shop. The barbers took their elevenses as they worked, so it was not unusual to see a man biting into a meat sandwich which he held in one hand while the other used the clippers to nibble away at the customer's head. Edward remembered the boss's words soon after he had started: 'This is an 'igh-class place. See you keep it that way otherwise you'll sling your 'ook.'

Edward's mind went forward a few years. What he lacked in education he would make up for as a businessman! As soon as he knew enough about running a barber shop he might be able to open a little place of his own. He was bound to get trade because people were always wanting their hair cut and their shaving done. Half of his mind settled on the secret idea of being his own master at nobody's beck and call, but the rest of him was in rebellion because the barbering trade meant you couldn't have many evenings to yourself. He had become interested in cricket and discovered a scratch team that played one or two nights a week, down on the recreation ground. There was a church team he wanted to join if they would have him ('I'll keep quiet about my eye then they'll let me in ...'). Being tied down to a job dragged him away from things. It would not be much use talking to Pat about it; he'd say cricket was only a game and it didn't earn you a living so it was best to concentrate on working.

A few days later he asked to be let off earlier than usual. His boss said it would be all right 'so long as you don't go making an 'abit of it'. Edward was off, sprinting through the streets towards the recreation ground. Near the gates he found a dozen young lads discussing positions and was just in time to adjust his headlong rush to a leisurely stroll before they saw him and started sizing him up. They were only too glad to enrol him. They accepted him without question, not even asking his name. He was second bowler. While he was waiting, he watched the others, studying their style. And then he was in!

His heart pounding, he caught the cricket ball and rose to his feet, uncertain of what was expected of him but knowing that he must put up a show. Retreating from the crease, he rubbed the ball up and down the side of his trouser leg to rid it of dampness and then, sighting himself, he broke into a run, raised his arm and let fly. The ball went wide. There was a total silence from the others until it was retrieved and returned to him. He could see the batsman standing there, a superior smirk on his face.

He quickly went back to his former position and tried again. At the last moment the ball slipped. Another failure! Next time he shut his almost sightless left eye, relying on the right one. This time the ball was nearer but still it flew away, wide of the wicket.

He desperately shouted out that he would be better in a moment. *Just one more try? Please?* The leader turned to his lieutenants, some of whom shook their heads. There was no room for a dud bowler in this team!

By now he was really unsure of himself. If he did not bowl straight next time they would never speak to him again. You had to be fit to get yourself accepted, but once you were in they stuck by you. He had heard plenty of tales about them, enough to want to belong.

While they were debating at one end of the pitch, he squatted down, trying to size up the uneven roll of the pitch. Next time he felt sure he would have that ball dead on the wicket. But would they allow him to try?

The leader swivelled round and waved at him. 'Go on – what you waiting for, you spud basher?'

Relieved, Edward went through the motions again, taking a shorter run this time, and the ball left his fingers with whistling velocity, heading straight towards the wickets and making an alarmed batsman step forward and barely deflect it into the slips. Another inch and he would have been out.

Next day, as he mixed the lather and saw the first bristling customers settled, Edward whistled to himself. Even if it were only a scratch team without proper fixtures, they had taken him on.

In some ways he knew how right Patrick was when he said life was not all games, but Edward was working on his mind, reading everything he could get hold of in hopes of making use of it later. At work he was not quite as sure of himself. Watching his boss, it seemed that these self-glorified men with their own businesses to look after did not get more than a whisper of fun out of life. Was it better to have security in a proper job and spend your spare time doing what you wanted to do or what?

Edward's boss was himself a cricket enthusiast. He admitted that the boy worked hard and was entitled to some leisure, so it became a toss up between increasing his pay from five shillings a week to six-and-sixpence and making him work longer hours, or else pegging it at five shillings and letting him get away early a couple of nights every week. In the end cricket won.

Julia noticed the change in him. When she tackled him about his left eye and how he managed at games, he claimed that he was a new sort of bowler who used only one eye! He invited her to go and watch, but she never appeared at the recreation ground because she knew nothing about cricket. Her only game was keeping house. Under the stress of trying to keep track with a growing family, she was prematurely old and bent. It was one of the penalties of motherhood. Sometimes, when they were all out, she sat down with a cup of tea and the cumulative weariness of the day came over her as she dozed off in her chair.

As Julia grew more tired, Edward seemed to become more energetic. Evening games throughout that summer brought an elation which he had never before known. Only one thing marred his fun, lack of money. Where the rest of the gang could afford to take their train and tram trips, he always had to bow out, muttering that he could not afford it.

'How much is it?' he asked uneasily, knowing it was bound to be too much.

Bert, the leader, eyed him mockingly. 'Only fourpence. You broke, Paddy?'

'I'm broke,' he confirmed.

Bert turned to the others. 'Paddy's broke. He says he's broke.'

They were planning to go by bus to a place about five miles outside Canterbury where a stream was thick with trout. Bert knew all about fly fishing and had enrolled them in the expedition so that they would be able to bring a fat catch home for tea. This appealed to Edward but not to his pocket. He had already asked Julia for money but she did not have even a penny to spare, so he was forced to drag himself back to the park to announce that he would not be coming.

Still protesting that fourpence was little enough for such a good day out, Bert led his flock away. None of them looked back. They filed out of one gate while Edward headed for home where he might be able to console himself with a book. Money was not all that important to him so long as he had something to read. All the same, the idea of having a fat trout on his plate for tea was not quite as easily dismissed, whether it was poached from protected waters or not.

Everything seemed to be summed up in this one word, money! You could barely breathe if you had no money. Why were some people better off than others? What was it that enabled fellows like Bert always to be flush when he, Edward, worked twice as hard yet had nothing?

His own earnings, still five shillings a week in return for the favour of getting off early for cricket now and then, were always swallowed up by family demands. Julia occasionally returned sixpence or a shilling to him to spend as he pleased, but that happened rarely enough. It was not exactly poverty, it was the *being without* that riled him. It was not as though he wasted money. He always tried to make good use of it. He had just discovered one or two second-hand volumes for a penny each on a street stall and persuaded the man to put them to one side until he could afford them. The trouble was he wanted them *now*!

'He's a great reader,' Julia used to say out of her thin gentility.

'He's learning, is he?' friends asked, quite impressed.

She nodded. 'Like his –' She had to check herself. Any mention of the Corporal's name might lead to probing questions. A neighbourly inquisition could destroy all the walls of sham respectability. Only one of the children knew everything, Patrick, and he was not, thank God, a talker The others would know soon enough, but in the meantime she held on tightly to the masquerade.

The months went by without Edward displaying any real ambition beyond barbering. Patrick felt more and more worried because his brother failed to show signs of wanting to get on in life. He spoke to him as frequently as possible about it, not that it did any more good than cause Edward to promise to think it over. In the end Patrick decided to force the issue. 'There's a post for a junior now. You can have it if you'll apply,' he said.

Stripped to the waist, washing himself in the kitchen sink, his mind full of the game they had just played on the recreation ground, Edward spluttered: '*Me?*'

'Yes, you. Are you listening Eddie?'

'Yes. Go on.'

'It's – it's a small job, nothing big about it. Just about suit you.' Patrick realized his gaffe. 'What I mean is, you'll have a chance to make something of yourself. It'll help Mother, it'll be more money.'

Flinging out an arm for the towel, Edward surfaced, his eyes twinkling through the suds. 'A lot of things pay more than barbering, Pat. You think I'd really like clerking?'

'Try it anyway,' Patrick suggested. 'If you don't like it, you can always chuck it. Nobody's going to make you stay on if you don't like it.'

Edward carefully twirled the corner of the towel to a point and cleaned out his ears, rubbing them until they glowed. He threw the towel on to its nail, drew on his shirt 'And you'd like me to try for the job –'

Gesticulating, Patrick retorted: '*Try?* I'm sure you could have it if you'd write a letter of application.'

'I'm not much good with letters. What do I say, please can I have the job my brother told me about?' There was a mocking light in his eye.

'That's how not to get it,' Patrick pointed out. Perhaps he was wrong after all.

No more was said about it, but Edward went to the sideboard for paper and pen and ink and settled down to please his mother and brother.

The National Telephone Company accepted the new recruit. He was given a chair and a desk and the regulations to read. It was difficult to get genuinely interested in this alien business; his mind kept going back to barbering where everything had seemed so concerned with real life.

In the first week his brain would not juggle with figures. He sat there, staring haplessly at all the columns, wondering what to do. Presently two and two began to make four and even if he made some errors he showed that he was capable of going through the motions with deceptive efficiency.

You sat here all day, writing down figures and 'using your brain' as they called it, and in the end they paid you more than you could make out of barbering.

Edward's pen faltered, stopped, but he dare not lay it down because somebody was always watching you to see that the affairs of the National Telephone Company maintained a businesslike impetus. His head cautiously turned to look out of the window. This was not so very different from school. Every office was like a classroom and most of the senior clerks behaved like schoolmasters (even Patrick was getting that way), and keeping the ledgers was the same as one unending arithmetic lesson.

'Eddie –'

He turned quickly. It was Patrick, smiling at his brother's absorption.

'How are you getting on?'

It took an effort to force the words out. 'Fine. I'm grand. It's very interesting.'

Patrick returned to his own office, feeling gratified.

Edward still played cricket in the evenings, noticing that the rest of the gang were starting to look up to him now he had an office job. Bert's terrifying habit of deriding him because he was only a lather boy came to an end and there was respect in his voice when he realized that Edward was able to sit at a desk all day long and get paid for using his brains. Edward tried to talk them out of it. They were angry because he did not want their respect, only acceptance. In the end he and – surprisingly – Pat joined St Gregory's Cricket Club. Within a few months Edward was captain of the Saturday Team.

Julia felt more settled and her worries abated. There was even some talk among the children of her marrying again, but she told them to mind their own business. There was nothing in it! The story grew out of a meeting she happened to have with a labourer who came to the cottage to do a job for her, putting up some shelves to make a few coppers because he was hard up. After packing up his tools, he sat down and had some tea with the family. After he was gone the girls started giggling over the idea that he was going to be their new dad, but it was only childish invention. Julia took it in her stride, and quickly denied it. She was not going to marry again, not for all the tea in China. Exchanging looks with Patrick, she knew what he was thinking: the Corporal must still be alive – somewhere. Besides, she had other things on her mind, like Edward.

She noticed how fast he was growing now. His chest was filling out and standing six foot one he was getting to look just like the Corporal, but thank God without the Corporal's moodiness and bad tempers. She found herself wanting to forget that Eddie was her favourite, because it looked so bad in front of the others. Many a time she slipped a little extra on his plate.

'Why can't the rest of us have it?' Jess, hard voiced in comparison with the rest, had a chilly imperious air which often frightened Julia. She pointed rudely at Edward: 'He's always getting the odds and ends!'

'Shut up and mind your own business!' Julia whirled on her. 'If you'd mind your own business we might all be a damn, sight happier in this house!'

Nora put in slyly: 'But Jessie's right, Mum.'

'I know I am!' Jess said smartly.

'Quiet!' Patrick lifted his hand. 'If you don't shut up, you can go and eat outside.'

Edward, Patrick observed between mouthfuls, was doing very well. He had taken it upon himself to report progress in the office and Julia enjoyed hearing all about the routine. It was a foreign world to her. She knew nothing about offices except what Patrick told her.

'He'll be on double entry work soon,' Patrick said. '*Won't* you?'

Edward nodded. 'Suppose I will really.'

'It'll be a leg up for you,' Patrick thrust out.

'Yes, suppose it will.'

Patrick stopped eating and laid down his knife and fork. 'What do you mean, you *suppose*? Of course it will! You've got to be more positive if you want to get on, Eddie, I'll tell you that.'

Edward managed to keep his face straight for a moment and then laughter came. His humour caught hold of his sisters and they tittered infectiously. Julia was amused and could not help smiling. The only straight face belonged to Patrick. Rivalry and affection collided head on until Patrick felt like throwing something at Edward. Then the laughter stopped as Julia motioned the girls to get on with their meal. After a moment or two Patrick lifted his own knife and fork. Tension fled.

The ledger lines were always waiting, looking like the plan of some interminable railway journey across a plain. Edward's eyes became blurry looking at them. What was there in all this that satisfied people? Patrick talked about it as though it were some sort of Holy Grail, an almost spiritual ideal towards which the clerk-penitents must struggle on their knees. But then, the dependable Patrick made such a god of work!

It became practically impossible for Edward to understand how very useful all these compiled figures were to the National Telephone Company. He gained no satisfaction from completing one page and then turning over to a fresh one. A million unanswered questions flew about in his mind. What happened to them all when they were full up? Were they placed in some library for students to examine? *Exactly how important were they*? It was the sort of question nobody ever asked in the stuffy clerical atmosphere. Nothing happened here where even the upraised voice was an exception and the day's excitement was the cup of tea put on your desk by a red-faced office boy. In wild moments he thought of swapping jobs with this undersized youth for the fun of it, then a memory of Patrick's expression when first he got this job filled his mind's eye and he sighed and settled down to it again. He had visions of himself flinging down his battered pen and shouting *I've finished with all this daftness – FINISHED!* When he confessed his feelings to Julia she did not, as he expected, explode and condemn him, but half-admitted that she understood how he felt, but he must never give it up unless he felt completely sure of himself. *Never!* It was a word with a funereal sound to it ...

Beneath his generally calm exterior she knew there must be currents which he found it hard to harness. After some months of office life he was beginning to look pale, despite frequent games of cricket and outings. He acted so listlessly when he came home at night, as though he no longer cared about anything. Surely a boy could not change so quickly unless there was something wrong. She made up her mind to speak to Patrick about it. He might not like her criticizing office life but he must face up to the fact that Edward looked peaky and the cause was probably that office.

While she was looking for a chance to tackle Patrick, Edward came home early one afternoon and ran straight up to his room. His stomach was churning painfully, he could neither sit nor stand. When he propped himself up against the wall it was an effort to draw breath. As he grappled with a reality grown misty his knees buckled and he collapsed on the floor, the everyday things spinning round and round in a sickening vortex. Only the sound of his mother's step on the stairs pulled him together. By the time she entered he was apparently on his hands and knees, pulling the violin case out from under the bed.

'Eddie '

'Yes?' He did not dare turn. She would soon notice how pale he was.

She took his head in her hands and gently turned it towards her. 'You're not well, now are you? It must be that old malaria or something.'

He did not answer or resist. What was the good of going over it all again and trying to explain that the office was stifling him, that he could not stand it much longer? The only way to get something done was to talk to Patrick. But it was a very thin hope.

That night, when he felt slightly better, he took Patrick on one side and tried to tell him exactly how he felt about carrying on with the job. His elder brother's attitude was at first one of disbelief. He just could not comprehend the mentality of anybody who would not make an effort to create security. Bad health could surely be overcome? Edward was at first courteous and then belligerent as he waded into the argument. This time he had to win

'There are dozens of young chaps, better educated than you are, who'd give their right arms for the job,' Patrick managed to answer.

'They can have it!' Edward said angrily. Patrick never would understand, but they must above all remain good friends, that was very important because his elder brother was the only person to whom he could talk, even if they did not speak the same language. He had a feeling that he might need him in the future.

What Edward really desired was not to be so speechless when faced with Patrick's apparently irrefutable arguments. Could education give you some strange gift so that you could fight back with words? He had already tried studying elementary logic and rhetoric but neither seemed any good in a domestic situation. Patrick was almost determined not to listen, not to understand, that was the trouble. What price all those books he had bought with hard-earned pennies? There was a sixpenny dictionary, full of words, and he had spent night after night going through it. He wished that he could have produced some of them now, neatly woven into a strong argument to make Patrick see that office work was no good to him. But everything he said sounded weak and stupid.

Presently Edward decided to go down to the recreation ground to try to pick up a game of cricket. As he passed through the familiar gate he could see the gang standing sturdily in a group, just as they always did. They waved for him to hurry. Feeling better here than he did at home, he trotted across the turf. At least they were accepting him again.

There was one bat, one ball and one leg guard. It limited the game, but to make sure that everything was quite fair they went through a complicated routine of drawing lots for first man in. There was the equally difficult business of preparing the lots to be surmounted first. Edward retired behind a tree to a place where the long pale swathes of grass grew. Plucking a handful, he counted out one for each man, nipped one shorter than the rest and then stepped out again, hand outstretched for first pickings. The lucky batsman grinned and loped off to take up his position before the wicket.

When it came to Edward's turn to bowl, he picked up the ball and let fly. After captaining St Gregory's he was getting good at it, and he could feel the power of his muscles passing right down his arm and into the ball.

'Cor – watchit! What a zinger!'

But somehow their enthusiasm did not bring any warmth to him. While they debated whether to have another game before the sun went down he stood apart, noticing a cool breeze which made a restless sea of long unmown grass round the pitch.

He left them to it and walked back through the outskirts of the town, whistling to himself and keeping one eye open for Grace Wimsett.

Grace was his own secret, shared with nobody and but for a boy called Powell he felt that he might be walking her out by now. But Powell was the snag, he was always there, making her laugh whenever Edward desperately wanted to make an impression on her. He was always hoping that she did not notice how shabby his suit was, how worn the collar and cuffs of his shirt. Powell was better dressed, more self assured. To make it worse, he worked in an office a short way down the corridor. There was no way of avoiding him. He was supposed to be one of the company's bright boys.

How did you make a hit with women? Edward's greatest ambition was to have Grace Wimsett consider him a man of the world, but she never reacted the way he thought she would. Her placid disposition and manner made him want to shout in her face. Greater than his irritation was the attraction, so always went on hoping that she would fall for him.

He cut through a passageway near her house. It would be dark soon, then there would be no chance of seeing her because her parents kept her in. He did not want to go home without seeing her. It was worth waiting.

By the place where the posts stood to prevent horses and carts passing through, he suddenly saw her small plump figure under a gas lamp. She was only about five foot six and beside him looked like a midget, but that did not matter. What was important was her reaction when he appeared. He walked on quickly until he was only a few yards away and then saw that she was with Powell. *Again*!

He waited until Saturday, knowing that she always went shopping for her mother and then headed towards the main street, moving along the edge of the pavement and staring over the heads of all the women who thronged the shops. She must be there somewhere! With her mass of auburn hair she was easy to spot. He went up and down the street twice and then found her standing on a corner. Great heavens, she was with Powell again! This time he felt no inclination to slip away unseen. One thing was in his favour, he thought, his height. He could easily bowl Powell over if there were any trouble

But nothing happened! He was all keyed up for a scuffle and showed it, yet Powell grinned at him as he approached and after saying good morning and putting his hand up in a cheeky salute to Grace he was gone, leaving Edward alone with her.

'Hello!' He started to make conversation when it struck him that he should deal with Powell once and for all. 'I'll be back ...'

Pushing through the shoppers, he caught up with him. There was no means of going round his feelings, so he came straight to the point. He squared up to his astonished rival and blurted out: 'If you ever take that girl for a walk I'll kill you!'

In the next week or two he seemed to be bumping into Powell everywhere, and was ashamed to discover that he was not such a bad type after all. For one thing, he was a great reader, and went through novel after novel. He was always talking about books.

'Don't you find anything interesting in novels, Eddie?' Edward shook his head. He had no time for fiction. 'The only book I read is the dictionary ...' he asserted.

'Really?' Powell glanced at him.

'I read it every night,' Edward added in a determined voice. He wanted to like Powell, who obviously had an insight into things and knew what was what, but Grace still stood between them. After threatening him with a quick death if ever he as much as looked at her again, he felt foolish and tried to make amends. Powell laughed it off. Quite obviously it did not matter to him one way or the other.

'What else do you do besides read the dictionary?' he queried.

Edward told him about St Gregory's cricket team and how well it was coming along now they were getting fixtures with others in the neighbourhood. And he had just joined the Terriers, too. The first parade was next week. He was thinking of taking up the bugle!

'I used to bash a drum in India ...' he said.

He went on talking about his early days, about how he found the kettle-drum and the Jew's harp, but he did not mention his father, except to say that he had been a soldier.

'Why don't you come down to Whitehall? I'm practising my bugling there ...'

That weekend they met again, Edward with the bugle wrapped up in a brown cloth bag, and they walked towards a remote spot beyond the area known as Whitehall. The bugle was no instrument for practising indoors, it made such a terrible din, but out in the fields you could blow your lungs out and nobody complained because few heard.

'Why don't you come back with me? Have some tea if you like,' Powell said carelessly. He was interested in getting to know Edward better and noticed how cleverly he avoided talking about the family. The only person he ever mentioned was Patrick.

They arrived at Powell's house. Throughout tea Edward was very quiet, barely answering questions or joining in the general conversation but it was obvious that Powell's mother liked him because she told him to come again whenever he wanted to. After the next visit, just as he was departing, she thrust a brown paper parcel in his hands. 'They're a few things we don't really need ...' Her whisper did not reach the kitchen. 'You have them, Eddie.'

On the way home he tore open the corner, curiosity eating him. The next moment he came to a stop. They were clothes! Mrs. Powell had given him clothes! He sat down on a low wall, staring at the things, all neatly folded up and well-laundered. They must be Powell's cast-offs! He felt like hiding them under a bush or a tree, anything to prevent Julia from seeing them, but the next moment knew that the parcel was too bulky for easy concealment. If he left it lying about for anybody to find, it might find its way back to Mrs. Powell. In the end he dragged home miserably, holding the string between his fingers and hoping for a last-minute miracle. The miracle did not happen. As he expected, Julia fastened on to it, untied the string and rolled it into an economical ball, and then spread all the clothing out on the table. He saw her mixed expression, knowing exactly how she felt. After some hesitation she laid everything out to air and did not refer to the matter again. Every time he went to work wearing one of Powell's laundered and mended shirts he took care to avoid him. Kindness often contained unintentional cruelty he was beginning to find.

And after a month or two neither he nor Powell had any further interest in Grace Wimsett. Edward's spare time was now taken up with the 2nd Home Counties Field Ambulance, RAMC, Territorial Unit. Clad in the thick, prickly, brown serge, he could hardly reach the drill hall quick enough to bring out his bugle, give it a gale of a blow and hear the echoing noise it made among the metal rafters. He found a new world in which everybody was equal. The well-dressed chap you saw out in the street was just the same as you as soon as he put on the uniform, that was the beauty of it. You could talk on equal terms to any of them.

Being a part-time soldier did something else for him, it helped him to stand on his own two booted feet and make up his mind to ask for a transfer to outside work. It was time he cut adrift from Patrick. There was one other reason of even greater importance: he wanted to work in the open air.

First thing one morning he walked straight out of his office and started down the long corridor towards the door marked 'Manager'. As he passed Patrick's partition he sensed that his brother's eyes were following him, filled with curiosity. Perhaps he ought to call in and explain what was going on? Patrick would only ask about it later. The next minute he went straight on.

In the normal way, he would have avoided this brown varnished door because it represented momentous things, the sack for some, promotion for others. It was a door which symbolized drastic decisions.

He paused, going over what he intended saying, and then knocked hard and decisively, breathing deeply, hoping that Patrick would not take it into his head to come thundering along at the last moment to demand what was happening.

The first thing he must explain to the manager was about his health. For once he was glad of his sallow skin because it would bear him out. He looked ill, although he felt all right at the moment...

'*Come in!*'

He might let out a few deep bronchial coughs to help things along? It was hard to cough convincingly. He had tried it earlier that morning and realized that it would fool nobody.

'Come in!'

With a start he turned the handle and entered the overpowering room with its dark furniture and church-like atmosphere. No wonder some chaps looked changed after all this!

The manager was sitting at the far end, under the window, his face in shadow. Nearby sat a secretary. Edward was counting on being alone so that he could plead his case properly. The presence of the young girl behind the typewriter put him off his stroke.

'What do you want?'

The words came out like a prison sentence. It was all Edward could do to plunge into his explanation. Halfway through his stumbling speech the sun hit the window, blinding him for a moment and he had to lift his hand to his forehead. It was very difficult to see how the manager was taking it. Had he done the right thing in coming in here in the first place? It was beginning to look unlikely.

The manager straightened his waistcoat, pulling at the points which stuck out at an angle over his large corporation. This would have to be thought about. But supposing Mannock was *always* going to have bad health, what about that? Working outside in all kinds of weathers was not the best way of improving your health, now was it?

Edward shuffled his feet. This was difficult! Perhaps he could have a try at it if that was not putting the company out, he said hopefully.

Transferring from the office staff to the outside staff was very irregular! How old was he?

Seventeen, Edward said.

Yesssss, seventeen! Well, there were age limits for outside men, did Mannock realize it? We will have to consider it.

Keeping the elation out of his voice, Edward said thank you and got out as fast as he could, but on his way back to his desk he scratched his head, wondering if he really had done the right thing.

There was no sign of Patrick. He put his head over the frosted glass but the office was empty. It was lunch time so Pat must have gone out for a walk.

His feet making an empty sound on the bare boards, Edward returned to his desk, opened a drawer and pulled out his sandwiches. He then produced a newspaper and spread it across the anonymous face of the ledger. He did this every day, enjoying a read while he munched his way through the thick sandwiches supplied by Julia.

Some chap called Rodgers had flown across America from New York to Pasadena, making several forced landings. It had taken him eighty-four hours and two minutes' flying time.

Edward re-read the report, feeling mildly interested and wondering what it must be like to be in the air all that time. Presently he turned the page to look at the photograph of Rodgers's machine. It was wonderful how a thing like that could get up into the air at all, let alone stay there! It looked so clumsy, though from what he had read it seemed that the fellows who built these flying machines had studied birds and were trying to imitate them. Rodgers's machine was not at all like that fat old crow which nested near the recreation ground. Between innings during the cricket knockabouts Edward often stood watching it as it swooped down to ground level to pick up some tidbit. It was quite tame and he was able to stand close and observe it strutting about.

He finished his sandwiches and then went out to the corner shop for a penny bottle of lemonade. On the way back he met Patrick.

'What did you do this morning?' Patrick tried to keep a hectoring tone out of his voice, but he was obviously bursting to know the news.

'Asked for a transfer. I want to work outside.' Then Edward noticed his brother's beaten expression. 'I'm sorry, Pat. I've tried, but it makes me feel so ill being in there, you know that.'

'Mother did say something about it.' Patrick's voice was faraway, as though he did not want to know about it. It was as he had feared for some time. He knew all about his father and he knew that his mother did not want Edward to go that way.

Two weeks later Edward's name was crossed off the clerical staff list and placed on the roster for duties outside with the riggers.

CHAPTER THREE

It was really quite an art keeping the steel scaling pieces straight while you shoved first one and then the other into the splintery timber of the pole. When you were halfway up and your hands in their leather gloves felt as though they were breaking, you could throw your head back and stare straight up into the clouds. If there were a wind tearing at you, trying to throw you down, it was like being aboard a schooner bound for the Indies. Then all of a sudden you remembered that you were supposed to get up to the thin crosstrees and throw one leg across and then connect those two wires so perfectly that not all the weather in creation could break the joint. Down below a couple of fellows waited, stamping their feet in the cold, laughing up their sleeves at you because you had volunteered to go up and do the job but it was a darned sight warmer scaling the pole than standing about down there!

'You be long up there, Paddy?' The nickname had quickly replaced the more formal Edward.

Another few inches, the spikes giving you plenty of purchase, and then you could get your knee across the lower crosstree and rest for a minute, looking down at them and grinning. At first it seemed a terrible height, especially when a keen wind was pulling and pushing from all directions, but you soon got used to it. Most of all you appreciated the keen tang of freedom. It was the low whistle of the wind in the wires, it was going from one place to another in the truck, drinking tea out of a mug and listening to the others talking.

His hand went up to feel for the pliers.

They drove back along the long straight roads towards Wellingborough, his new home, where the outskirts were grim, smoking, metal smelters. He found nothing pleasant about the look of the stark stone walls of the leather workshops and tanneries. Had his heart not been set on making something of himself climbing telephone poles he felt sure he could get a job in one of these solemn-looking places and earn good money at it. If that failed he might even work on the land. For miles round there were farms and he often looked at them from the truck, noticing the slow pace of life as men moved cows from one pasture to another, manured the fields, went along at the traditional pace of the farmworker. Wellingborough, Northamptonshire, was not every man's dream of Eden but it might do for a year so so.

The old restlessness still came but it retreated faster now that every day was so full. Under the influence of a timesheet he got to know the real meaning of self-discipline and to suppress the desire to move on and do something else. There was no real reason why he should do any more moving, because he was sending money home to Canterbury every week. He could almost hear Patrick's voice as it droned on through that sermon on security and a pension after thirty-five years' service.

The lorry wheels spun round as they started their long haul into Wellingborough. They were early tonight, a change from all the other times when they rolled into the town just as crowds of people poured out of the factories, slowing them down with a grinding of gears, giving them a chance to lean out and poke fun at the girls. To Edward it was not quite seemly. Beside the others he felt ignorant when it came to girls. Whenever they discussed their adventures he was always the silent one, preferring to concentrate on other things but still quietly amazed that they could even find time to take girls out when there were so many other things to grip the attention. He had already seen most of the things worth looking at, including St Luke's Church, Norman and Early English. He went there to stand in the cool of the nave on hot summer evenings. Very few girls would want to share moments like that!

As soon as they had put the truck away he shouted good night to the others and walked with a springy step towards his lodgings at 184 Mill Road. He was glad that he had left the other place, just round the corner in Eastfield Road, and come to the Eyleses, a good old-fashioned couple who regarded him as their own son.

He had met Jim Eyles as the result of a boil on the neck. Booked to play cricket for the Wellingborough Wesleyans, Eyles was in agony. Although he tried to break and drain the boil he met with no success. The time of the match drew nearer, so in desperation he turned to Edward, whom he knew slightly and liked, to substitute for him. When Saturday came and Edward drew a nought, Eyles, sensing his need for companionship, said: 'What about coming and lodging with us?' Edward, who missed home life to a certain extent, jumped at the chance and moved in. Eyles was to become a father-figure to him.

From such a cosy atmosphere he wrote reassuring letters home to his mother, putting her mind at rest and bolstering her happiness by saying that he had everything he wanted. After the hurly-burly of Canterbury the placid atmosphere of the Eyles's household took some getting used to. There were so many unexpected pleasures, like being able to talk to the Eyles and know they were listening.

He had a quick meal, then went upstairs to change into his thick khaki serge uniform. Sitting on the hard chair, he slipped his metal buttonstick under the RAMC badge and started rubbing the brass, humming quietly to himself as it glowed under the duster. Now that he was a senior NCO he had to put a little more spit and polish into the job of being a part-time soldier. It could be a damned nuisance except for the chance of meeting other fellows.

Before going out he found a few moments to read the paper.

'LARGEST SHIP IN THE WORLD ABOUT TO SAIL.'

The unsinkable vessel, built in the Belfast yards of Harland and Wolff, a honeycomb of luxury, including the 'Cafe de Paris' dining salon with its banks of exotic plants, was about to take to the ocean. What a marvel it must be!

Jim Eyles watched Edward's expression change as he grew interested in the news.

Titanic, forty-six thousand tons of unsinkable metal, was about to cross the Atlantic. It was unbelievable! Eddie should take a look at the passenger list, all printed in that small type at the bottom of the page.

Colonel and Lady Astor; Guggenheim, the banker; Jonheer Reuchlin, one of the Holland-America line directors... Eleven honeymoon couples were aboard, too.

It was a wonder such a big ship could float at all!

Ruminating on the wealth between the decks of the *Titanic*, Edward went into the backyard and pulled out his old bicycle. Pushing it through the narrow entry, he steadied the machine at the kerb and then set off for the barracks. It would soon be time to go to camp, and there would be a chance of meeting some of his old friends, including one or two from Canterbury. The focal point of the Territorial year was the annual camp and they always tried to bring as many companies into it as possible. Even if it rained all the time, it was still worthwhile.

When Edward started totting up the way he spent his spare time, he always seemed busy. There was the RAMC, and the Wesleyan Cricket Club where he was wicket-keeper. He enjoyed squatting behind the sticks, waiting to make a swift catch or crash the ball down on the wickets to send the bails flying. What he was really interested in was the Parliamentary Debating Society, because it brought him out of himself. He had just been elected secretary of the local 'Labour Party' and discovered in himself an aptitude for laying down the law. This was, they said, 'the Irish in him', and as a result the 'Opposition' was always pulling his leg about it. He often felt like asking them if they really believed in what they were doing, backing the Tories, but that would not have been within the rules. He acknowledged that he had a more passionate love of Socialism than any of the others realized. No matter how rough a man might be, if his heart were in the right place then he was all right! Had he been able to meet Keir Hardie, who was under fierce fire from the right wing of the Labour Party, he would have shaken him by the hand.

Pedalling on towards the drill hall, he forced his heavy Army boots down on the narrow pedals, trying to pick up some speed because he did not want to be late. At the next Labour Party meeting he would raise the question of the new spread of the Independent Labour Party.

His mind still on Hardie, he parked his bicycle against the drill hall wall, and remembered reading about Hardie's alliance with Edouard Vaillant to call a general strike through the Socialist International in the event of war. A strike of that size might be the wrong thing to do, it could lead nowhere. Brushing himself down and correcting the folds above his puttees, he felt that his allegiance was to the uniform, not Hardie's latest declaration. All the same, it would be hard to desert that tough old Lanarkshire miner. But the way the Germans kept rattling their cavalry sabres showed how prepared you had to be. Being an instinctive Socialist could put you in some difficult positions.

As he entered the drill hall to start greeting his friends he wondered what personal politics would mean if trouble between England and Germany did happen. A lot of people would laugh in your face for even suggesting that a war could break out, but none of them really bothered to study the papers and try to put a construction on the trend of events. All they did was swallow whatever was ladled out. Some commentators were now concentrating on the tall stack of treaties which had been signed by the great continental powers, and many of them seemed to think that nothing could possibly go wrong while all those signatures were neat and tidy. Dealing with the honourable heads of state of such settled and reliable areas as Belgium, Prussia, Holland and France could not be compared with keeping order among the squabbling Balkan states, where cordite was always a familiar smell in the air.

Sniffing at the pleasant combination of saddle soap and leather in the drill hall, Edward moved forward, listening to some of the jokes and ribaldry. He found it hard to understand the brutal sexual humour of the average ranker. Out of uniform, he knew them as tradesmen's assistants, craftsmen, mostly men who earned a living by serving others. Once they got into khaki they changed. Something made him want to step aside from them while his Socialist belief in the importance of the ordinary man forced him to try to take part.

Parades lasted only an hour or two, and they were then free to go home or to the pubs. He preferred to slip away. Pub talk was no different from drill hall chatter, and he saw no point in wasting time.

A blue mist hung over the lower land as he pushed the bike up the hill and coasted down the other side. In the evening light he noticed an increase in the number of lambs in an enclosed pasture as he flashed by. Spring was a good time to be alive! You became more alert, more sensitive, you paused and listened, and you could almost hear the old earth creaking as all the new growth started shooting up.

Round the rough brown boles of the elders, near the river, straight pale green shoots were starting to show. He often fingered them, appreciating their texture as he sat looking down at the quiet stream, waiting for a fish to push up its nose. He could smile at it now, but he had one memory of the rough face of the water bailiff who caught him red-handed as he cast his line into a stretch of protected water. The bailiff bawled crudely as he crashed into view. *Protected*, he shouted. Challenged by Edward, he grunted that it was owned by Sir Somebody-or-Other, who certainly did not want all the rif-raff chucking their dirty old lines and hooks in his preserves.

'Get out! Go on, bugger off!' The bailiff waved his arms about, prepared to fight.

Edward suggested that if he used a more reasonable tone he might have achieved more, but seeing that he was adopting such an ugly tone he could go and jump in the lake and Sir Somebody with him!

The bailiff charged him, making animal sounds. His fist shot out and if Edward had not been quick to move he would have ended up in deep water. In the next moment Edward managed to circle round him and throw a strangling bear hug.

'I'll have you up in court for this... you...' The bailiff's face was blue with bad temper and shock at being assaulted.

'You made the first assault,' Edward reminded him firmly.

'This length o' river belongs to'

'It belongs to nobody. It was given by God. How can you argue about it?'

'You talk like a Socialist!' he grunted, rubbing his sore wrist when Edward released him.

'I *am* a Socialist!' Edward yanked the line out of the water, noticing that the fly had been nibbled and regretting that he had not seen the trout in time. 'Anything wrong in that?'

The bailiff started to explain that you heard a lot of things about these Socialists, and none of it good. Socialists didn't know their place, that was the trouble, and

England would be a better place if young chaps spent more time thinking about keeping to their place in life

Tucking his last piece of equipment into a canvas rucksack, Mannock stared the bailiff in the eye for a moment, not bothering to hide his quizzical grin, then started tramping back the way he had come. As soon as he reached a bend in the bank, he shouted: 'I'm still a Socialist. Give my regards to your master ...'

The incident stayed in Edward's mind. Why did that water bailiff seem to personify the ignorance of the working classes? It was all wrong! With a stout loyal spirit like that a man of his sort could become a fine Socialist. Surely he could believe as passionately in the working class cause, the righting of indignities and injustices, as he did in his master's interests. It must be a question of a dull brain and settled wage.

The Eyleses watched his development, and they could not help wondering what was coming next with him. To them he seemed to be a young man who never did anything by halves. There were times when he seemed so restless, and even his long trips out over the countryside did nothing to ease him. It had for some time been obvious to both of them that something was worrying him. It never occurred to them that it was the cosy security of their house which was in conflict with his growing restlessness.

At last he exploded his bombshell. He said that he was thinking of going abroad by working his passage.

Abroad? Now? They were staggered and perhaps a little hurt. It didn't seem the right thing to do with all this trouble going on, had he thought of that? Yes, he said, he had but it made no difference really.

The Eyleses were such good kindly people that he did not want to hurt them by appearing to reject their hospitality. In weekly letters to his mother he had often referred to them as his 'second mother and father', a sentiment which seemed to come quite naturally to him. He had never known a home such as they offered him, and the physical break was going to hurt all of them. When they asked him what he was going to do he was diffident about discussing his plans in detail and it took several days before he really opened his heart and told them that he was desperate for money. He diffidently hinted that what he needed was a loan, not very much but just enough to take him by the cheapest possible means, perhaps a cargo ship, to a foreign country.

They sat listening to him, stifling all their objections and knowing that they must do anything to help if it made him happy and helped him along in his career. When they pressed him about his intentions abroad, he said: 'I'm going to become a successful engineer, tea planter or rancher.' Smiling faintly at their undisguised credulity, he added: 'I feel it's the duty of every man to try to raise himself to whatever heights his ideals take him, whether they're spiritual or worldly. It only requires determination to try ...'

They nodded. Perhaps he was right, but it was so difficult to reconcile a discussion like this in the ease of the parlour with all the hardships he may have to endure while pursuing the lively fox of ambition. Did he realize what he was up against? He looked so young and unblooded, sitting there, and stumbling through his philosophy of life. They knew that his experience was limited to Canterbury and Wellingborough. He was popular in the Terriers, and everybody said he was a good chap. But all that was not enough! It might quite be another story when he stepped ashore at the other end because he would be a stranger there

They agreed to lend him the money. They had to. It was a case of the heart ruling the head. Jim Eyles appealed to his own brother to make up the sum, but in the end it was done and the cash paid over to Edward, who promised to give it back out of his wages as soon as he got a job. He started preparing for the trip, not very sure exactly where he was going until he heard about a cable-laying contract in Turkey. He would work his passage!

He went to see his mother and Patrick, then solemnly shook hands with each of his sisters. To them it all seemed a bit of a lark, their Ed going off like that. Patrick was serious, he did not think it right. Edward should be careful, he must write frequently. Some terrible things happened, and with the Germans being in such a state it could mean trouble.

Edward went aboard the tramp steamer and a few hours later watched the quay vanish into the mist. There was a strange stillness about it all and the February air carried sounds so that they had a new sharpness. A gull standing on the foremast, started hawking at the top of its voice like an aggravated pilot, determined to get the ship through to the open sea without mishap. Edward craned forward to make out its shape and as it clattered away with a clicking of wings felt the link being severed. Something like a shiver of fear went through him as he went below to the hot little cabin. Relaxing on his bunk, he thought over the past...

...it was queer about chaps like Patrick, standing there with their neat haircuts and good suits, shoes and faces shining, all wrapped up in their safe cocoons. They were like some of the people H G Wells wrote about in *Ann Veronica'*... old-fashioned people... knew right from wrong; they had a clearcut religious faith that seemed to explain everything and give a rule for everything...'

...Wells was a good Socialist; he knew a thing or two when it came to people. Edward remembered Mrs Miniver who said in *Ann Veronica* that everything was 'working up' to Socialism and the men and women in the movement would some day make history.

Edward yawned and fell asleep.

The rusty freighter moved on through seas which after a few days became placid. One meal followed another, all composed of solid food badly cooked, but Edward did not care so long as they kept on moving towards Turkey. He would have lived off ships' biscuits and salt water for the sake of being able to get there. He started blessing the day he broke away from the cosy life at Wellingborough. The only painful episode, which remained disturbingly clear, was that farewell meal with the Eyles, but despite the nostalgic sadness which he felt when he remembered their kindness, he was confident that he would some day sail home prosperous and let them see that their faith in him was justified. It was somehow different with his mother and Patrick; they would take whatever he said and think, '*Ah well, that's our Edward*' and leave it at that. The Eyleses were different, quite different. Perhaps they were more human.

In a letter to them he found it hard to control the nostalgia which crept into his brain as he sat there, pen in hand, doing his best to portray himself as a self-reliant man of the world. 'How I long to have a night with you and the old piano...' and then he recovered himself and passed on to the future, the tough, uncompromising future which he wanted to grasp with both hands.

There was time now to have a systematic think about politics. He knew that he would always be a strong Socialist, but wanted to ally political strength with a religious conviction. Christ and Buddha, Shelley and Tennyson, even old Keir Hardie, they seemed to be imbued with that divine spark which made them stand out like great leaping flames above the smoking smoulder of ordinary men.

He paced up and down the airless cabin, glancing now and then through the porthole to the sea, which washed by almost at eye level.

The real trouble was that men enclosed themselves and would not come out. In Socialism he saw the prime mover of a completely open and free society without any distinctions. In the golden age you would be able to go up to a man and talk to him as an equal even if he did happen to own the big house in the wood at the far end of the village. You could always do that with ordinary people like the Eyles, but the big chap looked at you as though you were mad because he was frightened of being contaminated by your ideas.

Remembering the water bailiff, Edward had to admit that it worked both ways. The gentry infected the working classes. What was worse, the working classes seemed to enjoy being infected! It would be interesting to see what sort of conditions prevailed in Turkey.

When he arrived in Constantinople with only fifty shillings in his pocket there was very little time to investigate social conditions. He had to get a job almost at once or starve. Fifty shillings might keep him going for a couple of weeks, but he had no idea how much it would cost to live in this noisy crowded city.

He seized on the first idea that came into his head, telephones, remembering the government cable-laying job. Visions of riding the range or planting tea on vast estates with small armies of coloured men to do his bidding dissolved when he examined his finances. It was going to have to be bread and butter at once. Ideas must be left on the shelf.

He examined the stained pages of his pocket diary. It was now February 1914, and by the end of the year he would probably be doing so well that he would be able to look around for something more to his liking. The thought of the eleven months of hard work did not deter him. A lot could happen in that time ...

The next thing, after finding somewhere to leave his small amount of luggage, was to find an Englishman to talk to. Once he did this he was sure to find a job.

He set out to scour Constantinople in the beating sunshine, walking slowly from one street to another, scanning notice boards on all the office buildings. Several near-English sounding ones he rejected as being risky, and then, quite by accident, he found one which said *English Telephone Company*.

Climbing up the wooden stairs he quickly smoothed down his hair and wiped the perspiration off his face with his handkerchief. At the top he discovered several doors, each labelled in English and Turkish, but none of them looked right, so he walked on down a corridor, hoping to meet somebody.

Somewhere in the distance he could hear the spasmodic tapping of a typewriter. He wanted to avoid secretaries, they always fobbed you off, he knew that from experience.

Near a bend in the corridor he halted in front of a door marked 'Manager', breathed deeply, knocked and marched straight in. Without examining the man behind the desk he rattled off the fact that he had been working for the telephone company at Wellingborough, omitting to lay too much stress on the fact that he had done practically nothing but climb telephone poles, and saying rather saucily that young men of resourcefulness and initiative were needed in these overseas areas. After all, he *had* managed to work his passage out from England and that took some doing.

The silence which followed showed no signs of abating. He looked fixedly through the window, counting minarets, wondering when he would be sent clattering down the stairs. Impressed, but hiding his feelings, the manager slowly lit his pipe and drew hard on it, his shrewd eyes following the thick stream of blue smoke as it eddied up from the briar bowl. After laying the matchbox down on the desk, he grinned. Edward's face remained straight as he explained that he had heard about the contract for the Turkish Government before leaving England.

It was a strange coincidence, the manager finally said, that Mister Mannock had chosen to walk in at that precise moment, just when there was a first-class crisis on. Although the company had managed to open up a number of new exchanges and lay just so much cable, using the existing manpower, the pressure was being put on by the Turks to complete the balance of the now overdue contract. The trouble was there were simply not enough men to do it! If he had everybody working round the clock – impossible with skilled labour! – the contracts would never be met within the time limit to which the company had agreed. What they really needed was a sort of junior supervisory man to go round and check on things and see that all the jobs were being carried out correctly. But before anybody could be appointed – and here he stared pointedly at his caller, who now felt more at ease – they must be sure that whoever did the job would serve a short 'apprenticeship' to get acquainted with local conditions and some of the problems. There were plenty of problems.

Mannock started at once, and was immediately fascinated by the activities of a company which managed to persuade a handful of Englishmen and the quarrelsome Turks to work together. Work was confined not only to the city districts, it spread into the rural areas over hundreds of miles of the most desolate face of Asia Minor where outposts had to be linked up. Because the lines passed over uninhabited areas it meant going out and living rough for days at a time, shepherding a work gang and trying to urge them on to get the jobs finished. In desperation Edward bought a phrase book and stumbled through the idioms to try to make himself understood. Turkish was, he quickly realized, one of the most difficult languages, and his life became a running battle against the determination of the gangers and his anxiety to satisfy the company.

Beyond Constantinople rocks and the sun were the enemies, combining to cloak a man in heat of unbelievable humidity one day and arid dryness the next. Even the slightest effort called for vast reserves of energy. He felt that he must go on with it, all the time conscious of the gangers trying to cheat him. He did not want to lose his temper with them, it might mean a mass walk-out. Some of the English overseers tried bullying them with the result that the gangers never worked at all. Some slunk away and were not seen again until payday, others were smitten with sudden deafness.

The work went on right through the spring of 1914 and into the beginning of a summer of ever-increasing heat, but he had not been able to save enough to move on. It would be hard to leave now, despite the oppressive temperature and the aggravation of conditions. While he had tried to remain detached, he was soon caught up in the job, feeling that he must contribute something definite towards establishing this network of communications. There was after all a great amount of satisfaction in watching the figures on the office progress board change from day to day as new exchanges and links came into commission.

And then it was June, hotter than ever, bringing dysentery and fever to the Europeans.

On June 23rd the Archduke Franz Ferdinand was also feeling the heat as he travelled from Vienna South Station towards the Balkans with his entourage. That night he grumbled about the failure of the electric supply when he planned to spend the evening reading official reports on a large number of subjects. One in particular interested him. It was about political troubles in Bosnia and Herzegovina, an insoluble problem caused by the 1906 annexation.

A member of his suite knocked and came in with several candles which he carefully placed in holders on the wall. Upset by this disruption of his routine, the Archduke started to prowl about, the sheaf of reports fluttering in his hand. 'This is beginning to look like a catafalque!' Before the man could escape he ordered him to put out all the candles except one. The reports would have to wait unless the electricity supply came on again.

The train started gathering speed. A wagon axle which had been causing trouble ever since the start of the trip was now repaired. The driver told the fireman that they would make up the schedule during the night.

Edward wiped his face and compared curses with one of the English wiremen about the climate. It was a bit too much today, but they must finish off this stretch. His colleague lit a cigarette, flicking the match towards the Turkish workers, who lay like logs in the shadow of a village wall. They were on strike, an unofficial protest against – the way they were being driven. Neither Edward nor his colleague felt inclined to argue with them. There was not a great deal to be done and it was easier to finish it off between them than run any more blockades of violent language and angry gestures. The Turks were a strange race, Edward mused, always shouting the odds, and they certainly disliked the British. As far as he could make out they preferred the Germans and only by a financial fluke had the British secured this contract.

He started sorting out the tools and fitting them into the scarred hide satchels. The Turks made no move to help him, although this was part of their job.

Sometimes it was hard to be a Socialist.

CHAPTER FOUR

...I'm not climbing telegraph poles now. No more climbing irons for me! Diagrams and a blue pencil! But my feet, eyes and heart ache!

He rounded the letter off with a few more thoughts, sealed it up and addressed the envelope to Mr and Mrs Eyles in Wellingborough, then went out to the post office. It was true that within the last few weeks he had been elevated to the status of an 'office man' and it meant that no longer did he have to go out with the labouring gangs. But mental work, checking documents and keeping things moving was, he soon found, more wearing on the health than sweating under the Turkish sun. It reminded him of his early days in the office at Canterbury. Although pen-pushing was never his forte, he had to make the best of it.

On the way back from the post office he paused at the stationers to buy the latest English paper, already nearly a week old but about all you could get in Constantinople. He hunted through the pages for any development in the Central European situation.

News of the murder on June 28th, 1914, in Sarajevo of the Archduke Franz Ferdinand and his morganatic wife, the Duchess of Hohenburg, had lain dormant for about four weeks. Apart from a few lines after the first wrathful explosion of public opinion, the subject had withered. Only when you took the trouble to examine the growing situation – and few people could be bothered doing that – did you start feeling somewhat apprehensive. Ever since hearing about it Edward had been telling people that Ferdinand's death might lead to something of enormous proportions.

His eyes did not miss a report about the peremptory note sent by the Austrian Government to Serbia, demanding reparations for the death of Ferdinand (but how could you make reparations for shooting a man to death?) and asking for certain safeguards for the future. The Serbians were placed in a difficult position. Nevertheless, to appease the ranting Austrians they made a reply of a sort.

Whenever he tried to talk about the stretched tension in Europe with some of his younger colleagues, Edward was usually cried down. Who wanted to chatter about politics in this heat? What between labour disputes and all the different pressures exerted by the Turks on the company to get the job done, the international situation was not really worth a brass farthing out here. Sometimes they did listen quite patiently to his careful voice as he explained what the Serbian-Austrian wrangle could lead to, but then there would be an outburst of laughter and he had to give up. They were too young. At twenty-seven he felt practically ancient.

His loyalties were strangely divided by a kind of political and personal mitosis. So many things were happening in the world that it was impossible for a man of his sort to isolate himself. Enough heat had been generated in Ireland to make him angry with the British, the more so since Ulster had proclaimed her right to resist any usurping of her authority by an Irish national parliament. Edward went to great lengths to understand the Irish question, but in comparison Europe was far more important.

What price Socialism at a time when the politics of the thick-set, heavy-blooded men of Europe stood so many worlds away from the volatile appeal of Keir Hardie's creed? Edward had often considered his Socialist orientation in relation to England, and it seemed that he must discover the heart of it, something through which he could drive his stake of belief and say 'This is my political faith'. He had become a man of causes without any particular cause to which he could adhere. The knowledge troubled him as he lived and worked in the vacuum of British society in Turkey.

A friend who listened to his doubts told him that if one country stuck out its tongue at its neighbour, the rest followed suit. Countries were like children.

Edward stared at him in surprise. 'You think it's as simple as all that?' he demanded belligerently. 'Just sticking out tongues?'

'Well, there might be a bit of stone-throwing, too.'

'There could be war as easy as that!' Edward snapped his fingers.

'We'll just have to wait and see, won't we?'

His place in the telephone company was of such importance that he was often called into the manager's office to give advice about certain matters. One day he was asked to wait until a conference finished, so he settled on a chair outside the main office, pulling a book out of his pocket. As he sat there, reading, he could hear upraised voices followed by a period of silence and then a fresh outburst, most of it in rapid Turkish. About half an hour later the disputants trooped out, half of them Turks and all looking grim. None of them even glanced at him.

Edward entered a conference room thick with tobacco smoke. The manager waved him to a seat, exhausted but just able to lift a limp hand. 'I'd trade this job for anything they've got to offer back home.' He yawned and stretched, passing over his tobacco pouch and watching Edward fill a pipe. 'Don't you ever feel like that, Eddie? Ah, but I was forgetting, you came and you asked for this. I was *ordered* to do it. One volunteer's worth ten pressed men …' He took a hold of himself and brightened up. 'How're things in your department?'

Edward admitted that he was happy enough so long as the work could be kept moving. And, of course, he had other interests, horse-riding, croquet

'Aye, so I've heard,' the manager put in dryly, holding a match to his briar, then tossing the box across. 'The lassies –'

Embarrassed, Edward abruptly changed the subject. As a matter of fact, he had taken to wearing a gentleman's wedding ring to keep the 'lassies' at bay.

'Well now, we'd better get down to these progress sheets.' The manager flattened them out and started comparing the figures with Edward's information.

Quite a lot of the work was practically finished, but that did not mean the end of the contract, because there were some troublesome clauses about maintenance and the training of Turkish personnel to take over when the English company completed the installation. It was not going to be very easy, recruiting the best men for such involved work in a country like this. They settled down to discuss the problem.

Later, as they adjourned to a nearby bar for a much needed drink, Edward happened to remark on the international situation. Mention of it brought the manager to a stop and he looked pained. 'Now, don't start telling me this is going to affect us, Eddie, because I won't believe it! It's a lot of political nonsense, like old women haverin'...'

Edward produced the latest newspaper and ran his pencil round a report about a telegram which had been sent from London by Sir Edward Grey, the Foreign Minister, to Sir Edward Goschen, the British ambassador in Berlin. Although it was in hopeful terms, there was an underlying note of trepidation if not actual fear. Grey was no fool, he knew the Germans through and through. The situation was making strong men weak, and the Franco-Russian alliance existed as the great touch-fuse. In the middle of a situation in which so many nations were tensely poised came France's statement that she would have to act in her own interests. The game of demand and surrender between countries went on.

'Trust Grey to look yellow – he's a Liberal!' exclaimed the manager, a Tory supporter.

And then the Germans started to mobilize. Edward was among the first to go and see the manager when the news came through. It was impossible to get an answer to any questions. The manager said philosophically: 'I've thought about it, too Eddie, but no matter what sort of an optimist you feel like being, you've got to admit that part of Turkey is friendly towards Germany. If the Germans invade Belgium it'll spread.'

'What about Turkey, then?' Edward asked.

'Shotgun wedding between Germany and Turkey I expect.' If Turkey did go into wartime partnership with Germany it would obviously be a poor prospect for everybody in the English colony. One solace, if it could be called that, was Turkey's insistence on the early completion of the telephone contract. They needed communications now and the English were probably the only ones who could finish the job. The manager told Edward that they might just possibly be safe from any interference, but it could not be guaranteed. The Turks generally fired first and then asked questions.

Hanging suspended by a thin cord over this brewing maelstrom, Edward half regretted coming to Turkey in the first place. Had he still been in England he would have joined up at once in his old Territorial Army company, which must by now be geared to the emergency. He was still on the strength, though his name had been placed on the suspended list to cover his absence abroad. All he could do now was wait, and the waiting made him bad tempered and angry over the antics of the old careerists of European politics.

On Sunday, August 2nd, 1914, German and French troops marched. The European frontiers were quickly fenced with soldiers, standing like hounds ready for the unleashing.

Edward was standing near the croquet court with a pretty English girl. He had known her for two or three weeks and she seemed to like him. This was her fourth attempt at light romance. All the others had limped to a stop, partly because of his blunt attitude towards such matters as excessive education and an objection to the strict class levels which held the English colony together. Ordinary girls called him moody while the more perceptive ones considered him interesting but hard to understand.

He was about to hit when he noticed the figure of the company manager hurrying through the ranks of deck chairs, waving to him. He gaily waved back and served the ball. The next moment a loud and urgent shout made him stop the game and rush to the edge of the court. The very air felt tight.

'*It's started*,' the manager gasped, catching his breath after running all the way from the office.

Throwing down his mallet, Edward at once went and changed, then rushed to telephone company head office to find the place thronged with employees, demanding news. There was very little news to give. The situation was still hazy. One thing was firm enough: Britain, France and Russia were all standing together, and from the tone of the latest ultimatums it appeared that Asia Minor and Northeast Africa might soon become battlegrounds.

'Enver Pasha's behind this. Look at all those German officers he's got in the Turkish Army!' somebody exclaimed. 'He's a damned fox!'

Enver Pasha was the army commander and leader of a splinter group in favour of opposing Britain and her allies. He had entered the army in 1896 and rose to be military attache in Berlin, where he gained his affiliation with Prussianism, which created in him a duality of militarism and politics.

Eight days later an incident took place which seemed to signpost the future.

On August 10th the *Goeben* and *Breslau*, German naval vessels, sailed into the Dardanelles. They had been charged with the job of harassing the British trade routes beyond the Suez Canal but a miscalculation threw the operation out and they were detected and chased by a British naval vessel, HMS *Gloucester*, whose smoke the Germans mistook for that of a squadron. *Goeben*'s captain suddenly altered his plans and raced at full speed for the shelter of the Dardanelles, closely followed by *Breslau*. Both were cutting through the water at about twenty-eight knots and the *Gloucester* could not get close enough to head them off. A few salvoes did only minor damage and the Germans fired back with eleven-inch guns to some effect.

Safe in Turkish waters, the crews and officers of the two German ships were feted as heroes by the Turkish military authorities and most of the population turned out to welcome them. One of the captains was received in special audience by the Sultan. The incident was just what Enver Pasha needed.

Edward watched it all with mixed feelings, hearing later that the allied ambassadors in Turkey had sent a message to the Sultan which said that by international law *Goeben* and the *Breslau* must depart within twenty-four hours, otherwise they would have to be interned.

The Turks must now finally make up their minds whose side they were going to be on in the war.

Some hours went by before the Sultan informed the allied ambassadors that he had *bought* the *Goeben* and *Breslau*, and they were now his property. After such a long delay in receiving an answer, it was not difficult to detect in this coup the hand of Berlin. Alone, the Turks would never have been so smart!

Edward was one of many who thought that Turkey must side once and for all with Germany. Within a few days of the sudden arrival of the Goeben and Breslau, representatives of the telephone company went to meet the Turkish authorities. When the British firmly asked permission to pack up and go home the Turks did not know how to deal with the request. One section was all in favour of letting the British go, another wanted them thrown in prison. The Turkish press was now enthusiastically pro-German and public opinion, easily swayed in a backward country, soon viewed the British colony with primitive hostility.

Some people did carry on with their work, Edward among them, although none of them could be paid because all the banks were closed. The war was now beginning to make itself felt and food had grown short. When criticized for working in such an intolerable situation, Edward said that the contract between the company and the Turks had never been rescinded or cancelled and it should be completed. He made several mild enemies but did not much care how they felt. His best friend was a hollow walking stick full of gold sovereigns as insurance against the unknown future. He was waiting for something to happen. One day, when he and the rest of the staff were asked to attend a special meeting in the manager's office, it did.

There was very little joking as they filed in. Men chewed at their pipe stems, blew their noses loudly, lit cigarettes and stubbed them out a moment later. Discussion was stilted.

The manager entered, followed by a worried-looking Turkish Government representative. The manager spoke first. He said that every employee should get out of the country as quickly as possible and return to Britain, but this might be difficult for two reasons, the first being that the Turks wanted the contract completed, and the second that the Germans had assumed control one hour ago. They said that the British must finish the job.

While the room shook with protests the Turkish representative tried weakly to explain his Government's point of view. Where defiance had been mild it now rose to a savage howl. Edward joined in. He saw no reason why they should work for the Germans. His loyalty towards the company was instantly dissolved in an acid hatred of the men responsible for this situation.

In a deadlocked atmosphere all work on the telephone installation came to a stop. Edward went to his apartment and packed a case, ready to get out as soon as the chance materialized. During the waiting time he wrote a number of letters, one to the Eyleses in Wellingborough and others to his mother and Patrick in Canterbury. It was all he could do at present and he wanted to reassure them that whatever they might read in the newspapers, the real situation was not quite so bad as it might appear.

The Germans now began to import bullion into Turkey while trying to talk a reluctant Grand Vizier and Sultan into cooperating with them. Under Enver Pasha the Turkish Army could be built up on large gold reserves, but the heads of the Turkish state refused to agree to the virtual takeover. The Germans, aided by Enver Pasha and Talaat Bey, told the stubborn Grand Vizier that he must resign, and it soon appeared that the Germans were impatient to use the Turks in an offensive war in the Middle East theatre. The Sultan and Grand Vizier were standing in the way of military progress.

Writing home practically every day, Edward told his mother that there was very little chance of getting out of Turkey at the moment. For days he tried to work out a method of getting an emergency telegram to her, but it was one of the small ironies that while he knew the communications system backwards, there was no small loophole through which he could slip a message. The Germans were beginning to arrive. Their eyes were everywhere. It looked like a military occupation.

In November the British Minister, Sir Lewis Mallet, and his staff packed their bags and left Constantinople.

'Let's wait and see what happens now.' The manager's eyes went from one anxious face to another. 'They might chuck us out. That would suit us all. We'll get back to the old country somehow and we know what to do from there …'

That night they were arrested and imprisoned. The Turks did not bother giving any reason, but they later discovered that while the Turks had tried to get them out of the country a German general countermanded the arrangement. Lugging his suitcase along through the darkness, urged on by the sharp prodding of a rifle barrel, Edward swore and cursed as he held on tightly to his 'savings bank' cane which might still come in useful. Without the calming influence of the others he would have turned round and converted the ignominious march to the bastille into a free fight.

Sitting in the cold stone cell, he tried to organize a roll call, to find out who had been arrested. For some moments none of the familiar names answered and his heart sank. Down the corridor there were some women. He could hear the old ones crying while the young ones comforted them.

He went to the bars and shouted heartily, 'It'll be all right. Don't start worrying about it!'

Someone in the next cell growled: 'You're an optimist, aren't you?'

'I'm an Irishman so what else can I be?' Edward wiped cold sweat off his face, bunching a grubby handkerchief in his fist. 'We're lucky. They've given us the best hotel.'

'Oh, dry up…'

Frowning, Edward went back to the stone ledge which was both chair and bed and started working things out, the precious cane across his knees. His thoughts churned round and round until he dozed off, sitting upright. In the middle of the night he suddenly woke up and said out loud: 'Damn and blast the Germans!' then went off to sleep again.

The Turkish conception of imprisonment was based on a primitive desire to humiliate and annoy the prisoners. In the next few days it was perfectly obvious that they could not expect any measure of understanding or kindness from the slouching turnkeys. Edward cited what little he knew of the rules of war to them, but they took no notice except to spit in his face. When the cells fell into a filthy state, he protested again, and this time it had some effect. They were all moved into fresh cells and once more left to their own devices. The health of some of the weaker ones was beginning to deteriorate.

Stories of Turkish behaviour filtered down the long grey corridor. Some of the young women had been molested by the guards. The older women were segregated and refused special toilet facilities. Morale was falling.

Feeling faint and weak after the poor diet, Edward spent feverish hours rattling the bars until an officer appeared. He stared into space as the haggard-faced man protested about the treatment of the women.

'I want a visitor,' Edward added.

'Visitor no allowed.'

'I insist. I want to see the governor.'

'Name of your visitor, plis…'

Edward gulped and leaned against the grille. 'Ali Hamid Bey. He worked with me in the telephone company. You needn't worry, he won't pass me a file.'

'I will inquire.' The officer walked away. There seemed very little hope that the English-loving Hamid would be allowed to enter the prison, let alone talk to any of the British prisoners. But after a few days Edward was roused from his sleep and looked up to find his old assistant standing on the other side of the bars. It was a grand reunion for both of them. Hamid was ashamed of what had happened. After working with the British for so long and being well paid he was quick to condemn the attitude of his countrymen.

'Thank you very much.' Edward grasped his hand through the bars. 'Can you help us?'

Hamid shrugged. 'I will try, sir.' It was obviously impossible to say too much.

'We need food. Anything at all, so long as it can be eaten. And news. Can you find out what's happening?'

Hamid frowned. 'Sir, I do not understand this war. It is going on now and that is all I know. I am an ignorant man ...'

The Turks could not hope to confine them to the cells indefinitely. A few deaths might cause trouble with the Americans who had set up commissions to hold a watching brief on what was happening. Cut off from the world, Edward wondered if there were any slight chance that some diplomatic pressure could be brought to bear, perhaps through the Americans, to improve the situation. There were rumours that news of their imprisonment was known outside, but as yet nothing had happened.

Suddenly the Turks decided to move them into a camp. This was certainly better than the cells, if only for the slackening of security. The bars were replaced with barbed wire and they were given a little more liberty behind the entanglements. Edward could not rest, nor could he be as philosophic as the others as he prowled about like an angry tiger, stopping now and then to have violent arguments with some of the men who a few weeks ago had been his colleagues. They looked strangely placid as though the predicament could not be helped. It was all Edward could do to resist taking them by the shoulders and shaking them out of lethargy into reality.

His burning mind consumed his physical health and like some of the others he broke out into ugly sores which quickly went septic for lack of washing and proper dressings. When they did report sick they were given a cursory treatment which did not help. The sores spread to their arms and legs.

Returning from treatment one day, Edward met the girl with whom he had been playing croquet when news of war came. He halted, grinning and patting his soiled clothing. 'Hardly white flannels, are they?'

She shyly shook her head. 'Hello ...'

There did not seem much more to say until he cracked a joke about the situation and told her that he had been ragging the doctor. A guard knocked him across the ear and it was bleeding slightly, but he disregarded it in his satisfaction of pulling Turkish legs.

'I'm getting up a concert tomorrow,' he said airily. 'You must come along and enjoy yourself.'

'*Concert?*' She looked aghast as though he proposed going boating.

'Nothing else to do is there? Thought we might all sing 'Rule Britannia' and 'God Save the King'.'

'The Turks won't like *that*.'

He started on his way towards the tent. 'I know,' he said cheerfully. 'That's why we're going to have a concert.'

They were both right. When the Turks heard the familiar songs being bellowed out, led by Edward, they could do nothing about it except make threatening gestures. There was no rule to prevent prisoners-of-war singing. Soldiers tried to break up the 'concert party', but Edward quickly re mustered his singing group and laughing audience in another sector of the camp and the singing started all over again.

A few evenings later, in his wanderings round the entanglement, he came on a weak place in the wire. It looked like a good bolthole.

Without sharing his secret, he managed to squirm out when night came and walked into Constantinople to try and locate Ali Hamid Bey. The risks were enormous. With Germans and Turks in the streets he could be shot down without being challenged. By this time he was known as a troublemaker and Turks and Germans alike would be glad of any excuse to get rid of him.

By dodging through the network of back alleys, he soon found his bearings and finally edged into Hamid's home, prepared to wait until dawn if he happened to be out. Fortunately his old friend was in. The two men sat talking for a time until Edward remembered the terrible shortage of food in the camp. He said the men with whom Hamid had worked were literally starving because they passed most of their rations over to the women. Hamid said no more. He rose and filled a small sack with bread, cheese and cooked meat and then gave it to Edward, dismissing the grateful thanks.

The trip back through the sweltering night was easy and Edward was in the camp well before dawn, hugging the sack of food to his body. After roll-call he quickly shared it out, making sure that the larger part went to the women. He had just finished his mercy mission when he was called to the commandant's office. Swaying weakly from a sudden paroxysm of dysentery, he was told that he would be punished severely if he broke out again. They had seen him issuing the food and deduced that he must have been out to get it. A few nights later he managed to stagger through the wire for a second time, stumbling through the city to see Hamid again. This time he could barely manage the weight of the sack of food, light though it actually was. As he crawled back to his tent he was halted by a guard and searched.

They put him in solitary confinement for a few days in a tent apart from the others. A nest of septic sores under his armpit made him sweat as the poison filtered into his bloodstream. Lying on a rough bed, he managed to keep his spirits up by singing as loudly as possible. The rest fell silent, listening to him. He may have been a crazy Irishman to the cynics, but to others, including a solid contingent of women, he was nothing short of a martyr, and some of them smuggled letters out to friends in Britain, mentioning his refusal to be downed by the sadistic Turks.

Malnutrition and the sores which would not heal nearly killed him.

Punishment diet was designed to make a man weak and barely keep him alive. He gulped down whatever they brought him, lumps of black bread coarsened by the addition of bad flour and a bowl of warm water with grey dust floating on the top. Most days the temperature was so hot that he could barely manage to muster enough saliva to chew the bread. The only way it could be forced down was by making a dark revolting mash of it with the water. As he crammed it into his mouth with his fingers, watched by an amused guard, he shut his eyes and tried not to gag.

'England is finish,' the guard grimaced, rolling his eyes. Smiling weakly, Edward lifted his hand to his nose and extended the fingers.

One day, as they were marching him to the latrine, he caught sight of some Indian prisoners in iron cages, open to the beating sun and without any protection whatsoever. Some of them were hurling defiance at a Turkish officer who was passing, and Edward cheered them on. 'The English will come,' they yelled to him. The sight of their miseries swept his own condition out of mind. Yes, the English (and the Irish!) would come. God knows how long those Indians had been there but their spirit did him a world of good.

By now used to the humiliation of the guards staring at him as he used the latrine, he got on with his toilet, his mind dwelling more on the sight of those Indians than on his liquefied intestines.

'England finish,' one of the Turks said. It was becoming a cliché with them.

Mustering what strength he had, Edward lifted his arm as though to land a blow to the chin. The guard flinched and he roared with laughter. As long as the Turks jumped when they saw a bunched fist the war had not even started.

The punishment period did come to an end and he was unceremoniously pitched into a tent with several Englishmen. After fending off their welcome, he lay back wearily, listening to them discussing the chances of an early finish to the war. One fellow thought it would be all over by Christmas with the Germans beaten hollow. Such a comfortable attitude of complacency did nothing to soothe Edward. Arguing in a voice made faint by punishment, he declared that the war would go on. It would take more than talk to smash the Germans. What other news was there?

One said: 'I hear we might be part of an exchange-prisoner scheme before long.'

Edward sat up, his eyes open wide. 'What do you know about it? Tell me ...'

The Germans and Turks had agreed with the English to swap one prisoner for another, and negotiations were still in progress, but there was not enough solid news to be able to count on it.

At dawn one day a senior Turkish officer came round, selecting prisoners by sight and telling them to pack any belongings they had. At the other end of the camp the same thing was happening to the women. So it was true, there *was* going to be an exchange! Laughing with relief, Edward started throwing his few things together and lacing them into an old piece of canvas, keeping the stick full of hidden sovereigns to one side. The officer watched him for a moment and then, knowing his record, barked out: 'We leave you here. Next time, maybe.'

As the process of selection went on day after day, Edward felt they must be victimizing him because he was passed over every time. While his mind railed at the unfairness of it, his physical state grew worse. He had a recurrence of the boyhood malaria which he caught in India, and it left him alternately sweating and shivering in an empty tent through the long hours of the night. So few of them remained that the camp was a ghost town, its derelict tent flaps flapping in the night breezes. He gave himself over to prolonged nightmare...

Such hope as did remain materialized in the shape of three men who came and stood at the entrance of the tent. He could hardly raise himself up to meet their calculating eyes. Two he recognized as Turkish doctors, the third man was a complete stranger in civilian clothes. The Turks spoke quickly, discussing him, until the third man broke in, obviously exasperated.

'This man is sick,' the senior medical officer explained in Turkish.

'I'd like to hear that in plain English.' He swung round to Edward. 'I'm the American Consular agent, sir. We're acting for the Red Cross.'

'Glad... glad to meet... you,' Edward whispered.

'I'll try and get you on the next draft out.'

One of the Turks interrupted: 'Health of this man bad. Left eye no good.' He tapped his own left eye to illustrate. 'No good to British Army.'

It took two ghastly months to travel through Bulgaria, Syria and Greece before there was any sign of Edward's ragged, pale-faced contingent embarking on a boat for England. Most of the time passed as a bad dream for him, but as soon as he was on his feet he worked hard at cheering up the others.

In quiet moments, as he sat reading and impatiently waiting for the future, he could still hear the voice of that anonymous American who had succeeded in making the final arrangements for his repatriation. His last words were challenging: 'It's all your war now...'

In 1915, the fangs of war were reinforced with a foul breath which eddied out from the guts of the destructive monster that made nation fight nation. Gas was used by the Germans at Ypres and bad feeling about it was prevalent by the time Edward landed in England, a tall, emaciated, sallow-skinned wreck of a man with burning eyes who had to force himself to walk upright. During the journey several doctors had inspected him and said that he must rest and get some good food when he got home. His reply took them aback. He said that his only intention was to get into the Army and start destroying Germans. His apparent lust for killing sprang out of his hatred of what they had done in Turkey. But it went deeper than that, because he blamed them for demolishing the delicate building called civilization. News that they were using gas appalled him and reinforced his determination to start slaughtering as many as possible.

After making inquiries from the military authorities he found that it would be possible to make his way back to his former unit in the RAMC and rejoin. Some of the men to whom he spoke seemed to think that he should first take a rest, but he turned them down flat. He was actually quite fit, he said, and defied them to contradict him.

It was a good job none of them saw him stripped. His ribs stuck out and his belly was flat with a stretched appearance caused by malnutrition. The septic sores had gone now, but he was so thin and starved looking that only a cheerful manner and the constant assertion that he always looked 'like this' carried him through.

After making a quick round of visits to his relieved family – except Pat, who had joined up and was in France – he went to Ashford and found the familiar unit sign sticking up by the roadside. Some documents which he had collected in London and at Wellingborough were going to be handy here. Brushing back his hair with his hand, he made for a but marked 'Orderly Room', banged on the door and walked in, conscious of his down-at-heel civilian clothes in a sudden environment of khaki. Most of the men were strangers to him.

A man was sitting behind a table, patiently marking some forms. He did not look up, but Edward recognized him at once as Wyles, an old friend. On his sleeves were three stripes.

'How's the sergeant?' Edward asked quietly, stifling a laugh.

Wyles looked up and dropped his pen, ignoring the blot which formed. Leaping out of his chair, he pumped Edward's hand. 'Mannock! Eddie Mannock! I'm blowed.'

'You look just the same,' Edward said, overwhelmed. 'Can I sit down?'

'Where've *you* been?' Wyles pulled out a packet of cigarettes. 'Oh, I forgot – you're a pipe man. Gosh, you look a bit worn out, Paddy.'

'I've been travelling. Turkey, Syria, Greece – oh, all over the place. Now I've come home if I'm wanted.' He paused, then said darkly, but still grinning: 'Even if you don't want me, you've got me.'

'I think we're going to need everybody.' Wyles looked serious. 'It's getting bad out there, it really is. I've been over, so I know about it. We're in reserve here now, you know.'

'I've heard about it,' Edward said. He gestured. 'Still, we'll bash 'em between us, won't we?' He brought out his papers. 'Some of these might not be in order. Don't let that worry you. We'll straighten them out. You're the chap to have them, are you?'

Wyles went through them. 'What we need is a transport sergeant here. You'll get the job. Yes-s – you're right, these papers are out of date!'

Edward stood up. 'You sort them out anyway.' Then with genuine warmth he clapped Wyles on the back. 'Where's the uniform store? Let's get started.'

'Round the corner. The CO is Major Chittendon, by the way.'

But if he wanted to be within earshot of gunfire he was soon disappointed. A big percentage of the war was now seaborne, and while he was busily trying to keep abreast of progress in the comparative calm of camps at Ashford and later Halton, near Tring in Hertfordshire, he discovered that the accent on land operations lay with the Russians. Reports on the battle of Bobrka, eighteen miles south-east of Lemberg, flowed in and large headlines announced the Russian capture of 1,600 prisoners while the French took some trenches in Gallipoli. The British were attacking on Achi Baba in Gallipoli and going through hell.

To his dismay Edward discovered that some of the men whom he had known well in the unit at Wellingborough during the halcyon days of parades twice a week and camp once a year, did not welcome the chance of going to France at all. What on earth was wrong with them?

As a result of this and other discoveries, he suffered a bad period of introspection. While in that Turkish concentration camp he made a strong personal vow that he would get out and start killing Germans as fast as he could as soon as possible. He would be a lethal machine, backed up by the great spirit of the fighting British. But now he looked about him, the regional peace was almost pastoral! The men were living a wretched mockery of war. He tried very hard to understand why they should be more interested in individual welfare than in a state of affairs in which their own countrymen were daily being killed in France. After all, they were still Englishmen and the same sort of men whom he had known before. Or had he himself changed in some way? He was older than most of them, more experienced, *but why couldn't they start hating the Germans?*

It was worse in the evenings after parades and duties. In the barrack huts and tents the men lay about like dummies, absorbed in their newspapers or playing hypnotic games of cards which continued until all hours. As he watched them, his brain urging him to do something about it, he suddenly remembered the mock parliament which he joined back at Wellingborough in 1911. With a man called J. T Johnson, he helped to form the 'Wellingborough Parliament' as it became known within the YMCA. He and Johnson sat for two Irish boroughs, Waterford and Belfast, and in due course the office of Secretary passed to him. He remembered how pleased he felt to be called 'Mister Secretary'. When he went to Turkey he had to pass the job over to Johnson, but he still recalled with exciting clarity the amount of interest which the parliament used to evoke.

Doing the same thing in an Army unit was not easy. When he outlined his idea to the others they looked at him as though his brain had caved in. Politics, they pontificated, got us into this war, so what was the point of stirring things up? The less said about politics the better.

In desperation, he went to see Sergeant Wyles about it. Wyles laughed. Surely Sergeant Eddie Mannock didn't expect everybody to follow him first go off, did he?

'It's not that at all, it's the bloody apathy among them.' Edward flung himself down on an orderly room chair. 'How can these chaps believe in anything while they think like sheep?' He leant forward: 'I'll tell you what happened? I was sitting in the but talking to them about it, and first one then the other brought up some objection or other. The rest of them followed on.'

'Like sheep,' Wyles suggested.

'*Exactly* like sheep.'

'You're a Socialist, aren't you, Eddie? Oh now, don't start preaching at me! You know how I feel about it! They know you're a Socialist, too. Why don't you try some other tack?'

'There is no other tack for me,' Edward came back at him. 'Everybody should be a Socialist.'

In the end he did get his mock parliament going and the men joined in, first one and then the other. What tickled and attracted them was that they were allowed to 'represent' a definite constituency, in many cases a town they had never even visited, but the distinction was there, and Edward encouraged it while he himself took his 'seat' as 'Hon. Member for Newmarket'. This was in deference to his knowledge of horses and his fondness for riding.

'We are fighting for the freedom of civilization,' he declared, 'and we must fight to the last man...'

When the parliament was in full session the words came hot and strong. His speeches were based on the platform of Socialism, and so eloquently did he lambaste Tory members that the uproar attracted the attention of passing officers. Edward Mannock's political turn of mind was certainly making its presence felt.

Everything he ever thought about or believed in as far as Socialism was concerned now came to the surface. Up to this moment he had found it hard to make himself felt as a personality, and most people tended to regard him as a likeable, quiet young fellow with a hidden strength, but as 'M.P. for Newmarket' he felt that he could, in fact, have stood for the Westminster Parliament and got in with a majority!

If the excitement of the mock parliament filled his leisure time, he had to deal with his conscience when on duty, especially after his section was transferred to the Army Service Corps. The unit had not operated under conditions of active service up till now, but rumours said that they would soon be shipped to France. At this point he had to reconsider his aims. If they went into the front line it would mean dealing with wounded ally and enemy alike. His memories of German and Turkish behaviour were too recent to agree with that. He must be more positive about the future. It did not take long for him to reject the idea of ministering to wounded Germans. The only good one, he told himself, was a very dead one. There was no niche for a cosy-minded humanist when it came to fighting the Hun.

His application for an interview with the Commanding Officer was granted and he marched in to put his case. They knew one another sufficiently well for Edward to speak frankly. The major listened intently, nodding patiently from time to time, then said, 'I suppose you've taken into account that somebody has to look after the wounded, Mannock? I mean, if all of us wanted to fight – and perhaps we do at heart – there wouldn't be any Medical Corps, would there?'

'It's a matter of conscience with me, sir.'

'Conscience?' The major frowned. 'This is the very unit for a man with a conscience.'

'You're thinking of another sort of conscience,' Edward replied earnestly. 'If men want to look after the sick and wounded, that's up to them, but I don't. I'm sorry, but I can't feel their way about it, I can't do it. I'd just feel like –'

'What do you want then, Mannock?'

'I've just told you, sir, I don't want to nurse sick and wounded Huns. I want to fight them.'

It was a difficult and thorny interview. Trying to put aside the fact that he felt slightly nettled, the major examined the application again. The man certainly had his mind made up and while he appeared to be a rational, sane human being it was obviously no good arguing the point any longer.

He noticed that Mannock wanted to be considered for a commission in the Royal Engineers, and without a doubt his pre-war experience in telephones would be useful there, especially when it came to wiring up a sector. One thing in his favour was his family background, because his father had been a regular. It was no use wasting the urge to get out there and do some real fighting.

The major said: 'All right, Mannock, I'll forward your application.'

'Thank –'

'You'll probably have to go to Fenny Stratford for an interview with the OC of the cadet unit there…'

Later, when he wrote to a friend, Edward said: *'I'm going to be a tunnelling officer and blow the bastards up. The higher they go and the more pieces that come down, the better!'*

Hard on the heels of this came his promotion to sergeant-major. To him it seemed an irony that they were promoting him for doing precisely nothing. Life had been so completely uneventful at Ashford and he knew that better men than he were already fighting in France. The elevation in rank did not give him any easy moments. It was incompatible with his radical political beliefs and while he did not actually refuse to become a sergeant-major he never did anything to use his new status.

While waiting for the Fenny Stratford interview he went back to his studies of the war situation and felt angry with the Clyde shipyard engineers who had gone on strike to ban overtime and demanded tuppence an hour more. Politics was a game divorced from the exigencies of war. He decried the shipyard personnel for their selfishness and thought they ought to be called up.

His feelings about the war were at a high key and he was among the first to applaud Asquith's announcement about the complete blockade of Germany in which no goods of any kind must enter or leave the country. This was it! The Jerries would see what we were made of!

And then he was off to the Royal Engineers Signals Depot at Fenny Stratford. Apart from one visit and a short interview he had no difficulty about transferring to the Royal Engineers. There were rumours that they might be asked to play a part in the setting up of Lloyd George's National War Workshops plan in which the Government would have powers to commandeer factories and if need be divert them to make munitions. The Royal Engineers had the biggest available pool of skilled men. When Edward heard this his heart sank. He had to avoid being drafted to a factory at all costs. His aim was to be trained and then go straight out to France.

Fenny Stratford was not the bustling centre he thought it would be, and he failed to find any great ambition among the cadets to breathe fire down the necks of Germans. Once more he was outnumbered and smothered by indifference and badinage, this time from well educated young men. He soon felt his position keenly. Whenever the question of education came up, he dodged the issue, saying that he had received his schooling in the university of life.

They were all on probation pending their final interviews. The time passed slowly and only a few men per day were called for a discussion about their capabilities, so Edward passed the time talking to the others and reading. He had brought a case of books with him and, as usual, used the long hours to shut himself away in the pages. He noticed with some irritation the usual preponderance of uniformed dandies who fancied their chances. He was ten years older than any of them. Why did some men merely want a commission without having to work for it? He knew the answer, it was a mixture of egotism and a desire to cut a dash with the girls. Any hint of snobbery or class distinction made him writhe with contempt. He went back to his books, speaking even less to them and waiting only for the interview.

The day his name came up on the noticeboard happened to coincide with the fact that he had put his one pair of boots in for repair. His only available footwear was a pair of wellingtons. He sat on the edge of his bed and slipped his feet into the cold rubber and strapped his spurs on over them. Ignoring the amused stares and caustic remarks of the others, he plodded across to the assistant adjutant's office and tapped on the door with the shaft of his riding whip.

Lieutenant J E Buchanan, the assistant adjutant, was an efficient officer who was helping the adjutant out with some of the interviews. He attempted to view each applicant for a commission in as helpful a light as possible. Whenever a man seemed to be made of the right stuff he finished the interview quickly, marked his papers and affably wished him luck. In the main, candidates ran to a set type with a good education and sometimes – but not as often as he wished – a real instinct to lead men. That was the devilish part of his job, finding out whether a man could earn the respect of others.

'Enter!' Somebody was knocking damned hard on that door! If it were a member of *the* Mannock family he was certainly running true to type.

In marched a man wearing wellingtons and spurs with a riding whip, instead of the usual swagger cane tucked tightly under his arm. Buchanan's first thought was to reprimand him for being improperly dressed, but it was all he could do to repress a smile. What a get up! But he was obviously a good soldier, you could see that much from his bearing. 'At ease, sa'nt-major.' These RAMC chaps were supposed to be eccentric, but *wellingtons and spurs*!

'Sergeant-major Edward Mannock, that's you, isn't it?'

'Sir,' Edward said decisively.

Buchanan, his contained hilarity dwindling, leaned back in his camp chair, thinking, What a grave and dignified type! and met the applicant's eyes with some seriousness. It was very difficult. 'I somehow seem to know your name, Mannock. Are you any relation to Frank Mannock?' The idea seemed preposterous, because Frank Mannock was the direct opposite, suave, debonair and so cultured.

Edward thought quickly. There was a branch of the family in London and he had met some of them just before the war, but it was a misty recollection. 'Yes sir, he's my cousin.'

'Really? I've often been in his home. He lives in Putney, doesn't he?'

Edward refused to thaw out his reserve for the sake of family connections. 'Yes, sir.'

'I know your cousins Pat and Charley, too.' He chatted on for a few minutes about the family, but Edward said very little, perhaps fearing that his father's name would be brought out. At last Buchanan suggested: 'I suppose we should get on with what you're here for.' He rifled through the file, scanning a confidential report from Edward's commanding officer. 'So you're in the RAMC, are you?'

'Yes, sir. Transport section.'

'Good. And what have you been doing before that?'

'I was outside engineer in the telephone company, sir.'

To Buchanan this was almost incredible, because he knew the London Mannocks as well-to-do professional people. This one was certainly different. He nodded. 'Ah well, I daresay the Royal Engineers will be rather in your line,' he pointed out. 'You'll be able to keep in touch with the sort of work you did in civilian life.'

Edward was about to inform him that this was absolutely the last thing he wanted while the war was on when he changed his mind and said instead: 'Possibly, sir.'

Buchanan was secretly amused by Edward's almost angular attitude, but he decided to let it pass until later on when the younger man would have lieutenant's rank and they would be able to chat about things on more equal terms. There was, for instance, a most strange link between them, for a cousin of Buchanan's father about the middle of the last century wrote a book about the Bronte family and Haworth parsonage, and the name of one of Edward's great-uncles appeared on the flyleaf as a subscriber.

Being recommended for a commission was not the same struggle in wartime as in peace. Edward was as good as in. Buchanan terminated the interview with the remark: 'You will have about three months' training here.'

Attempting to stamp his heels together and give a smart salute as he said thank you, Edward felt the full scrunch of wellington rubber and remembered what he was wearing. It was difficult to make a composed exit, for his heart was singing with triumph. He shut the door quietly and then broke into a cumbersome trot, back to the but to tell the others the great news.

After the first month's training he was used to the idea that things were not always quite what they seemed in the Army. Men with ferocious expressions on their faces during bayonet drill turned into meek lambs once they appeared in the Mess. After disembowelling straw-filled sacks they quietly sipped their mild-and-bitter and talked about nothing but cricket or the girls they knew. Edward was stunned. These were officers in training, yet like the RAMC lads at Ashford few of them had any real ambition to get at the Germans.

By June his final acceptance was gazetted. As the Germans pierced the French lines in the southern part of the Caillette Wood, his initial *joie de vivre* wore thin, especially when the papers reported a struggle 'of unprecedented violence' in which hundreds of men were killed. His own small victory in gaining final acceptance as an officer in the Royal Engineers seemed small indeed, and hopes which had been building up over the last few weeks fell as he studied the syllabus of studies and training which stood between himself and the real war.

It was not enough to have the volunteers for dangerous work, they told him, because men must be trained to a peak of efficiency. Even the rough and tumble infantry had to go through it, and while everybody naturally deplored the setbacks which were now appearing in the newspapers with frightening regularity, it would be quite useless to ship untrained soldiers and officers to the front. The mortality rate was high enough without giving the Germans the chance of raising it.

This kind of truth was a particularly bitter pill for Edward to swallow. Brushing aside studied opinion, he started casting about for the chance of getting over to France quickly, but it was quite hopeless. Wherever he searched the answer was the same, the training period must come first and while they appreciated his spirit he must also realize ...

Chopping and changing was beginning to give him a bad name. Older officers who had forgotten the impetuosity of their own youth said that Mannock was unstable and probably unsure of himself. Why should a man ask for entry into the Royal Engineers – and get a commission to boot – and then start playing hell about the war? His habit of speaking out created quite a few enemies, especially when he put in a dig or two about the automatic privileges which came from the public school system. The phrase 'an officer and a gentleman' was enough to enrage him.

Edward was in a thoroughly defiant mood by the time the leave roster was pinned up on the board, and he made up his mind to get out of this doughy free and easy atmosphere for a week or ten days by going to Wellingborough and quietly enjoying himself despite a chronic lack of money.

Taking as little kit as he would need, he made his way early one Sunday morning to Bedford station and exchanged his voucher for a ticket at the booking office. There was time to spare before the train was due and he passed it by pacing up and down the platform, letting the heat of the summer soak into his skin, yet no matter how hard he tried the idea persisted that it was more difficult than he ever dreamed actually to play an active part in war. Landed in a backwater like Fenny Stratford, where so many men acted as though the conflict was a million miles away, it took an effort to remember what had happened in Turkey.

The platform was practically deserted as he slumped down, immersed in his own racing thoughts and the discontent which never seemed to leave him. Sitting on one of the hard wooden seats, he stared hard at the permanent way, noticing how the sun shimmered on rails the colour of gunmetal. Up on the station roof some birds squabbled over a few crumbs.

He closed his eyes until a train came in.

He stood up and went to a point near the barrier, watching travellers descending. He was about to go back to his position further along the platform when he suddenly saw a familiar face at an open carriage window. It was an old friend, Eric Tomkins!

The sight of that face created a sudden host of memories which went back all the way to those early days in Wellingborough when, for a spell, he used to travel to work at Northampton. Somehow or other he always seemed to get into the same train carriage as Tomkins and they usually chatted during the journey.

They shook hands, laughing with excitement, and Tomkins exuberantly hurried him across the station yard and into the railway hotel. He shouted for some beer for himself and lemonade for Edward, whom he knew to be a teetotaller, and then sat down, gazing at him with amazement. 'Just can't believe it's you!' His eyes went to the pip on his sleeve. 'And going up in the world, too, eh, Ted?' He was one of the few to use this name.

Edward lifted his glass, grinning shyly. 'Not exactly,' he said. 'I'm trying to do something about this blasted war, that's all.'

'Aren't we all?' Tomkins toasted the meeting and set his beer down with a clank. 'I'm in the Flying Corps, you know. But never mind all that for the moment. Tell me where you've been since I last saw you.' After Edward described Turkey and the adventurous trip home, Tomkins sensed that he was all bottled up and burning to discuss his feelings with somebody. He went on nodding his understanding, eager to help but still willing to let Edward take his time over it.

'How are you settling down to service life?' he asked at last.

Edward made a face. There was a short silence while he marshalled his thoughts, then tried to explain exactly how he felt about the war. What he wanted was action, not this constant grooming and having to listen to useless lectures, he said. It was too much like sending an old soldier to learn how to march and salute.

'Why *don't* you put in for a transfer?' Tomkins suggested. 'Ask your OC to move you down to Netheravon. That's where I am, on Salisbury Plain.'

Edward thoughtfully lit his pipe, not caring to commit himself on the spur of the moment. He had had enough of asking for transfers and knew how fed up they must be with him. He did not tell Tomkins this, because there was no time now and the story would only sound involved and perhaps a little silly.

'Why *don't* you come into the RFC?' Tomkins urged. 'I think you might like it.'

This time the idea went home. Edward looked pensively into his lemonade, swishing it round and round as though hoping to see an answer in the pale fluid. He cleared his throat: 'Quite honestly, I don't think I'd make the grade,' he confessed.

'Why not? Other fellows have done…'

'Ah yes, I daresay they have, but I can only see out of one eye. It makes it difficult. Anyway, tell me about the RFC What's it like?'

Tomkins pulled no punches as he described the hardship and the unremitting toughness of the training. Aircraft were still fairly new in the military service and they were very clumsy things to handle. They had done very well in France but the Germans knew a thing to two more than the allies and more often than not outnumbered the British by ten to one. It was amazing how quickly scientific fighting technique was developing.

'What about the chaps you're training at Netheravon?' Edward asked absently. 'How do they get on?'

Tomkins shook his head, looking gloomy. 'Very high mortality rate, I'm afraid, Ted. It's all so chancy, you know, when you get a machine up.'

They went on talking, and from time to time Edward asked a number of questions about flying and looked thoughtful. His hand went unconsciously to his left eye as though he had only just become aware of it as a serious disability. It was ludicrous to think of a one-eyed man flying an aeroplane, let alone trying to shoot up the expert Germans. Already they were beginning to be labelled 'aces' with their high-powered rate of gunfire and finely calculated manoeuvrings against the British and French.

'Well,' said Edward reverting to the subject without much confidence, 'it wouldn't be much good to me, Eric, would it?' He went on to explain what happened in India when he was about six years of age. As Tomkins rather selfconsciously leant forward to look at it, he added, 'Oh, it *looks* all right, but it isn't any use.'

Tomkins had never even dreamt that Edward had but one eye because he carried himself so confidently, as though in full possession of his vision. It was amazing! He remembered the days when Edward got on the train and settled down to read all that small print in the book he was usually carrying. A man must have a fierce determination to learn if all he had was one eye.

As Tomkins said, it was impossible to transfer from the Royal Flying Corps to the Royal Engineers, otherwise he would do it cheerfully, so they could go through the war together. The only alternative was for Edward to try for the Royal Flying Corps. It might come off, it might not, and blow that defunct eye! Edward nodded as though thinking of something else.

Edward spent his leave quietly, looking up one or two friends in and around Wellingborough, going to see the Eyleses for a talk about old times and savouring his own private memories as the hours fled by. He wanted to get back because he had an idea.

A few days after he returned to the boredom of Fenny Stratford he ordered the back numbers of certain newspapers. When they arrived he took them into his barrack hut and sat on his bed, searching for various reports, although most of what he wanted to know was printed prominently on the front pages. The name Albert Ball was practically daily currency in the popular press.

Captain Ball was the nineteen-year-old Nottingham son of Sir Albert Ball, once mayor of the city, and he was doing incredible things with aeroplanes in France. Some reports called him a modern hero, others thought that he was the allied answer to German air might. He was supposed to be more than the equal of Oswald Boelcke, the German inventor of planned group combat flying.

Edward neatly folded all the papers together and stowed them away in his locker. He was very thoughtful. Against the rattle of newspaper superlatives he could hear Eric Tomkins's words with terrible clarity. What they amounted to was the fact that *the mortality rate among trainee pilots was comparably higher than casualties at the Front.* Yet Albert Ball's handling of those diabolical self-willed aircraft showed it could be done because he was clearly having a terrible effect on German morale – and he was only nineteen years of age!

What really gripped Edward's attention and magnetized his imagination was the fact that Ball was repeatedly called a 'lone flier' who used his skill and wits against what often appeared to be the weight of the entire German Air Force.

For the next fortnight Albert Ball had no greater follower than Edward. The more he read about Ball's exploits the more unsettled he became. Up till now the Royal Flying Corps had limped along on a steady stream of volunteers from the Army, some of whom were gross misfits who would never fly, while the rest did their best and went west in a few weeks. The essence of learning how to handle an aircraft lay in trial, error and spunk, but you needed something much more besides, a knowledge of guns and how to handle them in a tight corner.

His relationship with members of the unit was courteous but no more than that. He did not go out of his way to make friends with any of them, except Captain Buchanan with whom he had many talks. The rest considered him an odd sort of chap without much 'go' or jollity in him. He disregarded their veiled criticism, did his best to keep up with his training and dutifully sat all the examinations, many of which were hard going. But for his years of spare-time reading he might not have got through at all.

The three months came to an end. Everybody awaited the appearance of that fateful list of names which would be pinned up on the noticeboard.

Edward wandered towards the board, impelled by a natural curiosity to know whether he had come through. A crowd of young faces turned as he approached.

'You're in, Eddie...'

He nodded and did not share their high spirits. He was in all right but to what end he did not want to consider, not at this stage.

Going into the Mess a few minutes later, he bumped into Captain Buchanan, the assistant adjutant, who wryly remembered the wellington boots and spurs, and stopped to congratulate him on his success.

'Now you can get on with the job, Mannock,' he said, tapping out his pipe.

Edward gave him a steady look. 'I'm going to apply for a transfer to the Flying Corps,' he said.

Flabbergasted, Buchanan drew him round the corner, out of the way of the others, knowing already that it was useless to argue if Edward had made up his mind. 'Good Lord! Why do you want to go in for this – this new-fangled flying business? Why not stick to the Royal Engineers? It's more likely to help you get back into your civilian work afterwards.'

Edward poked sharply at a windowsill with the end of his cane. 'But that's not what I want.'

Buchanan disregarded his remark. 'Besides, you're too old. You're about thirty, aren't you? They want *young* men in the Flying Corps. It would be a foolish thing.' He hesitated: 'You know that saying about old dogs and new tricks, don't you?'

Smiling, Edward did not bother justifying his decision. He could not argue with people who would never appreciate his frame of mind. Buchanan was a kindly fellow but he just did not *see*.

It took some days before he finally sat down with a sheet of paper and a pen to draft a request for an interview with his Commanding Officer. This was the sticky part of it! How many times had he asked for a change so far? First at Canterbury when he went to see that frightening manager, then once or twice in Turkey, once in the Army... It would not be surprising if he were turned down on principle! What they wanted in the flying game was the man with a firm mind, not a gadabout...

The Commanding Officer did not take long with the preliminary talk. Captain Buchanan's note had convinced him that Lieutenant Mannock was not completely happy about being in the Royal Engineers. While he did make a conscious effort at joining in with the others, his heart was not in it. Such a man was better off elsewhere. Knowing the truth, the Commanding Officer felt some regret at having to let the strapping, six foot one Irishman go, because he was so obviously a tough, resilient character who would do well if only he would buckle down to it and not worry too much about what he called 'red tape'. The interview was therefore brief.

Was Mannock quite sure of himself?

Yes, sir...

Did Mannock realize the amount of trouble these transfers caused? There was all the administrative work and then he must not forget the expense of being trained from scratch in something entirely new.

Of course, sir...

How could you argue with such a man? It was odd, but looking into Mannock's fresh, open face you could almost see a smile there, as though he knew he was getting the better of you. Damn it!

The Commanding Officer hurriedly scribbled *Recommended* on the application form and rang for his orderly while Edward began to thank him.

Just before dismissing him, the Commanding Officer puckered his brows: 'Tell me, Mannock, have you ever seen the inside of one of these aeroplanes?'

Edward coughed loudly to cover his confusion. Well, no, he hadn't, not exactly, he said. But he had watched them flying over Bedford. When he was off duty he lay on the grass near the barrack hut, watching them circling overhead ...

'Blasted dangerous things,' the Commanding Officer said gruffly, showing due loyalty to groundhog soldiers like the Royal Engineers.

Edward departed, his head in the clouds.

Already the Royal Flying Corps with its rising mortality rate was in the position of having more men than planes, said the cynics. Its history was that of a 'Fred Karno outfit' in which Army personnel decided that this flying game must be a jolly jape. Edward's interest matured at a time when most of the laughing was over and men and machines were settling down to a long and scientific war. Netheravon and Uxbridge, the two main flying training centres, were a cross between the Army and something which might or might not eventually become an officially recognized branch of the fighting services, although new pilots still tended to stroll out to their waiting machines wearing spurs. Already some incredible rumours surrounded the RFC It was alleged that General Trenchard, in 1912 an instructor but now commandant of the military wing, would not permit British pilots to take parachutes up with them for fear they might be tempted to use them as an 'escape' route if they turned yellow. The Germans had parachutes which they frequently used, but British pilots could do nothing but cling to their machines and trust to luck, often surrounded by hungry flames and the final explosion as the fuel tank burst in their faces.

This grisly rumour had little effect on Edward. He was by now possessed by the idea of being able to sit in the cockpit of a single-seater Scout (later known as the single-seater Fighter) and fight his own war in his own way.

Waiting to be called for examination, the feeling that his future must be in flying stronger than ever, he studied fighter tactics from the few aviation magazines then available. von Richthofen, the German ace, Fokker, the Dutch aircraft designer, and men like Boelcke, who grouped fighter aircraft together into fighting units, represented the deadly opposition, while the British seem more inclined to fight their air war individually. Edward could not have asked for more.

One day, when he was studying an official booklet on the Royal Flying Corps, he came across the words: 'An air pilot must have 100 per cent eyesight.' The next moment he was laughing to himself. He could always tell them that he did have 100 per cent eyesight – in his right eye – but there was very little prospect of anybody sharing that particular joke.

He went on reading anything he could find about flying, and noticed some disparity in the newspapers' attitude towards the Royal Flying Corps. They lionized Albert Ball and one or two more, but they failed to take the main idea of the aeroplane as an offensive weapon seriously. This lack of responsible assessment was due only to a scarcity of writers who knew their subject. Their major emphasis was on the activities of land troops or sea engagements. The reading public at home gained the idea that military aviation was composed of a handful of devil-may-care young men who did nothing but haphazardly fly about in the sky and shoot at their German counterparts without contributing anything of tactical worth to the prosecution of the war. True, some of the British bombers had damaged German positions, but in comparison with the showers of hot steel which the allied artillery sent hurtling over the lines it did not mean much to the layman.

Before going for his interview Edward wrote to Eric Tomkins to say that his Commanding Officer had backed the application for transfer to the Royal Flying Corps, and, what was more, he had asked to be sent to Netheravon. Tomkins was surprised to discover that their talk had produced such quick results. He was not, however, destined to meet Edward again, because postings for trainee pupils were so erratic that it was impossible to guarantee preferential treatment.

Edward arrived in good time for the medical examination. This was it! If he could get through he was quite certain that he would be a competent pilot in a month or two. His sublime confidence carried him along on a soft pink cloud all the way to the examination unit where he booked in and then started investigating the ordeal itself. It looked like being much more thorough than anything else he had ever experienced, and he knew that one setback now could condemn him to spending the rest of the war in the Army or, worse, a civilian! Already the idea of staying on the ground repulsed him, especially when he sensed the new atmosphere which pervaded the youngest branch of the services.

Hanging about the camp he found an incredible mixture of officers and rankers, many of them obvious misfits in search of a 'cushy billet', but how they thought they could achieve such an ambition in this notoriously breakneck business of flying puzzled Edward after he chatted with them. Quite obviously, they were not the stuff of which heroes, airborne or otherwise, were made!

The place was run with some efficiency, and he quickly discovered his name on a list near the Orderly Room which told him to report to one of the huts at a certain hour next morning. He carefully noted the exact time when he would be required and made a few more inquiries. Satisfied, he went to bed, making sure that he would be called earlier than anybody else.

After a quick wash and breakfast, he walked briskly through the camp to the medical inspection hut, knocked on the door and went straight in, shutting it tight after him. One glance was enough to show that it was completely empty. Everything had been prepared, the files were standing on the table. Of the medical officer there was not a sign.

Striding across to the wall, he stood right in front of the eye chart and started memorizing the exact order of the letters. From past experience he knew that people who tested eyes seldom went through all the letters, they generally asked you to read one or two on the lower lines until they could classify your vision. But it would be safer to memorize them all this time.

The lines of print stood out in implacable order, mocking him, as he gouged out their sounds and placed them in equivalent rows on a ledge of his brain. This was not going to be as easy as he had thought. There was very little time to test himself and find out whether his memory was working. He would just have to risk it. One slip, one letter out of place when he 'read' them to the doctor, and that would be that. He started again. The first four lines were simple, so he skipped them and went on to the lower ones, bending down to cram into his mind all the smaller type.

Once more, then he would feel quite certain of himself. He was about to go through them when he heard footsteps outside. Just in time, he stepped to a safe position near the desk as the medical officer walked in, apologizing for keeping him waiting. Edward said nothing, because if anything distracted him he might easily lose the thread of memory. The officer sat down and started sorting out the documents.

'You're Lieutenant Mannock?' 'Yes, sir.'

'Are your eyes good, Mannock?'

Keeping the tremor out of his voice, Edward shot back: 'Of course.'

'Sit down on that chair, will you? We'll just test them.' Lowering himself on to the plain kitchen chair, Edward waited for the ordeal to begin, anxiously willing the man to cover his sightless left eye first. It was a gift from the gods! He felt the slip of card cross his face, and set about rattling off the letters which he could see perfectly with his right eye, simultaneously memorizing lines on which he was weak. Without hesitation the medical officer covered his right eye, plunging him into darkness and he went through the rigmarole again, this time as fast as he could.

The doctor noticed nothing amiss as he wrote 'Fit for pilot' on the form.

The rest of the physical examination was nothing. His muscle tone, helped by riding and regular athletics, was superb. His build was excellent, if a little tall for climbing in and out of aircraft with small cockpits.

Muttering to himself, the medical officer agreed that he 'would do'.

Mannock's craving for wings and action was about to be assuaged in full measure.

CHAPTER FIVE

Edward reported to the Orderly Room feeling puzzled and worried by the command to put in an appearance so early in the day. Nobody knew why the Commanding Officer wanted to see him, and for the life of him he could not make even a wild guess at the answer to it. His flying training was going along fairly well, even if it did seem insufferably slow at times on account of pupils having to wait in a queue for their turn to go up.

He had been at Hendon, the Middlesex aerodrome, only a few weeks, posted into this new practical world after doing his classroom stint at No. 1 School of Military Aeronautics at Reading in Berkshire, and passing out with honours.

'What time will the C.O. be in?' he asked, casting about for a chance to escape.

A disinterested sergeant yawned: 'Dunno. Pretty soon, sir.'

Edward sat down, gnawing at the stem of his long, straight-stemmed pipe, still wondering what it was all about. If they had found out about his dud eye at least it meant the end of flying and probably every other kind of military service. From the beginning he had been extraordinarily careful to keep quiet about it, so there really was no 'reason

'C.O.'s just arriving now, sir.' The sergeant suddenly grew busy. As the Commanding Officer entered he said: 'Mornin', sir. Lieutenant Mannock for you.'

Edward jumped smartly to his feet. 'Morning, sir.'

'Come in, Mannock...'

They entered the inner office. The Commanding Officer left him standing rigidly at attention while he carefully hung up his cap and then laid his cane on a side table before seating himself behind a highly polished desk, staring at Edward as though in search of something. The longer he stared the more difficulty he appeared to have with his breathing while his face graded itself from pink to red and then went a riotous scarlet. At last he opened his mouth.

'You are, I sincerely hope, ashamed of yourself?' Every shade of anger appeared in the question.

Using a neutral tone, Edward asked: 'For what, sir?'

'*For what*? Good God, don't you know? Can't you even guess?'

'I'm sorry, sir, but I don't understand.' Edward's lips twitched into a half-smile which he quickly suppressed. It would not do to pull the leg of the Commanding Officer. 'Have I done something wrong?'

The interview was becoming more mystifying by the minute. Pupil pilots who managed to smash up valuable machines worth anything between £1,000 and £3,000 each were generally told off and the mishap soon forgotten, so it was nothing connected with flying, and in any case Edward had not damaged one of the precious machines since being here. Difficulty with landings and take-offs had already prompted one of the instructors to explain to him that this was common enough and he need not worry too much about it because it was only a question of getting used to judging the distances.

While his mind was busily reviewing the rest of the awful possibilities, the Commanding Officer bellowed: 'Lieutenant Mannock, as an officer *and* a gentleman, I think you must be devoid of the basic requirements. Last night, when I was returning to camp down Colindale Avenue, I saw with my own eyes an officer walking arm-in-arm with a young civilian female.'

'That must have been me, sir,' Edward said affably.

'It *was* you! I told my driver to slow down and I had a good look at you. I don't suppose you noticed *me*, did you?'

Her eyes were blue, her laughter generous, and under the circumstances it would have been ungrateful not to have taken her arm, Edward remembered fondly. Somewhere in *King's Rules and Regulations* it did say that a man in uniform must not behave familiarly with a female when in public.

'I apologize, sir,' Edward said soothingly.

'That's not good enough. I haven't finished yet, Mannock. Your – your *young lady* looked remarkably like one of those waitresses in the civilian canteen where you pupil pilots take your meals. Am I right?'

'Oh, quite right, sir.' A moment ago Edward had been ready to grovel, but when he realized exactly what his superior officer was insinuating his mind came to a brisk boil. He must be ridden with all the enormities of class distinction if he could not bear the thought of an officer walking out with a waitress, unless he had an inflated idea of the importance of *KR*s. It was time to take up the cudgels. 'Sir, I think that –'

'You are here to learn how to fly aeroplanes.' The senior officer pounded on his desk top. 'My God, no wonder the mortality rate is so damned high among you fellers!' He paused and then with inspiration shouted: 'Half of you must be thinking of women all the time you're up there.'

'Is that all, sir?' Edward felt that he must get out of the office or he would not be responsible for his actions.

'No, it is not *all*, sir. You took this waitress out, you were seen embracing –'

'Walking arm-in-arm, sir,' Edward corrected him.

'That happens to be technically embracing. I tell you, Mannock, if –'

By now practically overwhelmed by indignation, Edward could restrain himself no longer. With ironic politeness he said firmly: 'Neither you nor anyone in the British Army will prevent me from going out with the girl I love!' As the Commanding Officer stared, aghast at him for his lack of respect, he threw up a smart salute and marched out of the place, slamming the door hard behind him.

On the way back to his quarters he could not help laughing to himself. The girl certainly was a stunner, even if she did work as a waitress. What was wrong with being a waitress anyway? And that accusation of embracing…

The story of his unique reprimand went round the camp, helping to dispel some of the lethargy and boredom which afflicted so many of the younger men. That Mannock, the slightly scruffy specimen who always appeared in a Royal Engineers uniform full of creases, had been in a scrape just showed what a card he was, even if he did happen to be verging on thirty.

The 'external routine', as Edward disparagingly called it, lumbered on day after day, and then when the weather closed in, grounding the planes, there was always a lecture on navigation or fighting strategy to attend. Having had about as much theory as he could stomach, Edward was among the more restless, feet-shuffling pupils. All this talking about flying did not help a man as much as they thought.

One of the reasons for his dissatisfaction was that the authorities had recruited too many men far too quickly. Now that they found themselves with their hands full of expectant would – be pilots they did their best to divide them among the five main teaching centres, including the Bournemouth 'nursery'. What made it worse was the acute shortage of aeroplanes which led to so many men having to hang about and await their turn at the controls. At best, local administration was haphazard. Many pupils, especially the freebooters from America, found they had to fend for themselves as far as board and lodging were concerned. Problems of getting regular meals were solved by flocking *en masse* to the aerodrome restaurant which before the war had served amateur fliers and the beginnings of the commercial airlines. Practically everybody slept in civilian billets situated around the perimeter of the oval-shaped aerodrome.

As far as Edward was concerned, this situation was a powerful and painful reminder of all the time he had wasted since returning from Turkey. What made it worse was that no end was in sight. Granted, most of the instructors were as keen as mustard on their work, but they could hardly be expected to produce more aeroplanes out of thin air. Even one machine out of action had a crippling effect on the flying strength of the school, and this became more marked after the arrival of forty wild Belgians whose first thought was to get back to their own country and wipe out some Germans. They flew in fits of irascible bad temper, not the best quality for smooth landings and take-offs, and they left their mark on the number of machines laid up for repairs.

There was plenty of time for leave. Edward went home to Canterbury and while there searched out Johnson, who had been his fellow Irish member in the mock parliament back in 1912. Edward insisted that they have a little party with the boys at an old rendezvous, the Geasis Cafe, and to satisfy their curiosity told them all about his adventures in Turkey. In return they informed him that he had left the affairs of the parliament in such a frightful financial mess that they had to hold whist drives for six months in order to pay a printer who used to turn out tickets and literature.

Today, nearly half a century later, Johnson says: 'He had no idea of finance... (but) he was a very good fellow and very generous. We used to play together on two violins. He was very clever at extemporizing. He could harmonize any tune...'

Canterbury was full of memories for Edward, and he recalled the YMCA Bible class led on Sunday afternoons by Mr A Campbell, secretary of the local gas company. While Edward had the greatest respect for the occasion and for religious teaching, he could not resist turning every class into a loud political debate.

He decided to go round to the telephone exchange in search of familiar faces, and in one office discovered Powell, his boyhood rival for the favours of Grace Wimsett, five years earlier.

'But what on earth are you doing in the Flying Corps;?' Powell asked.

Looking round to make sure that he could not be overheard, Edward said softly: 'Well, I can only see out of one eye, but all I want to do is to get over the other side and bring down some of those bloody Jerries.'

It was a sharp change from the days when Powell had known him as a 'tall, sallow, reticent, serious-minded and modest fellow who would burst out jubilantly for a few seconds, then quite unexpectedly revert to his normal quiet manner'. So acute was the difference that many years later Powell said he always believed that Edward 'would do something significant'.

Back at Hendon Edward found things much the same. It was time to do something about it, and he was getting more and more fed-up with drawing approximately £250 a year for doing nothing towards the war.

He climbed into bed and pulled the sheets up round his neck, grumbling to himself to exorcize the devil of discontent. Just before he dropped off to sleep he groped for his cheap tin alarum clock and set it for ninety minutes earlier than usual. As soon as it tinkled next morning he slipped out, wearing shirt, trousers and crumpled tunic, and quickly headed for the hangar, whistling to himself.

It was one of those half-chilly mornings with clear air in which even the dull red cubes of the nearby suburban houses suggested a kind of excitement, and the hangars in the distance were like humped, brooding African animals, waiting...

Two mechanics in smudged overalls that matched the grey painted hangars, were preparing a plane for the day, working with the preoccupation of their kind as they looked into the intestines of the engine, like doubtful surgeons about to operate.

Edward moved round the tall hangar wall and found the side door made of metal. If you let it slip as you operated the lever latch it banged resoundingly, echoing drum-like in the space. He held it tightly and slipped in, glancing at the mechanics, who were still preoccupied with their work. Through the ranks of wings, wheels and fuselages of parked planes he saw the Caudron standing towards the front, its nose about fifteen feet from the open door, pointing straight towards the field. It would have to be the Caudron after all ...

This was a strange looking aircraft, French by extraction, and as hard as hell to handle because of a self-will which the designer had unconsciously built into the airframe. In the air it became a three-sided battle between airframe, engine and pilot, and only the pilot was predictable. Nobody trusted the Caudron, she won every time if a man were weak.

There was no other choice unless he asked the mechanics to push some of the others to one side and then manhandle a smaller plane into position. It was the Caudron or nothing. After a restless night he had no intention of giving up the plan because of such insignificant difficulties. Anyway, it was impossible to tell which planes were serviceable and ready for the air just by looking at them. If he started asking any questions now, the mechanics would only refer him to the daily report on the wall of the instructors' office, by which time they would be feeling suspicious.

All he could do was brazen the whole thing out at once. Going round to the other side of the Caudron, he lifted his foot and put it in the metal ring. One bound took him up on top of the fuselage. He put his legs straight out and slid smoothly into the cockpit. It was now easy to reach out and touch the rudder bar and his hands fell naturally to the joystick. An inch to the right and then to the left to make sure the ailerons were free, then he stared hard along the nose of the machine towards the open hangar door with its panorama of grass and tarmac stretching away towards the London – St Albans railway line. In the distance the orange-coloured wind-sock swung about, showing that he would not need to taxi very far before opening up for a take-off into the light breeze.

He leaned out of the cockpit and took a chance. 'Can you give me a swing?'

One of the mechanics came across, looking unsuspicious. After wiping his hands, he went through the ritual of 'sucking in' by turning the propellor. Then he paused and looked expectantly at Edward.

'Contact!'

'Contact!' Edward shouted, flicking on the ignition switch.

One final swing and the engine came vibrantly alive. Seeing the mechanic waving an all-clear to him, he started taxiing towards the hangar doors. He let her tick over just enough to provide impetus but not too much because she might easily tip forwards on to her nose and smash the propellor.

Straight out, past the ancillary workshops, the Caudron ran slowly until she was resting at the end of the runway, nose pointing into the wind. Edward idled long enough to run up the engine quickly in the approved drill then let her move off in a gathering speed. He knew this prelude to becoming airborne, but on most occasions he had to put up with the instructor pouring advice through the rear cockpit speaking tube. It was much more exhilarating when you were on your own because everything you ever learned had to come into simultaneous play without any prompting.

The tarmac was slipping backwards. The Caudron needed another two or three miles per hour before the elevator could be slightly angled to give purchase on the air.

He opened the throttle a shade more, waiting for the moment of intuitive confidence when he could put a feathery touch on the elevator and then wait …

Slight bumps in the tarmac juddered up into his sweating hands through the joystick. Any moment now all that would cease. It must, otherwise he would pile up at the end of the runway, near the thick hedge into which so many erring pupils had been catapulted. The hedge was a life saver he did not want and within the next fifteen seconds he expected to be able to look down on it as the machine took to the air. But how could you be sure at this speed?

She was up! First a foot, and then, when he gently pulled the stick back, the machine rose – three feet, four, and up to twenty, right into the safety margin in which the machine no longer felt difficult but became a mechanical bird designed by man and flown by man.

At about fifty feet he started the next phase of the climb, going up into the now chilly morning air with every confidence, banking gently, his one good eye fixed immovably on the wavering altimeter which gave only an approximate indication but was good enough for this sort of work.

The million and one tremors which had been passing through the Caudron's wooden airframe, testing each nut and bolt, every small joint, were ironed out as the engine settled down to its job.

More relaxed, Edward had time to look around the small temporary home made by the cockpit with its sweet cloying smell of hot oil and petrol mingling with the tang of the worn leather.

The Caudron flew on, the beat of her engine losing itself in the slip – stream of air which started somewhere round the nose and grew as it was thrown backwards in a widening swathe.

When the altimeter needle started flirting with the '100' on the dial he stopped climbing. This was high enough. Levelling out, he throttled the engines back, encouraging them to idle in their momentary achievement.

Down there lay the airfield, all the irritations of training, the apparently insoluble problems created by human personality. Up here everything became simple, just a man and a machine with all the sky as a jousting field. He knew too well that within three months this same sky, which stretched right across Europe, would become a field of thundering red-hot exhausts and killing gunfire.

He did not attempt any aerobatics. They did not teach you much in that line at Hendon, concentrating only on how to get a plane up in the air and bring it back safely. As he gently encouraged the Caudron to move round, noticing the distant horizontal line of the horizon moving in sympathy, he did not try to taunt her well -known sensibilities.

After another ten minutes of strict textbook flying, he nursed the plane into a perfect landing and left her stationed in a place near the hanger. He jumped out and went to the restaurant for breakfast, speaking to no one for fear of breaking the spell which the sky and the machine had woven between them. If he did not fly again for a week, a month, it had been worth it.

As he ruminatively finished his breakfast he received a message to say that the Commanding Officer wanted to see him at once. He nodded, realizing angrily that all his satisfaction was about to be blown to pieces by a ticking off, perhaps worse. It was the same senior officer who had earlier reprimanded him for walking out with the waitress. There was not much hope in his heart as he marched in and saluted.

'Mannock, you flew this morning without permission. *Why?*'

'I wanted to, sir.' He was about to explain his impatience with the tedium of having to wait for flights when he was interrupted.

'You wanted to, eh? Technically, you stole that machine'

'I had no –'

'Listen to me. You might have smashed the Caudron up. You could have killed yourself and perhaps other people. You are grounded. You men need some discipline.'

'I went –'

'*You are grounded.* That is all.'

It was a stupefying blow and a harsh punishment. Always contemptuous of artificial authority which seldom took any account of the individual, he found slight solace in the fact that pupil pilots were often grounded for short periods, and few of their misdemeanours could be called serious.

While his feet remained firmly stuck to the ground Edward started making inquiries about other flying schools, discovering that if he managed to find a vacancy elsewhere he was entitled to put in for a transfer, although he would need several watertight reasons for doing so. Before he could work out ways and means of getting away from Hendon, they restored him to flying training and a few weeks later, on November 28th, 1916, he received the Aero Club's proficiency certificate, No. 3895.

On December 5th, 1916, he was sent to No. 19 Training Squadron at Hounslow, Middlesex, and on February 1st, 1917, commissioned flying officer on probation, attached to Hythe Gunnery School. The fortnight he spent learning how to handle guns was the most difficult period of his service. It was no use trying to get away with anything here. Even if the flying instructors did not detect the fact that he had only one good eye, it would become evident when he got over to France on operational duties. He must prove to himself that he could do it.

Time was running short when he was posted to No. 10 Reserve Squadron at Joyce Green, an aerodrome squatting on a fork of Dartford Creek, which ran into the Thames Estuary. It stood in such a position that a pilot in difficulties who was looking for a forced landing, had the choice of the water, a tracery of deep ditches, Vickers's TNT factory or a sewage farm. The CO was a South African, Major Swart, with two flight commanders, Martin and Long, the chief flying instructor being Lieutenant Packe, a forceful individual with whom, according to one of the pupils, it was difficult to get along in any great harmony.

On arrival Edward examined the names of his fellow pupils, who included Thomson, from the 5th Suffolk Regiment, Tattersall, Wood, Martin, Skeffington, Hunder, Wadlow, Newton Jones, Graves, Coomber, Arberry, Chapman, Pryce Davies, Fielding Johnson, Hepburn, Bush and Lethbridge. Few of them meant anything to him. What he really wanted, was to meet a few fellows with actual experience of operational flying. He knew that a high percentage of the instructors and officers in charge of home establishments were derisive of pupils, and lost no opportunity of running down the very effort of which they all formed an important part. Edward had had enough of it. He did not even waste his time arguing with the desk-bound warriors.

He had not been at Joyce Green more than a few days and was still settling in when he heard a rumour that Lieutenant J B McCudden, MC, MM, *Croix de Guerre*, would soon be arriving to give instruction in handling a spinning machine, general aerobatics and some of the special information necessary for getting out of tight corners when in combat. The newspapers had already made much of his record. Like Edward, he was a self-made man.

While Edward eagerly awaited his arrival, McCudden was elsewhere, making arrangements for his spell as a teacher, and to a friend he wrote: 'I reported to the Wing at Maidstone and was told to make my headquarters at Joyce Green for the time being. I was allotted a Bristol Scout for my work, but as it was not yet ready, I used a DH2...'

He had not been at Joyce Green more than a day or two before he was putting on regular shows and demonstrations for the pupils, dropping from 3,000-feet and holding the DH2 in spins while the tyros stood on the ground, fascinated by the sight of the plane's axis with its spinning wings. It was fantastic, the way McCudden handled the machine, but few of them felt anxious to try and imitate him because what he did seemed to invite a crash. The pupils, he remarked, 'regarded the machine as a super death trap, not knowing that in its day the DH2 was one of the best machines in the RFC...'

Looking at the other training machines, Edward saw a Henri Farman, a Vickers Gunbus, both dual, and the FE8, a pusher. There was also a spare DH2, like McCudden's.

Experience showed that out of this selection, only the DH2 would be suitable for what he had in mind.

Taking the chance of questioning McCudden, Edward introduced himself before the ace became involved in his new duties. He announced that he was very keen to learn all he could as soon as possible. McCudden took to him at once and they spent several hours discussing the peculiarities of the various planes, Hun strategy and the situation in France.

'Can you give me a bit more about spins?' Edward leaned forward expectantly.

Would it be a good idea to tell McCudden about his eye? He decided against it. McCudden might feel duty bound to mention the fact that they had a one-eyed pupil under training to Major Swart. It would finish things off completely.

McCudden was talking: '...if you want to remain the boss, in control, you have to hang on. You have to wait till the moment the machine is trying to turn itself inside out and throw itself into the ground...'

This was exciting stuff. Edward listened to every word of it, oblivious to the laughter and chatter round the bar. The DH2 was supposed to be a helluva plane to handle, McCudden said, but that was one of the fairy stories which had started and now everybody believed it. There were compensations, because if the DH2 was as tough as people reckoned it was, then if a man mastered it early on he should be able to handle any machine.

That evening Edward went walking by himself across the lonely Essex landscape. As he turned back, he could not help studying the layout of Joyce Green, the cluster of tin huts and hangars which was now his new world. An idea was gaining substance in his mind. He did not want to share it with anybody, not even McCudden.

Next morning he spoke to McCudden again as they walked towards the hangar and dispersal point, their flying helmets dangling from their fingers, jackets slung casually over their shoulders. Edward brought up the question of spins.

McCudden looked serious. 'Mick' – this was the name by which he was now known – 'don't try any of those turns below two thousand feet or you'll get into a spin and crash.'

Now more sure of himself, Edward argued: 'But surely it's possible to get out of a spin even if you *are* a bit low?'

'It isn't safe with the DH2 below two thousand feet...' The day's tuition proceeded. Pupils took off and landed with regularity and the atmosphere grew warmer. Edward went up several times on routine flights, practising his turns and behaving like a model pupil. It was not time yet. When he was rid of that man in the rear cockpit he would be able to get on with it.

Just before noon he climbed into his machine again, wriggling his seat hard down on the leather-faced cushion. He was alone now and the DH2 was all his. He was beginning to love the DH2 because the cockpit stood so well for'ard, giving the pilot clear visibility with the mainplane behind him. There was enough resilience in the construction to impart confidence. Unlike some pupils, he did not regard the short fuselage, which finished just aft of the mainplane, as risky or unsafe. The total weight of the airframe and engine was only about 800-lb. unloaded. It lifted superbly, doing about ninety-three mph at sea-level and with a ceiling of 14,000-feet.

Acrid blue fumes blew out of the engine vents as he revved up the Monosoupape 100-horse-power engine. The plane lurched forward, confidently gathering pace. Sitting quite comfortably, Edward checked over the different points which were needed for a classic take-off, smiling to himself when he thought about what would be happening in the next twenty minutes. He was out to prove McCudden wrong by spinning at a safe altitude – provided the twenty – eight – foot wingspan did not break off and dump him in the middle of the sewage works! He reasoned that the 228 square feet of wing area ought to support him in the spin.

With the joystick held firmly so that the DH2 climbed steeply, he noticed a few unusual quiverings of the structure, but dismissed them. The DH2 was full of grunts and groans when forced to do something contrary to her nature.

Streamers of cloud came out to buffet him. He laughed as he recalled his first experience in cloud when he felt afraid of hitting something. Now, after only a month or two of constant flying at three different schools, he did not give a damn about cloud, only about the machine and its performance.

The cloud was dense here, thick and white, a strange world of its own. There was no sign of the earth.

He shoved his legs out to their fullest extent, hardening the soles of his feet square with the pedals. Then he deliberately put the DH2 into a rapid spin just as the altimeter registered 1,500-feet.

The plane came fluttering out of the cloud, looking helpless and stricken. As the stalled Monosoupape engine emitted an alarmed stuttering noise men in the hangar and huts on the aerodrome came running out. A fire orderly dutifully clutched his extinguisher and started trotting towards a point where he thought the machine might strike the earth.

'My God, he's going to crash. He's out of control!'

His teeth clamped firmly together in a grimace of determination, Edward shut the throttle and assessed the DH2 as she did her worst. There was a tremendous reverberation throughout the cockpit and it was hard to keep his hands on the joystick, trying to centre the controls. One quick glance over the rim of the cockpit told him that he was lower than he thought and must act rapidly within the next moment, but he still had about 300-feet to fall, in which distance the structure and engine would undergo its most severe test. Every nut and bolt would take the growing strain. If only one snapped or was sheared, there would be a reaction and the rest of the plane would crumble.

'That fellow's a gonner!' somebody cried excitedly. Officers started running, then stumbled to a halt, uncertain where the crash would occur.

'He's not over here at all. He'll go into the estuary, poor blighter! We'd better warn them to get a boat out …'

'He's a bit over. He's – God, he's over the Vickers factory. *It's jammed full of TNT!*'

Nearing 200-feet, Edward tried to jerk the engine into action, waiting for the familiar cough and splutter as she fired. Nothing happened. The feed from the tank might be congested by clusters of air bubbles formed during the rapid drop. He tried again, willing it to start, cursing hard in the moments while his fingers fumbled for the switch. Perhaps the mixture was too rich to catch? Another few feet of this and it would definitely be too late to find out. Anything after 175-feet meant that the engine would be incapable of levelling the DH2 out. When that moment came and went a man could rely only on one thing, an absolute miracle.

When he took his bearings as the DH2 levelled out, Edward realized that he was no longer anywhere near Joyce Green, he was dead ahead of the Vickers factory on the far side of the estuary. He would have to force – land somewhere. From his earlier flying in this vicinity he thanked his lucky stars for remembering the grass which formed an apron around Vickers TNT sheds. Whether he could hold the DH2 back before she ploughed straight into that long black building was a question he did not want to ask or try and answer at that moment. He started on the descent…

Over at Joyce Green they were taking a rough and ready roll call, trying to find out who the new corpse would be. The only man missing and booked out flying solo was Lieutenant Mannock – 'Mick', that mad Irishman! Groups of pupils and instructors were watching, riveted by the fascination of watching a plane in what looked like being the death throes. It would not be long now.

One of them pointed and shouted as the DH2 sank from view behind the hedges. 'This is it!'

Rubbing his chin, McCudden walked away from the circle of pilots, waiting for only one thing, the soft thud as the plane hit the earth, followed by the crack of the petrol tank exploding and then, inevitably, the roar of the TNT sheds going up. Mick Mannock was certainly leaving this earth in a blaze of foolhardiness.

Landing on such a short strip of land was not easy. This was the first time Edward had been faced with the necessity of throttling back beyond the textbook rules as he worked to make the plane almost hover before putting the wheels on the ground, creating as much running surface as possible. Just below, only a few feet away, was a bumpy-looking, lawn-like stretch, but he knew there could be a pothole anywhere, perhaps hidden by some of the grass. If he hit it or one of those molehills which seemed to be all over the place the DH2 could trip herself and smash down, trapping him in the cockpit as petrol from a fractured tank leaked over red-hot fuel pipes.

He did not want to tax the engine too hard after its recent ordeal. Next time he asked it to perform it might not support him. A stall while trying to gain height for a second circuit would not be healthy. He had to land *now*, within the next few seconds because there was not even a thin hope left of getting back to Joyce Green.

Putting away the mental image of what happened when a wingtip snagged in the ground if a plane turned too low and too steeply, he concentrated on edging the control column forward an inch or less at a time. It would be damned easy to go into a disastrous sharp-angled dive.

The wheels kissed the grass and began to accept the settling weight of the engine and airframe. Looking straight ahead, he could see the doors of the shed coming closer, the warning marks on them getting bigger. He quickly closed the engine throttle and shut off the petrol before bracing himself. Luckily, the DH2 had no great impetus when moving under her own weight.

With a faint crunching sound, she slowed and stopped.

Edward levered himself out of the cockpit, perched for a moment on the side as he appreciated the soft still air of summer then slid down to the ground. He paced off the distance to the shed doors behind which was stored enough explosive to devastate a medium-sized town. Ten feet.

It took two hours for him to regain the sanctuary of Joyce Green. He went straight to his quarters and had a wash and brush up before walking over to the Mess. Now that he had proved to his own satisfaction that the DH2 was not quite the killer plane she was made out to be by the pupils and some of the instructors, he was prepared to help any of them towards a useful familiarity with the machine.

In the Mess a great wall of silence greeted him as he crossed the space to the bar and asked for a bottle of lemonade. Then he turned to look at them. 'What's wrong now?'

'That was a bloody stupid thing to do, Mick,' one man said huffily.

'What was?' Edward bandied back, an innocent expression on his face. 'I got her down safely. I'll pop over later and fly her back.'

One of the younger men pushed forward. 'You did that spin deliberately, didn't you?' he demanded peevishly. 'We're all told to avoid spinning but you have to go out and test it for yourself. They'll expect the rest of us to do it. You're a good chap, Mick, but if –'

Taken aback by the outburst, Edward felt an almost physical cross-current of opinion. He tried to calm it down by claiming that the spin was absolutely accidental. With so many experienced pilots present in the instructors' corner of the Mess, he did not relish appearing superior.

The DH2 came out of the cloud and then, for some rum sort of reason, went into a spin from which he could not extricate her until he was well down. That was reasonable enough, wasn't it? It was only by sheer accident that he had been so low!

They refused to listen. If McCudden happened to walk in he did not want to involve him in this ugly row, so he held his tongue, giving them time to split up into groups. Dinner, served half an hour later, passed in total silence and, feeling nettled, Edward took the opportunity of leaving before anybody else. He was still surprised by their behaviour but knew that he had to be careful because they were so touchy.

As he happened to meet McCudden he gravely thanked him for all his advice about spins, refraining from mentioning the incident. McCudden listened to what he had to say, his eyes twinkling. Already an ace in his own right he seemed to understand.

He had not been back in his quarters more than a few moments before he was asked to report to the Commanding Officer at once.

Major Swart was waiting for him, looking coolly formidable. Without beating about the bush, he told Edward exactly what he thought of pilots who deliberately endangered their own lives. And what about the Vickers factory? It would have been a disaster had the DH2 piled up in all that TNT

Edward started explaining that the disaster had not, in fact, happened. Everything was all right, except that the DH2 was awaiting collection.

Swart listened to him patiently. He knew that Edward had all the makings of a good scout pilot with the right sort of temperament, but discipline also had a place at Joyce Green and he did not intend to allow anybody to smear the name of the Royal Flying Corps. Vickers would probably kick up a fuss about it anyway.

As he listened to his Commanding Officer's reasoning Edward started appreciating the gravity of the offence. At the same time, what was the use of taking anybody else's word for it that the DH2 was deadly if it went into a spin. Surely these things had to be tried out?

The bombshell came when Edward had finished trying to justify his 'accident'. Major Swart said: 'I'm sorry to have to say this, Mannock, but you may have to leave us.'

There was a chilly finality about that sentence. Already the ranks of the Royal Flying Corps were being thinned out by dismissing men who would never make pilots, and the phrase 'temperamentally unsuitable for flying duties' was coming into regular use. There was no arguing with it. A man could finish flying one week and then immediately be remustered to ground duties or else returned to his regiment.

There was nothing for it but to start arguing and while the impassioned words came from his mouth he kept reminding himself that Major Swart's signature on a piece of paper could just about ruin everything.

'I'll have to consider it,' Major Swart said with dignity, refusing to be drawn. He looked out of the window and then back again at the culprit. 'Didn't you realize what you were doing, Mannock? I've seen planes come down here in spins and never get out of them. They end up as so much rubbish, man, and that could have happened to the DH2. I've stood at this window – are you listening?'

'I am, sir,' Edward said quickly. Was Swart weakening?

'I've seen them come down and that's the end of them. And, frankly, I don't believe it was an accident.'

Edward spent a sleepless night, worrying over what might happen. In the morning he was officially informed that he would after all be allowed to stay, but there was an innuendo in the message that he must in future watch his step, otherwise he and the Royal Flying Corps might not get on quite so well.

He was posted for a short period to an aerodrome near Birmingham, and with only a few days to go to Christmas he happened to be flying over Wellingborough when his engine cut out. Coasting down across the familiar countryside, he saw the playing field of Wellingborough School directly ahead. The machine settled on the turf and he jumped out, grinning. There was something in this situation that appealed to him, arriving out of the blue on the playing field of a 'good' school while he himself had had such a sketchy education. It was gatecrashing with a difference!

After apologizing for the intrusion to the school authorities, he telephoned his unit and was told that two mechanics would be sent as soon as they could be spared. Meanwhile, he should stay where he was. While waiting he strolled round to the Eyles's house to surprise them. They said that this was too good a chance to miss. He must try to stay for Christmas dinner. But Edward could not see much chance of it. The mechanics would be here shortly and then he would have to be on his way.

But fate was on the Eyles's side. As soon as the engine burst into life, one of the mechanics taxied the plane across the field – straight into a spinney. That settled it! Edward stayed on with a clear conscience and had Christmas dinner with the Eyles. The two mechanics remained with the plane, waiting for additional help and eating their dinner sitting under the wings after it had been served to them by G H Oxland, a master in charge of the junior school.

Captain Meredith Thomas, a fellow pupil at Joyce Green and Air Officer Commanding the Royal Air Force in India in World War II, later wrote about the days that followed:

'We shared a room and he told me many interesting stories of his pre – war life; it appeared to have been a hard one. At this time he was a staunch teetotaller and a fairly regular churchgoer, although during chats with him he professed to have no particular religion … we were great friends at Joyce Green and had many both amusing and serious talks when waiting in the cold on a petrol bin for a flight, but I cannot recall anything definite beyond our mutual disgust because of the manner in which the staff threatened the pupils, many of whom had seen pretty severe war service before transferring or being seconded to the RFC, whilst the Staff had seen very, very little, and in some cases none.

'My first impression of Micky was that he was very reserved, inclined to strong temper, but very patient and somewhat difficult to arouse. On short acquaintance he became a very good conversationalist and was fond of discussions or arguments. He was prepared to be generous to everyone in thought and deed, but had strong likes and dislikes. He was inclined to be almost too serious-minded.'

Edward's dislikes were founded mainly on his growing hatred of the Germans as he studied the progress of the war. News of the terrible hand-to-hand fighting by the allies against the Prussian cavalry renewed his desire to get over to France. The time must surely be soon?

Another friend of his, Captain MacLanachan, called 'McScotch' by Mannock, said: 'It was soon clear to me that behind Mannock's frank contempt of the Germans lay a deeper subconscious instinct of distrust and hatred of the aggressive bullying militaristic spirit of Prussianism which was linked in his mature mind with the memory of his early struggles... The tall, lean, Celt with the flashing eyes, not a little reminiscent of the young Bernard Shaw, hated all reactionism and anything savouring of red tape, officialdom and restraint of freedom. In a spirit not so well balanced and controlled he would undoubtedly have been a fiery agitator given to excessive wild spirits and extreme views... he referred to the Germans as 'swines' or 'hunerinos'... He had none of McCudden's absolute detachment about the enemy. He enlarged on Ball's intensity and dislike of the enemy to a degree of hatred in the deep and lasting sense that Nelson hated the French. Mannock saw the German not only as the enemy of his own country, but as a positive menace to all that he had learned was precious and ennobling for civilization. The freedom and security for which he yearned stood in danger from a German victory and was fed by pictures of his early life...

'Neither he nor McCudden had been to a public school, both being sons of Army NCOs, and whereas Ball had had an education which made him ashamed to express his hatred of the Germans in words, Mick had no such inhibitions. He was fighting for a cause, for a better world order, and he saw German militarism as the greatest obstacle to that ideal.'

It was his love of words and a feeling that some sort of record ought to be kept that made Edward buy a notebook into which he intended putting his serious thoughts. He had no aspirations to authorship, but he wanted to keep some kind of a journal if only for the satisfaction of knowing what day of the week it was. He had heard that when you reached France time did become muddled, and this was one way of keeping a check on it. As soon as he had passed out at Joyce Green and classified as a proficient scout pilot, he went to his quarters and started packing. The empty notebook lay on top of his kit until he had finished folding up his spare shirt and uniform, and he carefully put it in with his few items of personal association. He then packed his violin. It might be useful, he thought.

His posting orders read: MANNOCK, LT... CLARMARAIS, NEAR ST OMER, N FRANCE. He stood staring at it for a long time. This was it. Active service at last.

In the last days of March 1917, he arrived at the town of St Omer in northern France where the British had their headquarters, together with No. 1 Aircraft Depot, and on April 1st he wrote:

> Just a year today I received my commission, and a year to the day earlier I was released from a Turkish prison. Strange how this date recurs. Let's hope that a year hence the war finishes, and I return for a spell to merrie England... Landed at Boulogne. Saw the MLO and discovered that I was to be away to St Omer the following day at 3.45 pm. Rested and fed at the Hotel Maurice. Quite a nice place as Continental hotels go. Wisher, Tyler and two more strangers (RFC) kept us company. Rotten weather. Rain. I'm not prepossessed with the charm of La Belle France yet.

There was nothing much to do but wait until the next day, when he wrote:

> Breakfasted on coffee and omelettes. The Eternal Omelette. By the way, they are good. Left at 4 p.m. Quite punctual. Arrived at St Omer at 8.30 p.m. feeling very fed up and tired. Rotten journey at 2-mph. After portering luggage and practising my execrable French, reported to No. 1 AD. Orders to put up for the

night on our own. Proceeded by tender and devious means to Hotel de France. Horrible place – *dejeuner* worse – and filled with subalterns of all sorts, sizes and descriptions. No room for me – so to Hotel de Commerce. Small, cold room. Candles and damp sheets, ugh!

3.4.17: Rose at eight. The eternal coffee and omelette. Really the hens must be on war work. Tried to find the office again and subsequently managed to do so. Instructions to proceed to aerodrome. Met Lemon, Dunlop and Kimball on the way. Was catechized and placed in the School – on Bristol Scouts. Censored lots of letters. No flying. Billeted at YMCA in St Omer.

4.4.17: Did some flying today. Of course I expected to break something. U/C strut snapped but comparatively a good show. Nasty town. Mainly composed of estaminets, old women and dirty – very dirty – children. The streets remind me of Constantinople in their glistening filth. Went to the cinema in the evening.

5.4.17: Flying again. Did some stunts and got along well. I rather fancy the Bristol. Got a fresh billet today…

On April 6th, 1917, he joined No. 40 Scout Squadron, near Bruay, about nineteen miles north – north – west of Arras, in the coal – mining area. Here he shared quarters with Henry Jaffe, the equipment officer who took to him at once and later said that he was 'really a most unassuming person and inclined to be retiring and silent at times … we had a gramophone and there was a record by Kreisler – 'Caprice Viennois' to which he never tired of listening. He would invariably bury his face in his hands, being obviously much moved.'

Among the first men Edward met was his Commanding Officer, Major Tilney, who told him that he would be flying offensive patrols and going on bomber escort.

That day he was also introduced to his messmates, two men whom he had met previously elsewhere, Captain Mackenzie and Captain Dunlop. He was placed in 'C' Flight with Captain Todd as his flight commander. Todd summed him up as being 'like a highly – strung pedigree horse at the starting post.'

Feeling delighted but holding himself back because he was still very much a stranger here, Edward went into the Mess for his first meal with an operational squadron. Discovering a vacant chair, he bagged it only to find everybody watching him with a curious air of discomfort on their faces which remained until after dinner, then one of the pilots, a youth of eighteen or nineteen, broke the spell. 'Are you superstitious, Mick?'

'No more than anybody else. Why?' Edward's eyes stared back at them. 'We weren't thirteen at table, were we?'

'You were sitting in Lieutenant Pell's seat, that's all,' somebody explained quietly.

'Pell?'

'Pell was shot down just before you arrived today.'

Although the news was sinister, made more so because he had actually headed for a dead man's chair, it did help to cut the ice. It also represented a break with tradition, because pilots were not permitted to discuss death in the Mess, this being bad for morale. It was the usual story, the Germans had come out in a fast wolf pack, cutting Pell off and shooting him to bits. He was a damn good pilot, they said, but being a competent handler of aircraft and guns was not good enough these days. You needed more, a killing instinct.

He was surprised to find how very frank all these boys were about the situation. Very few of them were more than twenty-one. His stomach hardened when they told him that the majority of the German aircraft against which he would be pitted were faster and somewhat better than those of the allies.

Thrusting all these sombre thoughts away from him, he concentrated on the squadron's assets…

No. 40 Squadron was equipped with second-hand Nieuports, which had been used by the Royal Flying Corps since 1916, just over a year ago. They were built by the *Societe Anonyme des Establissements Nieuport* at Issy-le-Molinaux.

Edward tingled as he realized that Albert Ball had scored many of his greatest victories using a Nieuport.

Some of the older hands were quick to tell him that the machine had to be handled with a calculated, almost sublime, blend of brute strength, low cunning and plain, old – fashioned circumspection. One pilot said, 'It's like flying a feather'. Despite its faults, the Germans were already copying the nine-cylinder rotary Le Rhône engine which could lift the Nieuport to 10,000-feet in ten minutes.

As soon as he could, Edward escaped to the canvas Bessaneau hangars for a close look at the Nieuport. What he saw was an aeroplane in which the upper wing was nearly twice in breadth that of the lower one, called a 'stabilizer', supported to port and starboard by two V-shaped struts. The landing and flying wires gave the Nieuport a trim, almost demure, appearance, which became all the more pronounced when compared with her contemporaries, many of which suffered from the untidiness of their designers' minds.

Walking about in the hangar, he got into conversation with one of the mechanics, who knew the Nieuport inside out. He said that she had a kind of basic instability due to a sort of gyroscopic effect caused by the engine. To fly her well you had to hang on to the joystick all the time. If you neglected her, she tended to throw herself into the ground in a huff.

Digesting all this information, Edward was impatient to take a Nieuport up and test out the theories, but it was by now too late in the evening and most of the pilots seemed to be taking their ease after the day's operations.

He was inspecting the different parts of the camp when he spotted a sight which gave him a start of surprise, a full-sized tennis court with several players battling in an energetic game. The spirit of the Royal Flying Corps was to encourage men to take things easy when they were not flying. Some of them even cultivated little vegetable gardens or kept dogs in their spare time, and it was not unknown for the more eccentric-minded pilots to take their hounds with them on certain safe flying missions.

He went to bed, filled with an anticipation of what the morrow would bring.

7.4.17: First solo in Nieuport Scout. Lovely bus! tootled around and went as far as the lines via Bethune. Strange sight from above to see the flashes of big guns and note the *chevaux de frise* of salient, sap and trench. Feel almost at home on the controls compared to the Bristol.

There was a little more to handling the Nieuport than 'tootling'. Improperly or clumsily handled, the mixture levers, regulating the amount of petrol fed into the engine, could cause a sudden seize up, because they made the engine choke and stop dead. Edward was careful to obey all the advice given to him by other pilots and the mechanics. He did not want to go west on his first trip out.

The crucial test still had to come. The main purpose of the Nieuport was to carry armament. This was where he might be caught out with his eyesight. He planned to overcome his difficulties in the privacy of the sky itself, where nobody would be able to watch him. The gun, a single Lewis fitted on top of the centre section and firing over the propellor, had to be a friend to him. If it turned into an enemy the war would become a torture, not a crusade.

Sitting comfortably in the vacuum created by the slipstream, he leaned forward slightly and put his right eye to the ring sight, a metallic cobweb by means of which it should be possible to place a bullet within an inch of the intended place if he followed all the rules which had been drummed into him at Hythe Gunnery School. Drawing a bead on an imaginary point ahead of him, he put his finger on the button and pressed. A steady ratatat cut across the thrumming engine. He leaned back, grinning with delight.

It was some time later, when he met a New Zealander called 'Grid' Caldwell, nicknamed for his habit of referring to all planes as 'grids', that he came to know more about German tactics.

Caldwell said that in his experience the German Albatros Halberstadt could easily be outfought, not necessarily by the Nieuport but certainly by the SE5, unless the Hun pilot was particularly skilled at his job. The famous Fokker, on the other hand, could turn inside an SE5, so you had no alternative but to attack from above, then 200m up and gain height again before he could retaliate. When it came to the Fokker triplane, which Richthofen, the 'Red Baron', favoured, you really had to watch out, because it could turn inside an SE and also outclimb it …

They went on talking, Edward plumbing Caldwell's acumen about the Nieuport. The New Zealander was tremendously struck by the newcomer's almost animal-like ferocity of purpose. He obviously had no time for small talk and when somebody invited him to make up a doubles at tennis he quickly excused himself. He was not here to play games.

'He really hated the Germans,' Caldwell says. 'Absolutely no chivalry about him; the only good Hun was a dead one. I am afraid we rather fostered this bloodthirsty attitude…'

CHAPTER SIX

Although Edward later told his friends that shooting down Germans was 'as easy as piddling down a well', all his first attempts reduced him to frustration when he saw that even when you did have the advantage it was still damnably difficult, and he had to admit that the Germans were just as clever as the allies in a dog-fight. Part of the difficulty came from being involved in a fight in which ten or twenty planes twisted and turned about in the air, blending together to make their own aerial arena. How could you tell one from the other as they flashed past and you were busy looking after your own survival? This was something the flying schools never mentioned. Men with two good eyes found it hard enough, but in Edward's case it was harder because he had only one eye to use for all purposes.

There were diversions. Some pilots had hobbies, others drank and most of them were interested in women. Edward's love affairs involved the daughter of a local priest and then, when her father warned him off, a French girl named Odette, whose father kept a local estaminet. She was in her early teens and he could hope for nothing except conversation and kindness. He was her storybook hero and she adored him with the unspoilt devotion of a child. In his darker moments he knew how hopeless the relationship was. He was thirty while she was only a child. By certain crude standards he was hampered by his chivalrous ideas about women. With his halting French, they were drawn together in an idyll of friendship. He never mentioned her in his diary, which he reserved for details of his missions.

13.4.17: I went over the line for the first time. Escorting FEs. Formation of six machines together. Heavily Archied. My feelings were funny. A group burst near me – about 100-feet. I did some stunts quite involuntarily. Lost my leader and deputy-leader, but led the patrol down south. Returned safely after a very exciting time...

When pilots were flying at this pace, twice and sometimes three or even more times a day for days on end, strains quickly became apparent, even in the strongest men. Less than a week after that foray when he led the patrol back, he avoided looking in the mirror for fear of seeing how haggard he was becoming.

While he had always been anxious to put up a good show on operations, he knew that things were not coming up to expectation. The others were starting to murmur about the way he stayed out of fights when he might well have started shooting. Was he scared? Was he another yellow one? In fact, he was merely lacking confidence due to insufficient experience and practice. But once started the gossip went on and nothing could stop it except Edward's acquittal of himself. Nobody faced him directly with the charge that he was not doing his share. They preferred to watch and comment, that was all. But he was well aware of the hostile atmosphere and knew what they were thinking. He continued flying the Nieuport, though lacking his old confidence and telling people that it was a clumsy, heavy machine. They were sceptical. He was covering up

Not for a moment did he even hint what was going on in letters to his mother. About this time he wrote:

'Dear Mum... You will see from the address that we are prohibited from giving you the name of the place at which we are stationed, but I can say that we are in the actual thick of it, and I go across the lines every day (sometimes three times) when the weather is not actually prohibitive. The battlefields wear an awful aspect viewed from above – covered with shell holes and craters, which remind me of photographs of what the earth looked like at the very beginning of things. It's extraordinary how anything can live through such a bombardment. Just like a plum pudding with ten times too many currants and raisins mixed. I fly a machine on my own, and I can tell you it's very lonely being up in the clouds all by one's self, with the anti-aircraft shells coughing and barking all around one, and big guns on the ground flashing and spitting continuously. I've been over the German towns, but the Huns clear off almost invariably when they spot us coming...'

His anxiety knotted itself and settled in the pit of his stomach. While bullets seemed to be going straight to the mark, they had no effect. Was it his eye? If only he could get one Hun, things would look better, but he knew that his shooting was often wide and the difficulties of getting a bullet within ten yards of a fast – moving enemy plane seemed practically insurmountable. He knew the feeling of being badly frightened and was determined to overcome it.

Spurred on by his own resolution to do better in future, he walked out to where the Nieuport was waiting one day and took off. If he could put in an hour a day with the guns he might improve his marksmanship.

At about 700-feet he located the dummy firing area and climbed the Nieuport another few hundred feet until he was at a thousand. As he put the plane into an almost vertical dive he knew too late that something was happening to the machine. It was coming apart!

Sergeant Bovett, who was in charge of Edward's flight, described what happened. 'His bottom plane came off in the air, while diving vertically at the ground target. By skilful piloting he managed to get the machine down safely, but crashed it in a ploughed field without being hurt. It was a splendid effort. I saw the whole thing happen. When his rigger reached the crash, Mannock scared the life out of him by asking what he meant by it, but seeing the rigger's face drop to forty below zero, he burst out laughing and cheered him up by showing him the defective strut socket which had broken...'

Edward went into the Mess in search of Major Tilney, the Commanding Officer, and apologized for the accident. Tilney, the boyish-looking senior officer, could not help laughing. Crashed pilots generally raised hell about everything except their own flying. The truth was that the French makers of the Nieuport often employed unseasoned wood which was weakened by the insertion of screws. At one of these delicate stress points the break occurred.

After that things seemed better. He had been condemning himself entirely for his failure to shoot down his first enemy, but it appeared that he was not entirely to blame. Experienced observers said that the Germans were not fighting an aggressive air war. As soon as they sighted allied planes approaching, they turned tail and ran for home. The famous Richthofen circus was a myth, because they used tactics which split up allied patrols and then went for the weakest when he was virtually defenceless.

Discussing the atmosphere prevalent in the still new Royal Flying Corps at this time, Group Captain Ira Jones, who used to fly with Edward, said: 'Air fighting was generally looked upon as a game by most of the pilots; just like rugger. If one of the team in rugger is seriously hurt, he is carried sympathetically off the field, but the game carries on just the same. This spirit of 'carry on' found its counterpart only to a greater degree in the RFC spirit. This aggressively offensive spirit could not tolerate sorrow, for sorrow was liable to lower the morale. Though it might hide in the bosom of the RFC pilot, it was only permitted to exude in the secret seclusion of his sleeping quarters. In the Mess, it was an unwritten law for pilots to forget their sorrow and assume a cheerfulness which gave the impression of 'living for the day'...'

Edward wanted to live for that day and many more besides. He started taking what were considered extraordinary precautions with his plane and guns. He would not permit the armourer to sight the guns, always doing it for himself and fixing them closer than usual so that he would be able to get right on to the enemy before pressing the trigger. His eccentricities became a talking point. Nobody in the Mess guessed that he needed a better margin than any of them. A one-eyed man had to be careful.

On April 22nd the squadron moved to Auchel, then on to Bruay, about eleven miles behind the lines, which meant that they could cross into the German sector at 10,000-feet within ten minutes of taking off.

Although criticisms of Edward and his combat habits had been rife up to this time, they were not quite as sharp as they became at Bruay. Why was he always off alone, practising his gunnery with such determination? He could not shoot for toffee, some exclaimed. Others cynically pointed out that the frightened man is never quite sure of himself.

He did not miss the fact that most of them did not want to talk to him, and thought that he was an outsider only because he had not been to a good school. Many of his evenings were spent sitting apart from them, smoking his long-stemmed pipe and reading a book. He was always on the look out for a chance to fly, but if the weather were bad, the gossip-ridden atmosphere of the Mess grated on his nerves. There was no escape. Once he burst out: 'It's all very well for you fellows; you were born with a silver spoon. I had an iron shovel.'

The more elementary-minded ones guffawed at him, those with more perception suddenly knew the reason for his thorny personality. Perhaps one or two even guessed that his inverted snobbery had mated with a feeling that he was not doing what he had set out to accomplish in the war and it was having a bad effect on him. His Hamlet-like gloom was lightened only by the occasional rag, the rough 'rugger' played in the Mess whenever there was nothing else to do. But just as suddenly as he came out of his shell he wriggled back again into hiding, untouchable and remote, always on edge when roused.

The day must come when he would be able to edge into a flight and make that first kill! Until then he knew that he would remain only half a man in his own estimation. Ironically, on his next opportunity his gun jammed, as the following extract from his diary shows:

> 3.5.17: Two mornings ago, 'C' Flight escorted 4 Sopwiths on a photography stunt to Douai Aerodrome. Captain Keen, the new commander, leading. We were attacked from above over Douai. I tried my gun before going over the German lines, only to find that it was jammed, so I went over with a revolver only. A Hun in a beautiful yellow and green bus attacked me from behind. I could hear his M.G. cracking away. I wheeled round on him and howled like a dervish (although of course he could not hear me) whereat he made off towards old Parry and attacked him, with me following, for the moral effect! Another one (a brown-speckled one) attacked a Sopwith and Keen blew the pilot to pieces and the Hun went spinning down from 12,000-feet to earth. Unfortunately the Sopwith had been hit, and went down too, and there was I, a passenger, absolutely helpless not having a gun, an easy prey to any of them, and they hadn't the grit to close...

A day or so later he flew a voluntary sortie with Captain Keen and another pilot. No sooner were the three aircraft climbing than the third man turned back with engine trouble. This left Keen and himself. They flew on steadily, Edward watching the sky and from time to time glancing at his instruments.

Keen peeled off to westward. Edward decided to fly east. He was now at 16,000-feet.

He was still casting about in hopes of seeing enemy planes when three Germans suddenly came rushing in from above. He whipped his machine round to face them, knowing that the critical moment would come rapidly, because they were obviously out for a quick kill in the best German style.

He squeezed the trigger at what he believed was the right moment, but no answering blast came out of the barrel. It was jammed solid. Then, as he was desperately manoeuvring to elude the German bullets, his engine stopped.

Shrewdly observing his apparently irrecoverable situation, the Germans turned to close in for an easy execution, but Edward's mind was working fast and even as the enemy opened fire he side-slipped, then kicked his machine into a vertical dive. As soon as the Germans followed suit, he spun and then went into another dive, kicking the rudder from side to side and making it more difficult for his pursuers as they came streaking after him. Behind him their guns kept up an angry barking.

During his wild flight to safety he kept his eye on the British lines. Moment by moment he was getting nearer.

By the time he was down to 10,000-feet the Germans stopped firing. He was now close to the trenches and the Germans, discovering that they were almost over a hostile area, departed.

Alone now, he eased the plane into a shallow dive and tried to start the engine again. At 3,000-feet it spluttered and picked up.

Now that the danger was past his nerves played havoc until his entire body felt numb. He had to get out of this somehow. Assembling his wits, he turned to the east and started climbing. He was up to 12,000-feet when he suddenly saw an enemy machine, but when he realized that his gun was still jammed and the Aldis sight oiled up he turned away knowing, as he later wrote in his diary, that he 'hadn't the pluck to face him'.

Waves of sheer panic rolled over him as he flew away, wondering whether he would at any moment hear the telltale song of enemy guns on his tail. The feeling would not leave him until he sighted his own aerodrome and came in to land.

As the Nieuport's engine stopped and the propellor made its last sweep, he mustered all his energy and climbed out. As soon as he reached the ground his knees started shaking uncontrollably and he felt physically sick. He felt that he must never again have to face such an experience. He was useless as an air-fighter!

He was walking towards the huts when some small voice deep within reassured him. It was still a hell of a challenge. If he did give way now he really would be finished, once and for all.

Two mechanics passed him on the way to the Nieuport. His fitter looked at him searchingly, 'Any luck, sir?'

'What? Oh no, the gun's jammed.' He walked on and, when he saw Major Tilney, explained briefly what had happened.

Tilney nodded, apparently unconcerned but knowing in his own mind that Edward was still potentially better than any of them. It was a feeling he had had for some time. It was now or never with Mannock! He swept the rest of the explanation aside, and said: 'By the way, there's a new machine to be collected at St Omer. I want you to go over and bring it back.'

His casual manner did not deceive Edward.

As he was being driven to St Omer, he fought the biggest battle of his life. The shroud of fear which had engulfed him in the air was still there, and while the vehicle clattered over the badly – made roads he occupied himself with a savage grappling to get the caul away from his mind. It was only when they reached St Omer that he was beginning to feel slightly better, although this was not the end of fear, it was only the beginning of understanding what the fear was all about.

The white phantom of fright stayed with him for a long time, dwelling in his brain until he seriously questioned whether he was mad or sane. There was no knowing until the next engagement. It was not long in coming.

On this day, he was detailed along with some fellow pilots, including Cuddermore, Hall, Redler and Parry, to fly out on a balloon strafe. The mission would be led by Captain Nixon. It was going to be a pretty dull show, they agreed. But when they heard the briefing details, they changed their minds.

The approach would have to be at between fifteen and twenty feet, barely room in which to swing a Nieuport round. It meant flying through concentrated ground fire from machineguns and rifles. There would also be a 'flaming onions' – an incendiary anti-aircraft – which could be devastating in their destructive power.

Resolved to do his best, Edward took off with the others and flew until they were just above the balloon emplacement, and then, following Captain Nixon's instructions, they all managed to charge through the increasing hail from the ground.

A balloon came into his gunsight. He pressed the trigger, waiting for the gasbag to explode into flames.

It was a terrible anti-climax. He felt disappointed with it, with the fact that balloon strafing was not the kind of combat he wanted. True, he had got a balloon of his own, but that did not matter. A balloon was not a Fokker or an Albatros.

As soon as he landed he heard that Nixon had run into fifteen German planes, taken them on single-handed and fought like a devil until he was himself brought down after knocking over three of the enemy.

Still depressed, he was changing his uniform that evening, getting ready for his usual stroll, when he heard somebody shouting, 'Captain Ball's been shot down...'

So that was the end of Ball, his early hero whom he had never even met although he had wanted to so badly. He went on automatically brushing his tunic, trying to identify the emotion caused by Ball's death. They were sometimes wrong about these things. Planes were seen ploughing into the ground in flames, yet pilots often turned up a week or two later, having walked through the lines. He knew, finally, that Ball must be gone. There was some significant link between that fact and his shooting down the balloon. According to the others the achievement of bringing a balloon down counted as three German planes. Not that it mattered very much...

What he wanted was a German plane in his sights.

Two more weeks were spent in hard flying and trying to corner Germans. He could not claim any victories. In fourteen days he had been so close to enemy planes that he could have reached out and touched some of them. But just try and swing the Nieuport round and start shooting and all you hit was empty air! They were fast and wily and, he had to admit, very smart in their aerobatics. It was true what the observers said, the Germans were not fighting an aggressive air war.

Chances came and went like drops of rain on a window pane. A single enemy plane crossed the aerodrome at 18,000-feet, moving so lazily that Edward ignored the guffaws of the others and fled to his own machine. He flayed the engine until it was almost red hot in his anxiety to get after the insolent intruder. He had just reached 10,000-feet when he looked round at an empty sky.

The war was a baffling mixture of strict codes and cold-blooded freebooting. When General Trenchard came to No. 40 Squadron to congratulate them on their balloon strafe, he told them to shoot at the observers as well as balloons. It was a good idea to do the balloon first, then wait for the observer to start his parachute descent before shooting him to ribbons. Balloons could be replaced, observers were harder to come by.

The idea of shooting a defenceless man sickened Edward. He could not see himself following Trenchard's orders. It was so easy to say it, but harder to be the executioner.

Things did get better, although he never bothered claiming one or two possible victories, including a two-seater on May 25th and another on June 1st. They went into steep dives, but because he had not actually seen them crash he did not make much of it when writing his report.

He wanted to see some direction in what he was trying to do, yet it seemed there was a lack of signposts in this life. What was the ultimate goal? To shoot down as many Huns as possible? The phrase came back to him out of the recent past. He wryly discarded the words. They were still valid, but other considerations were beginning to creep in.

There was no accounting for the way a man was treated. At a time when he least expected it, Edward was promoted temporary flight leader because Captain Keen was still in hospital after a vicious bout of 'flu. Somebody, somewhere, must have thought that Mannock, the 'mad Irishman', had qualities of leadership.

It changed his luck. On June 7th he was able to write

> Many scraps and I brought my first dead Hun down this morning – over Lille-North. Have been up to 21,000 in the morning (3.30am) looking for the

early birds. Got rounds into a fat two-seater the other morning over Lens-Lietard. Sure I smashed him up, he went straight down without turning and I had to swing away to get out of the line of friend Archie… The push on Armentieres-Ypres sector commenced this morning. We escorted FEs over Lille on bomb-dropping business – and we met Huns. My man gave me an easy mark. I was only about 10 yards away from him – on top – so I couldn't miss. A beautiful coloured insect he was – red, blue, green and yellow. I let him have 30-rounds at that range, so there wasn't much left of him. I saw him go spinning and slipping down from 13,000. Rough luck, but it's war and they're Huns.

A few days later he engaged five enemy planes, shooting down two of them.

He was still an awkward man to get to know. New arrivals were mystified to find him treating them to about three weeks of silence and only a nodding acquaintance until he started asking them questions, sometimes very personal ones, in a sharp, brusque voice. Nobody guessed that he was in the grip of loneliness.

One man who did get close to him from the start was 'McScotch', who later remembered some of their times together.

'Mannock had changed into slacks and pale yellow socks and tie, which showed that regulations concerning dress were slightly relaxed at the front. His forage cap, soft round the edge, was poised jauntily on one side. His carriage was more alert and springy than it had been when wearing his heavy flying boots, but there was something ungainly about his walk, as if his ankles and knees were stiff… he had obviously shaved after dinner – a small trickle of blood was oozing out of a cut on his jaw. When I pointed this out to him as we walked along the dusty lane, he stopped, pulled out a yellow silk handkerchief of the same colour as his tie and carefully wiped the blood away, asking me, 'Are you sure it's all gone?'

'I laughed at his concern and remarked on his silk handkerchief. 'Your women friends evidently remember you.' 'They walked along together in silence until Edward started asking personal questions, demanding to know whether McScotch was a 'snob'.

McScotch felt amused. 'Snob? How do you mean? If you're thinking of social snobs, then I'm not. We each have our own particular form of snobbery: about intellect, character, ability, honesty and, I suppose, courage.'

Grinning, Edward clapped him on the back. 'Well answered! But snobbery is a nasty word. I only apply it to social and money snobbery – the empty social type particularly. There are so many damned social snobs about.' When he admitted how much he had always envied young men with a better education than he could show, McScotch tried to interrupt but was silenced by a now angry Edward. 'That's it, old boy! It isn't the school or the university, nor who your father is that matters, it's what you've got in your head and your guts,' he exclaimed.

McScotch was still digesting this when Edward explained that he was anxious to prove to the world the real value of what he thought lay within him. A few yards farther on he asked, 'Do you womanize?'

They were entering the village when McScotch said that he liked women, though not in the dark ferreting way of so many of the men.

'Now that I know something about you,' Edward said as they drew abreast of the estaminet, 'come in here and have a drink. I'm going to introduce you to a very nice young girl.'

McScotch came to a stop, shaking his head. 'I don't mind having a drink, but

Edward Mannock when under inital pilot instruction at Hendon in August 1916.

Mannock relaxing in a deckchair, St Omer, June 1918.

Off duty view of 85 Squadron pilots at St Omer, June 1918. From left: Dymond; Major Edward Mannock (OC Squadron); unknown; Callaghan; and Longton.

Mannock at Bruay in April 1917, when serving with 40 Squadron.

Mannock seated in a SE5 of 74 Squadron, about to leave for France on 31 March, 1918.

Mannock (left , at telescope) and Pettigrew of 40 Squadron, Bruay 1917, 'spotting' hostile aircraft.

Mannock when a Captain with 74 Squadron.

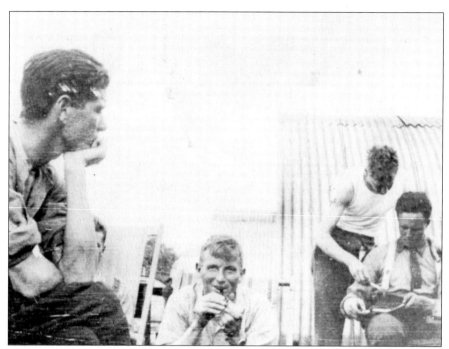

Mannock (left) with D C Inglis (lighting pipe), the New Zealander who accompanied Mannock on his last, fated sortie on 26th July, 1918.

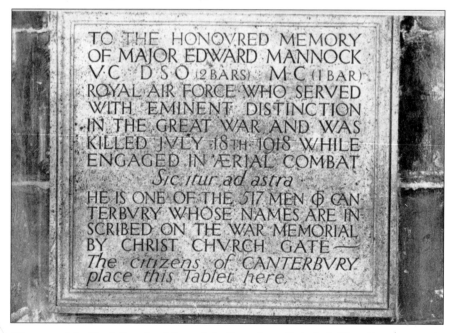

TO THE HONOVRED MEMORY
OF MAJOR EDWARD MANNOCK
V.C D S O (2 BARS) M C (1 BAR)
ROYAL AIR FORCE WHO SERVED
WITH EMINENT DISTINCTION
IN THE GREAT WAR AND WAS
KILLED JVLY 18TH 1918 WHILE
ENGAGED IN ÆRIAL COMBAT
Sicitur ad astra
HE IS ONE OF THE 517 MEN ⊕ CAN-
TERBVRY WHOSE NAMES ARE IN-
SCRIBED ON THE WAR MEMORIAL
BY CHRIST CHVRCH GATE —
The citizens of CANTERBVRY
place this Tablet here.

The memorial tablet dedicated to Mannock in Canterbury Cathedral. The tablet is incorrectly inscribed in that the date of Mannocks death should read July 26 and not July 18.

I'm not particularly keen on meeting girls.' He put a broad accent on the last word. 'I thought you weren't either.'

Taking his arm and almost dragging him through the low doorway, Edward burst out laughing. 'Come on, you fathead! This isn't one of *that* sort. She's the youngest, prettiest, sweetest and most innocent young thing you ever met. Why do you think I changed into slacks and shaved for the second time today?'

As they sat down at a table the French landlord hurried forward, greeting Edward, who said: '*Deux champagne avec cognac.*' It was a fluent phrase, one of the few which he could rattle off without stumbling.

The landlord bustled to a curtained doorway. 'Odette!'

McScotch gave Edward a dubious smile. The situation was beginning to resemble many others.

Edward groaned. 'Damned fool, giving me away like that! These French people are supposed to be so discreet and diplomatic – but just see what he's done!' He looked confused and a little embarrassed because others in the small room were now giving him knowing looks.

When Odette came forward all Edward's embarrassment melted. He was obviously infatuated with the girl and, after introducing McScotch as his ami and saying that he was an *aviateur fameux*, promptly forgot his existence as he went into an animated conversation with her, half in English, half in French. They were like children together.

What McScotch saw was a girl of no more than sixteen or seventeen, 'a really beautiful blonde with that ethereal look that only fair women can possess.' He was not surprised by Edward's affection for her, but at a loss to discover what he wanted out of it beyond friendship.

The lighter side of life was always clouded over by the shadow of German planes in their excursions over the British lines and then the quick dash for home, hounded by the savage Nieuports. Edward discovered that his reactions were keen: he was quick into the cockpit and faster off the ground than most of the others. Only one aspect of his personality still held him back, his inferiority complex. Was education synonymous with rapid success? he wondered. Supposing a man without much education put into the war the efforts of six men, what would happen then? Would it lead to success? Barring accidents, he felt that it should. Barring accidents...

He was out one day when he let the Nieuport go into a steep dive until she hugged the ground. His speed was about 120-mph and the plane was on top of her form. At this rate he would be over the aerodrome within a few minutes. He was steadying himself to lift her and make a banked circuit, then land, when he felt a double impact in his right eye and a spurt of pain which went right through his head. Clawing at his face, he tried to get out of the near-darkness caused by fluid as it streamed from the eye socket and down his face. He struggled to pull out a handkerchief, swearing at himself for not wearing goggles.

With his right eye practically darkened, he fished round for the grit or whatever it was, using a handkerchief bunched in his fist against the onrush of wind. The pain grew. The more he tried to get the particle out of his eye the worse the pain became, lowering a red-hot shield over the eyeball.

He tried to calm himself, but was aware of the urgent speed of the Nieuport. Flying blindly, he tried to keep the plane level for a few more seconds. He could not see anything except a milky film spreading over his vision.

The plane came arrowing low across the aerodrome, still moving at about 120-mph.

Pilots playing tennis dropped their racquets and raced to the perimeter, recognizing the machine. It was Mick, out on one of his mad stunts! There was some argument about it, because he had never been known to fly as riskily as this, reserving aerobatics for times when he needed them in a fight.

The Nieuport shot across the area, wobbling from time to time as though the controls no longer answered. In the cockpit Edward was staunching away the fluid as it blew down his face, making his cheeks icy.

Making one last effort, he partly closed the throttle and concentrated on feeling the wheels down on to the grass. The landing was an uncertain one, made more by instinct than judgement, and as it came to a stop he threw himself out of the cockpit and staggered into the Mess, the now saturated handkerchief held tightly against his eye. While a concerned officer was examining him, trying to find the grit, he suddenly went limp.

'Good God, Mick's fainted,' somebody said incredulously. 'He told me the other day he'd never fainted in his life.'

'He's for hospital. Some grit whacked him in the eyeball!' But it was not grit. Two fragments of steel had broken away from the engine cowling of the Nieuport. After two days they managed to get the second piece out. By this time his eye muscle was inflamed, but it was not so much this as the need to prevent them discovering his left eye was useless that worried him. Hospital depressed him. Lying in bed, most of his head enclosed in a thick white bandage, he was in darkness most of the time. Feeding himself was one problem which he conquered by using his sense of touch.

As soon as they discharged him, he went straight back to the squadron to find Major Tilney waiting for him. For one terrible moment Edward felt sure that he was going to tackle him about his eyesight, but the senior officer's mind was on other things. 'You've got three weeks' leave due to you in a fortnight, Mick. You'd better have it now. Do you a world of good.'

Taken aback, Edward was about to argue it out and say that he felt like flying at once when he noticed that Tilney was serious.

It turned out to be a holiday full of mixed emotions. When he arrived to see Julia, his mother, he discovered that she was drinking far more than was good for her. The feeling between them, once so strong and loyal, melted away. He had changed, so had she. In one drunken bout she accused him of not paying her enough attention. He rounded on her, roughly admitting that they had grown apart – but why should they stay together when she was in such a drink-sodden state?

She was an adept at angling for sympathy. Left with her two daughters, she cried that she could not really rely on Paddy, her eldest son. He had cut himself off from them and she was at a loss to understand why. Or if she knew, she did not admit that he viewed her drinking habits with distaste. Somebody else in the family once said that drinking was their hobby, forgetting that it is also a notorious Irish pastime.

Edward did not know what to do. He was aware that if Paddy failed to send the voluntary allowance on the dot, his mother wrote strong letters, almost demanding the privilege. When she was in a really bad temper she could sit down and write incredibly long letters about all she had been through for them. Her histrionics cut very little ice.

It was now obvious that Paddy had, by his own uncompromising values and strict morality, made a rod for his own back. Edward did not bother to discuss it with his mother. All he wanted was to get out of her sight as soon as possible and head for the more congenial atmosphere of the Eyles's house at Wellingborough. It was hard to leave her like this.

What was wrong with Julia Mannock? She was a hot-blooded Celt, given to bouts of emotionalism even at the cost of alienating her sons... and there was always the solace of the bottle when things went wrong, as they often did. She loved her Edward more than Paddy, but it was a love compounded of hatred and affection, a bond with a potential disintegration factor. She had never really got over the Corporal's liaison with the other woman, his steadfast refusal to return to a home in which the responsibilities were far too much for his limited mental and financial resources.

It had deteriorated into an unhappy family. Not only affected by the war, it was smitten by the peculiar blight which settles on some families like a curse. Edward was on the verge of leaving his own mother for good. He knew that things between his sister Jess in Ireland and her husband, Ted, were far from harmonious (they split up eventually) while Nora's marriage to a man called Llewelyn was also showing signs of foundering.

Now he took one look at his mother's drink-ravaged features and without feeling any emotion beyond one of relief caught the Wellingborough train. None of the ties seemed to mean much to him any more; he had been tortured on the rack of family loyalties too often. Perhaps he had wanted this break for years, from the time when he went to Turkey, to be on his own, self-reliant and in no need of any close emotional relationships.

The Eyleses understood him better than anybody else. He looked very serious as he said to Mrs. Eyles: 'I feel my age is rather against me in this new intensive form of warfare. But I think there's room for brains in this game. I hope to balance the weakness of the flesh by formulating tactics. I've spent hours thinking out schemes of catching the Hun since I've been home. You watch me bowl them over when I return!'

His next stop was London because he wanted to have a look at the RFC Club in Bruton Street about which he had heard so much. It would be a change to see all those pretty volunteer waitresses who treated visiting pilots with such good-humoured tolerance. The atmosphere brought everything back into perspective. As a stranger, he watched men with household names playing the fool and letting off steam. When some of the furniture was broken in a rag one night, they all trooped downstairs next morning to evaluate the damage, then clubbed together to pay for it.

He returned to France some days later with just one smouldering dissatisfaction in his mind. Since being in England he had noticed the vast number of charity bazaars which were being held 'in aid of our boys at the front'. Many of the organizers were, in his stringent opinion, shirkers who were intent only upon one thing, avoiding the real war effort. His dislike of them as a class interlinked with a boiling up of a violent hatred whenever he happened to catch sight of pictures of society people peacocking it in the pages of the 'best' magazines. It was all he could do to prevent himself from tearing them up and stamping the fragments of paper into the ground. He was still a cloth cap socialist.

As soon as he reached France he heard that McScotch was in hospital as the result of a collision. Still angry about the doings of 'Society', he went to visit him, and his heavily bandaged friend could only listen and nod his agreement as the voluble Irishman spoke his mind. At last, Edward said in quieter tone: 'But all that has nothing to do with us out here. We've got to get on with the work and leave the retribution till afterwards. Fellows like ourselves who understand what we are doing have got to put every ounce into it...'

Had he been able to talk more freely, McScotch might have questioned Edward's apparently solid belief that post-war society would be composed of men who knew what was what. True, there was a lot of Socialism being talked among the troops in France, but it did not mean they would go on being Socialists once they were finished with war. Edward seemed to believe that everybody held to his principles in the same way, completely forgetting that men could be very weak.

Edward's rich Irish voice tailed away and stopped as the ward sister arrived with some tea. His eyes followed her to the door. He was more like his old self as he turned to McScotch, who was watching his obvious emotions with a twisted grin on his plaster-crossed face. 'Look here, you old blighter, I know why you like lying here,' Edward blurted out. 'I'll have to see about having a spell in hospital myself!'

Returning to his sleeping quarters, Edward reflected that he was now in a position to test all those tactics against the Germans which he had so carefully planned in England. He was to discover that the transference of theory to a practical form was no easy step and met with no success.

Steeped in a new sense of failure, he did not feel that he wanted to discuss why things were going wrong with anybody, although, as he well knew, criticisms of his stubborn attitude were being made again. Nobody seemed to have a good word to say for him. He was puzzled and bewildered, and this time the reason for it was almost impossible to find. His total score was still only three. It stuck at that. He questioned whether to go and talk about it to the new flight commander, 'Zulu' Lloyd, then decided to wait.

One day, when he was feeling more confident of himself, he tried to join in a Mess discussion about tactics. He was full of witticisms and jokes, which dried up as soon as he uttered them. In the end, without another word, he swung away from that tight little circle, feeling the full force of being snubbed.

McScotch described it. 'One or two pilots even declared that Mick had 'stayed out' when the others went into scraps. They resented the development of his self – assurance and optimism.'

One possible reason for this resentment was Edward's essential jaunty 'Irishness' which, most of the time, was an act and a front to guard against depression. McScotch was still very new to the squadron, he had no way of judging whether the accusations of cowardice were right or wrong, so he steered a middle course while still remaining Edward's closest friend and without committing himself stuck to his opinion that he was not a 'quitter'.

'Zulu' Lloyd was not totally ignorant of what was going on. Soon after he took command of the flight somebody alleged to him that Mannock, if not exactly yellow, was certainly a bit of a funk.

'I was told that he had been in the squadron two months and that he had only shot down one single Hun out of control, and that he showed signs of being over-careful during engagements,' Lloyd said.

'He was further accused of being continually in the air practising aerial gunnery as a pretence of keenness. In other words (he was) suffering from 'cold feet'.'

It was time for Lloyd to tackle Edward about it. It was a difficult interview and one which Lloyd did not relish. Edward obligingly helped him out by admitting the truth. 'Of course, I've been very frightened against my will – nervous reaction,' he said quietly. 'I've now conquered this physical defect and having conquered myself I will now conquer the Hun.'

Lloyd nodded encouragingly. It made sense. He told Edward to continue.

'Air fighting is a science,' Edward said. 'I've been studying it and have not been unduly worried at not getting Huns at the expense of being reckless. I want to master the tactics first.'

Would the other pilots accept this excuse? It was doubtful, and so Lloyd decided to keep what Edward had said to himself and wait and see what happened. As it turned out, it was soon Edward's turn to defend McScotch in the face of squadron disapproval.

McScotch was one of several pilots who were mixed up with a series of hectic fights with the Germans some days after his conversation with Edward. He was in the middle of the engagement when he noticed with horror that the bolt of his gun had broken in two pieces. He flew away from the battle area, hoping to be able to reassemble the gun and then return. It did not work out as he planned. The bolt was beyond immediate repair, so he dropped the pieces in his pocket and flew back. He arrived to face a kind of jury composed of his own pilots. They were unanimously against him for deserting them at a time when the fight was warming up. Angrily, he tried to explain the cause. He could not be expected to stay in the middle of that maelstrom, a sitting duck, could he? They were beyond understanding, or so it seemed, and even the sight of the two pieces of the bolt which he threw down on the Mess table did nothing to pacify them.

Edward, who had been listening and watching, suddenly pushed forward, elbowing others aside. He glared at their disbelieving faces. 'Do you know Mac had the guts to dismantle his Lewis gun in the scrap?' he flared up at them. 'He came back here with a broken bolt in his pocket and his gun reassembled. If any of you has either the ability or the courage to do that you're a damned sight better than I think you are.'

Many years later McScotch reflected that on one occasion when Mannock's own gun jammed in a scrap he had carried on the fight armed only with a pistol, and added, 'I did not even have that...'

It was one of many flurries of excitement. With their nerves worn thin by the cut and thrust of the air war, pilots were always snapping at each other's throats, trying to break down reputations as they were made, so obviously jealous to the outside observer but potentially dangerous to one another.

It reminded Edward of his own mixed family life. He needed some relief from this kind of thing and Odette provided it, though not in the usual way. He knew that some of the others went whoring whenever they had the chance, but it was a deep-seated memory of his father's antics with other women which kept him celibate coupled with a kind of fear of women. Odette was still a defenceless, naïve child, and to her he was *mon brave aviateur*, an avuncular figure who cracked jokes and amused her. This was the way he wanted it, the way he tried to preserve it.

She cultivated a small garden at the back of the estaminet and it was here that Edward and McScotch spent many an afternoon, eating the cakes she made especially for them, sipping the wine she brought out. One day Edward clapped his hand to his forehead and exclaimed: 'I've got no right to be sitting here! I ought to be up there, waiting for the next two-seater that comes over!'

McScotch knew that he was thinking about the recent menace represented by the silver-painted shape of an enemy reconnaisance plane which had been circling, taking photographs to prepare the ground for the lumbering night bombers. Although haphazard bombing had little effect on the operations of the squadron, there was always a chance of a missile landing on top of the hangar and blowing some machines and part of the maintenance department to smithereens. Edward had already made a secret pact with himself that he would shoot the reconnaissance plane down if he got the chance.

Odette pretended to be annoyed. 'But monsieur deserves the tea I have made for him! Tomorrow I will allow you to go up and kill the Boche.' The seemingly innocent child's face held a picture of the sudden deaths which she had so often witnessed as planes came fluttering to the ground, blooming out a foul orchid of burning oil and petrol. The next moment she had recovered herself. 'You don't like to come here?'

Edward disregarded her question. 'But will you say that tonight when they come over and you all go up in the air – BOOF! – like that?' He was suddenly appalled by his own words for the effect they had on her. She was terrified. He took her hand. 'Little French Odette, we have come over here to fight the Boche who are destroying your country, not to have the honour of a lovely tea made by your sweet hands.'

He was at his most Irish. She did not quite understand what he meant, so, bringing out the pocket dictionary which he always carried, he started translating, word by word.

Strolling back with McScotch, he suddenly said: 'Don't you think we're darned lucky to have found a sanctuary like that? I'm going to shoot that Hun down next time. It'll teach them they can't come over here with impunity!'

The thought began to ride him. He had to get that reconnaissance plane. On July 15th he took the Nieuport up, letting the half-throttled engine hold it at 1,500-feet as he sat and watched the void between his own machine and the earth. He hoped that he was almost invisible to any German pilot, who would be more intent on getting pictures of the aerodrome than in fighting Nieuports.

If it did not come today, Edward vowed, he would try again tomorrow and the next day, and on and on until something *did* happen.

He was in luck. A German two-seater flew almost cockily across the lines, making a straight run for the aerodrome with a sureness which enraged Edward. In the cockpit the observer would probably be checking his camera sights now, preparing to get the photographs. He was not to know that he would never get home with them…

Edward permitted the German to circle the aerodrome and then, as he turned for home, put the Nieuport into the long dive which would bring him to a point of interception slightly above the enemy.

The Nieuport was gathering velocity now. The wind hissed through the wires, making them vibrate, gently at first and then ascending to a weird scream. He concentrated on the shape of the German plane as it grew by the second in his gunsight.

He shot the reconnaissance plane to pieces, riddling it with hundreds of rounds, pumping them into the engine and the bodies of the observer and pilot whom he could see slumped forward, their war finished. Something made him go on with it until his ammunition was practically finished.

The plane crashed near Avion. He made a note of the place. It would be interesting to examine it on the ground and see just how much damage had been done.

He landed in a riotously happy mood, buoyed up by his success. Commandeering a tender, he told the driver to go hell for leather to Avion. By the time they arrived and located the wrecked machine, his spirits had subsided and he tramped across the churned-up field in a serious mood.

The pilot was only an NCO The observer was an officer with a heavy pistol in one hand and the other round a shape which lay across his lap. Edward looked more closely, trying to make out what it was. The next moment he swung away, his face contorted with genuine grief. The observer had been carrying a small black and tan terrier for company. One of the bullets had caught it in the head.

He had himself driven back without a word. Feeling physically sick, he looked for McScotch and poured out a description of what he had seen. His friend listened with signs of a growing revulsion showing on his face, then shook his head. 'I'd never like to see the smashed up body of a man I'd killed,' he murmured.

Edward, his eyes softening, said: 'Neither would I, old boy. It sickened me, but I wanted to see where my shots had gone. Do you know, there were three neat little bullet holes right here.' He pointed at the side of his head, then fell silent, trying to calm his mind. 'No matter how much nausea it caused, I *had* to find out – and this one down on our side was my only chance. I've missed so many of them and I wanted to know for sure.'

He remembered the body in officer's uniform in the rear cockpit. 'Pity I didn't kill him instead of the poor pilot,' he said dryly.

This incident imbued him with greater confidence. A day later he brought down another German and the following week was able to report yet another one.

Although Edward's score was still low compared with many, his spirit and tenacity caught the notice of General Trenchard, who visited the squadron and personally congratulated him. It marked the end of all doubt and his critics became his admirers.

The new spirit which had entered into him was reflected in his diary entries. On July 20th he wrote:

> This morning we went out north as far as Armentieres, Keen leading a six patrol. Ran into three of the finest Hun pilots I ever wish to meet. Had quite an exciting and enjoyable ten-minute scrap. These Huns were artists. Do what I would, I couldn't get a line on them and it was six against three. Eventually, they drew off apparently none the worse for the encounter. I shall always maintain an unsullied admiration for those Huns.

But something was going on behind his back and he was blissfully unaware of it. General Trenchard was having an eye kept on him. Reports went regularly to field headquarters, detailing what Mannock was doing. The climax came on July 19th, the day prior to his encounter with the three Germans.

McScotch was preparing to fly up around the lines, looking for trouble, when Godfrey, the orderly room corporal, appeared, waving a telegram and searching for Edward. McScotch hung over the edge of his cockpit. 'Who wants him?' he shouted.

'Telegram, sir.' Godfrey was grinning widely as he held it out for McScotch to read.

Wondering what the fuss was all about, the pilot slid down to the ground and flattened it out against the fuselage. There were only seven words on it: *2nd Lieutenant Mannock awarded the Military Cross.*

Sharing Godfrey's elation, McScotch quickly glanced round the area. A few moments previously 'Zulu' Lloyd and Lieutenant Crole had driven by to ask him to go to Bethune for a drink, but he refused, placing more importance on his one -man trouble-shooting mission. This telegram altered everything. Now he *had* to go to Bethune because there was some shopping to be done!

He bellowed to Lloyd and Crole to hang on for a minute, then dashed into Edward's empty quarters, where he snatched up his spare tunic and leapt into the car, telling Lloyd to drive fast to Bethune.

Later that afternoon Edward landed from a sortie and pensively made his way to his quarters, ready for a wash and a good hot meal. Flying was a chilly business at present. He longed for a good hot French summer. He went into his quarters, slamming the door behind him, and started peeling off his crumpled flying suit. He was about to hang it up when he suddenly noticed his spare tunic hanging on the nail. It looked different. There was something over the left pocket.

McScotch's shopping had been swift and efficient. All he wanted was a strip of the coloured ribbon which represented the Military Cross. He talked a woman into sewing it on, then rushed back and hung it on the nail before Edward's return.

In his diary Edward gave the award one line, and some time went by before the *London Gazette* published the full citation, which ran: 'In the course of many combats, he has driven off a large number of enemy machines, and has forced down three balloons, showing a very fine offensive spirit and great fearlessness in attacking the enemy at close range and low altitudes under heavy fire from the ground.'

He never applied for his medals up to the time of his death, although he had several opportunities to do so.

McScotch said: 'What that official recognition of his valour and devotion to duty meant to Mick only his best friends knew. His serious patriotism had been sullied by his consciousness of what he had called 'snobbery'. The award half persuaded him that, after all, things might not be so bad. This acted as an encouragement, not to gain more decorations but to continue wholeheartedly to do his duty. In one way it helped him to get over the awkward transition that was taking place in his mind; it softened his bitterness and intensified his activities, giving him both actual and moral confidence in everything he did.'

But if General Trenchard and the others seriously believed that the Military Cross was going to allay Edward's fears and recurring depression, they were wrong.

CHAPTER SEVEN

If his crust of reserve remained intact, Edward was now showing more confidence in himself. Things had become a little easier to reconcile and understand, and the old trouble over his inverted snobbery was relegated to something deeper within him. And he had become part of the struggle, as his diary showed.

> 19 August, 1917: Had a splendid fight with a singleseater Albatros Scout last week on our side of the lines, and got him down. He proved to be *Leutnant* von Bartrap, Iron Cross, and had been flying for eighteen months. He came over for one of our balloons near Neuville St Vaast, and I cut him off going back. He didn't get the balloon either. The scrap took place at 1,000-feet up, well within view of the whole front. And the cheers!
>
> It took me five minutes to get him to go down, and I had to shoot him before he would land.
>
> I was very pleased that I did not kill him. Right arm broken by a bullet, left arm and left leg deep flesh wound. His machine – a beauty, just issued (June 1/I7) with a 220-hp Mercedes engine, all black with crosses picked out in white lines – turned over on landing and was damaged. Two machine-guns with 1,000 rounds of ammunition against my single Lewis and 300 rounds!
>
> I went up to the trenches to salve the bus later, and had a great ovation from everyone. Even generals congratulated me. He didn't hit me once.

Brought three Huns down during the Lens push. Great luck.

He was able to write about these incidents with the enthusiasm of a school cricket captain. Only a few months before it had been difficult even to think about them. He was in love with the air and came near to knowing affection for the enemy planes which came out to provide him with all his chances.

He was anxious to get at one in particular who flew under the nickname of 'The Purple Man'. This was probably Werner Voss, the greatest of the German air fighters who was reputed to use a purple-painted machine.

In one of his diary entries Edward wrote:

Ran into my old friend, the 'Purple Man' again a few weeks ago. No luck. He's a marvel. For ten minutes I was 300-feet above him, and he manœuvred so cleverly that I was unable to get my gun on him once...

The following incident occurred between August 16th and 20th, 1917. Edward and McScotch had been out together on an offensive patrol on their own. McScotch returned first and Edward arrived later, as his engine had cut at 10,000-feet on the German side of the lines. McScotch describes the incident as follows

It was still early when I recrossed the lines and, hoping Mick would see my machine in Mazingarbe,[1] landed there instead of returning to the home aerodrome. I was lying in the thick clover keeping a look-out when Mick's machine appeared, gliding towards the ground. His landing was much too fast, and to my amazement he ran straight into the haystack at the end of the field. I was ready to laugh at the sight of an 'old' pilot like Mannock failing to steer clear of a haystack, but, seeing him staggering from the machine holding both hands over his face, I ran over to him. He was trembling as I put my hand over his shoulder.

'Good heavens, Mick! What a damned silly thing to do,' was my way of expressing the sympathy I felt. 'Didn't you see the haystack?'

He stood silent for a minute, then took his hands from his face and blinked.

'No, that's the tragedy of it, old boy, I didn't see it. I can't see on that side; but it's all right, I can still see with my other one. I thought *that* was done in.'[2]

It became practically impossible for Edward to keep track of his own activities in his diary. Sometimes, after only a few hours' sleep, he had an early call and took off in total darkness to hunt for the 'early birds', the German pilots who set out on their missions before dawn broke in order to be sure of getting back again. He was at 18,000-feet at five o'clock one morning when his petrol pipe broke and he landed at the advance landing ground at Mazingarbe without mishap. 'My nerves seem better lately, for which I am glad,' he wrote.

Edward tried hard to hang on to his standards, but there were times when the effort tried him strongly. In one oblique instance he showed his real colours to his friend, McScotch.

McScotch was angry because his luck was not right. He had fired straight into German planes but often failed to achieve the effect he wanted. He was riled by the invariable enemy habit of using incendiary ammunition, and after seeing some of his friends sent down in a torch-like twisting he knew that he could stand it no longer. He would give them a taste of the whip.

His idea was to fill his drums with three types of ammunition, armour piercing, tracer and Buckingham (incendiary). Nothing was farther from his mind than any spurious morality in using this terrible concoction, but he did not miss the look in the eye of Davidge, his mechanic, who was a much older man.

'I'll do it if you order me to, sir,' Davidge said uncomfortably, 'but if you're caught with that ammunition on you it will mean death for you on the other side and a court-martial for me here.'

Frustrated, McScotch brusquely told him to forget it, then hurried across to the armoury to prepare the drums himself. He pulled out the different boxes and assembled the lethal assortment, then started packing the bullets into the drums, pausing to throw out the obvious duds which somehow eluded the inspectors in the British factories. A knock on the door made him pause. 'Who is it?'

Edward's voice said guardedly: 'Let me in. I want to speak to you.'

McScotch turned the key and Edward stepped inside, slowly shutting the door behind him. McScotch felt slightly guilty, as though caught doing something dirty,

---

[1] Mazingarbe was the name given to the advanced landing-ground.

[2] It was after this that Mannock explained to McScotch how he had 'passed' his eyesight test.

obscene.

'Your mechanic told me you were in the armoury. What are you doing here?' Edward was not quite certain of himself.

McScotch returned to the bench. 'I'm mixing some filth and corruption for the Huns,' he said, choking back a fresh wave of anger. 'I'm going to make sure of the next one I hit.' The silence continued for a long time, broken only by the methodical click-click as the bullets fell into place. At last, he looked up into Edward's suddenly haggard face. He was nervously pulling the strap of his Sam Browne. It lasted only a moment, but it was unforgettable. McScotch averted his gaze and started on the third drum.

'Look here, Mac, if you have any affection for me, you'll forget about last night and this morning and let me empty out that stuff.' He was referring to the recent deaths of two pilots, Rook and Bond.

The memory of the slaughtering of Rook, a likeable young newcomer to the squadron, was still fresh in McScotch's mind. He was out to avenge him, and this diabolical 'mixture' was one way of doing it. Rook was killed by German incendiary bullets; orders forbade the allies to use incendiary bullets, but he was prepared to forget the regulations.

Edward waited, his hand on his friend's arm, half restraining him, and McScotch detected a perceptible tremble. At last he threw down the ammunition and sat down on the wooden bench. 'It isn't poor old Rook,' he exclaimed hotly. 'They've never fired anything at me but incendiary, and two mornings ago I missed a two-seater. If I had had my drums loaded with this I'd have got him – properly.'

Edward did not say anything. His face looked drawn and full of sorrow and he could not find the words he wanted to utter.

McScotch went on. 'I'm out to do as much damage as I can and the surest way, no matter what it means, is the best for me. Besides, it isn't like you to care about how they die, as long as we kill them.'

A challenge came into Edward's eyes. 'Do you mean to say, Mac, that you would coolly fire that muck into a fellow creature or, worse still, into his petrol tank, knowing what it must mean?'

Not quite knowing whether Edward was trying to play on his emotions, McScotch started to speak, then gave up.

'Well, if I can't do anything with you, I may as well go and leave you to it.' Edward stood up, straightening his tunic. Then he hesitated. 'I'll give you one last chance. If you won't chuck it for humanity, will you for me?'

McScotch asked stolidly: 'If *you* will tell me exactly why you are so upset about it.' As he finished speaking he was startled to see tears in Edward's eyes, and it made him feel uncomfortable.

Speaking in a tight voice, Edward said: 'Because that's the way they're going to get me in the end – flames and finish! I'm never going to have it said that my own right hand ever used the same dirty weapons.'

McScotch quickly divined the complexity of mixed emotions which held his friend in their grip. Others did not guess just how pent up Edward was, and even to McScotch this was the first real indication of how he really felt.

'All right, you darned old sentimentalist, if that's how you feel about it, I'll empty my drums!'

'No, let the mechs do it.' Taking McScotch by the arm, Edward led him outside and they walked up and down for a time while McScotch chaffed him about his fear. Recent events had been a bit too much for all of them, he reasoned, and the sight of one's own friends going down in flames was not exactly calculated to inspire confidence in any of them. Everybody was more or less afraid they would go down like that.

Edward turned to him. 'No, Mac, they'll never be able to get you now; that's the way they're going to finish me. The other fellows all laugh at my carrying a revolver. They think I'm doing a bit of play acting and going to shoot down a machine with it, but they're wrong. The reason I bought it was to finish myself as soon as I see the first sign of flames.'

His plane had already been fired some time before, but on that occasion he managed to extinguish the blaze by clever flying, and when he landed he told the mechanic to put more tracers in his ammunition. 'I'll give the bastards set me alight!' he exclaimed. But that was away in the past, nearly forgotten.

To others he seemed at times to be so histrionic as to be untrue to the ideals which he preached, and he came in for some strong criticism as they grew to know him better. The feelings of others impinged on his personality, making him bitter or sullen by turn, and then as suddenly turning him into an almost cartoon conception of the mad Irishman.

His attitude to the Germans swung quickly from left to right. One moment they were 'Hun swine' without a grain of humanity in their tactics, the next moment he was trying to work out ways of killing them as humanely as possible.

Nobody really understood his outlook and few wanted to. The atmosphere of the Mess was one in which the pressures of war gave rise to many small nigglings and an irritating needling rather than vast heroics. Edward's occasional emotional outbursts did nothing but embarrass the others, even after he rose in rank and became one of their leaders.

In himself there was no calm, only turmoil. The rest might accept the war and air fighting as their lot in life, but at that point their consciousness stopped. Some pilots were just as unthinking as the Germans against whom they fought practically daily over the trenches. This mentality Edward abhorred; he could not believe that a man could be so unthinking and unfeeling. Even when the sky was full of savage bullets and a fight moved at more than a hundred miles an hour, there were moments when a man should listen to his inner voice. In the moments when he was on the ground, sitting in the Mess or hunched up in his cockpit, waiting for the take-off, he would cast about for some guiding principle in life. Ideals of all kinds intrigued him, but his lack of education and his unselective random reading did nothing to provide a true key to understanding higher thought and he was often angry with himself for not knowing. If only the hostility would cease! If only they were more friendly and accepted him!

He could not guess that his own shortcomings kept many away from him, although men like McScotch and a few more did genuinely admire him for his tenacity. He was one of another generation which had been at work when the war actually started, and came into the conflict in full maturity to find themselves surrounded by a phalanx of fresh-faced youngsters transferred from the regiments and already commissioned in the conventional mould of the well – educated Army officer. The time was past when he felt any antagonism towards men like these. He was older than they and even if he were continually fighting for mental maturity he still found it necessary to at least try to get close to them. They were young enough to need a teacher.

The chance came with his Military Cross and promotion to command 'A'

Flight. He did not know that their old habit of criticizing still remained, but in deference to his new responsibilities and decoration, the anti-Mannock lobby spoke out when he was absent, seldom to his face.

'What got him his decoration was the spectacular effect of a two-seater down on our side of the lines. Other fellows have done much more without getting any recognition,' they pronounced.

This was, of course, quite true. While decorations were supposed to be awarded for sustained heroism or gallantry, the British Army commands were in the almost embarrassing position of having to dispose as fairly as possible of a certain definite quota of medals throughout the regiments.

The Royal Flying Corps had not been exactly showered with glory. Their war seemed remote from the slogging of the allied infantry through the hungry Flanders mud. Nevertheless, the pilots had shown through numerous actions that air fighting could have a deleterious effect on the enemy, although daring aerial techniques like strafing and low-level bombing were not then regarded as being of very great use in comparison with the creeping barrage, the long-range bombardment and other more traditional devices.

The award of the MC to Edward seemed to some to bear out the idea that medals were sent up with the rations and issued in much the same way as meals. And there were other points of view about Edward the man which did not enhance his reputation.

'He's soft and panders to the CO and the staff while several chaps with more courage and ability avoid these non-combatant 'groundsmen' who give out the decorations and the promotion,' they said.

This again may have been partly true, but any 'pandering' on the part of Edward stemmed from a genuine desire to prove himself. A certain amount of showmanship was necessary, though he did not ostensibly court the notice of the 'groundsmen'. His character was such that they could not fail to notice him and in an environment where the majority of men had been through college a rough diamond would always create interest.

There were no grounds at all to support the accusation of pandering to 'groundsmen' – the non-flying and staff officers. For them he had only the disdain of the tough, old-fashioned Socialist comprising an unceasing antagonism and absolutely no respect whatever.

But any appearance of friendliness which a man might show towards senior officers was liable to be misconstrued in a service so notoriously rebellious as the Royal Flying Corps, which had from the first been viewed as a 'peculiar outfit' composed of eccentrics. Now that it had settled down to fighting its own war, the label stuck. Within the squadrons men gave the appearance of being bloodthirsty 'staunch fellows' and this was aided by the journalists who likened their exploits to those of privateers, pitting their wits against the Germans in a way so wholly individualistic that it touched on sheer madness. Early reports of fights in the air between unarmed machines, with pilots taking pot shots at one another with revolvers, still persisted, although by 1917 all aircraft were scientifically armed and had powerful engines.

Another criticism of Edward in No. 40 Squadron was: 'He's just a mad lone fighter who will only lose his head with success. He's not fit to command a flight.'

This was particularly cruel. None of his detractors even guessed that he had only one good eye. They did not realize, because he did not tell them, that judging distances, ranges and speeds with one eye was about one hundred per cent more difficult than with perfect vision. It happened to be one of the silent penalties which he must pay for bluffing his way into the Royal Flying Corps, and the time was past when he could openly admit his disability. His score was now nine, more than many of the others, and to have said that he had done it with only fifty per cent vision might easily have caused further attacks on his reputation.

To many he may have seemed to 'lose his head with success' whenever he came back to report a victory. In the heat of the moment he was naturally more ebullient than the others, some of whom cultivated a detached suave air and rather fancied themselves as 'knights of the air'. Apart from his underlying uneasiness at seeing a 'flamer', when a German went down on fire, Edward tasted fully the sweet fruit of victory, and the tang was intensified by a realization that he had accomplished more with one eye than others who had full vision. But the sight of him jubilantly bouncing across from his plane after landing to make a fuss over a claimed victory was enough to make many of the others huffy.

The remarks passed about his friend made McScotch feel uneasy. They might be partly right. To understand Edward one must know all his other facets. Although he had not told McScotch the whole story of his life – he never mentioned his family – it was obvious that the parts of his personality which jarred on the others must exist for a very good reason.

What really worried McScotch was the possible effect of promotion on Edward. The sudden elevation to a responsible position in 'A' Flight could easily have a bad effect on his unsettled mental balance, making him effervescent and over-enthusiastic. The true force of it would show only when he started leading them. When McScotch took off with the others in a great roar of engines the next day, his eyes were on his leader. In the next hour it would become easier to give a full judgement of Edward Mannock.

With the grass splaying out in waves behind them, the Nieuports took off, one by one. Those which became airborne first circled round, waiting for the others to join them. Higher than them all, Edward surveyed the field as his flock of war-birds gathered.

McScotch was one of the early ones up and concentrated on circling. It was going to be interesting, watching Edward in his new role.

When the flight was fully assembled Edward gave the sign and they set out in noisy formation, burrowing through the sky towards Valenciennes.

McScotch was vaguely disturbed. Valenciennes was about thirty miles beyond the lines. It could be a pocket out of which one might not easily slip if the Germans forced them into a difficult situation. Edward was pushing his luck, taking them over as far as this.

Flying steadily, but now at an increased speed when Edward gave the signal, the planes were in an arrow formation. Edward handled his Nieuport with apparent confidence. It was possible to assess a man's temperament from the way he flew, and today Edward was obviously on top of his form for this his first real taste of leadership.

They reached Valenciennes without seeing a thing. McScotch watched Edward circling, waiting for them to line up behind him. A disquieting thought was forming in his mind. Was Edward trying to lead all five of them into trouble for his own glorification, just to show off his new power as a leader?

The Nieuports went along obediently through skies disappointingly devoid of Germans. They returned by way of Douai and Henim-Lietard, again without seeing anything. Returning from north of La Bassee, they flew at about 13,000-feet with a thick bank of cumulus some 300-feet above them. Edward was leading for a time, but when they reached La Bassée he climbed away. McScotch and a pilot called Redler followed. At the lower altitude they could have been easy prey for the high-flying Germans.

With the Nieuport's nose arrowing towards the cumulus, McScotch waited until he was well into it before setting the plane for a new climb above the cloud bank. At any moment he would be in that other world with a sparkling blue sky and long visibility. This was the arena in which so much sky fighting was done, a testing ground of men and machines. In the lower altitudes, with the plane skittering and shrieking about over the trenches, air combat was different, demanding nerve-edge tactics. He was out to show Mick Mannock a thing or two, knowing very well that he might later be accused of bloody-mindedness.

There was no warning except a momentary thinning of the cloud, then the propellor ripped through the last shreds of white vapour. The sudden rush of light made him blink. Only half expecting to find the rest of the flight waiting for him, he glanced about. There was no sign of anything except two black specks which were approaching at such a speed that they could only mean one thing, the enemy.

McScotch managed to separate one of them and, in a shattering burst of gunfire, sent it down. The other moved warily away, heading for the German lines.

He looked at his wrist watch. Two and a half hours since take-off. If he could find Edward and the rest of them there might be a chance of some more action. The fuel level was going down steadily. There was only one thing to do. He headed for home, conscious of his 'crime' in cutting away from the flight. It might even teach Edward a lesson!

Landing at Bruay, he went straight to the Recording Officer's office and started filling in a form to claim his victory, quickly sketching in the details and a description of the area in the usual terse phrases. He was about to sign his name and blot it when he was aware of somebody watching him from the doorway. He slowly looked up and saw Edward.

Before he could say a word about having 'lost' the flight, Edward walked away, his flying helmet dangling from the fingers of his right hand, a hurt look on his face. McScotch felt a wave of sympathy and pathos. Edward might easily believe that he had openly rebelled against his leadership in front of the others. It was not really so.

That evening after dinner, when McScotch was sitting in his but writing a letter home, Edward walked past, dressed in a light-coloured shirt and slacks and carrying a cane, which was unusual for him. He dawdled for a time, evidently trying to catch McScotch's eye, so that in the end McScotch stopped writing and called out: 'Want your constitutional, Mick?'

'Yes, all right,' he said casually. 'If you want to come... with your flight commander.'

McScotch's lips puckered into a faint smile and the smile became a grin, then both men burst out laughing.

'I don't think a serious talk will do either of us any harm.' McScotch stood up and put his writing materials away, then reached for his cap.

'All right, then, old boy – but hurry up.' Edward started cutting at the grass with his stick.

They were halfway to the town when Edward burst out: 'You hurt me like hell this morning, Mac! Why did you leave the flight?'

This was Edward back in his old role, asking direct questions without beating about the bush. McScotch seriously thought of lying to save face, but the bluntness of the question took him aback and he had no alternative but to answer: 'Because I *meant* to hurt you.' He was now beyond worrying about his friend's feelings. 'You know how much I admire your courage and your ideas, and I was so glad to see you get your reward. But when I saw the change that had come over you I began to feel that the ingenuous fellow who took me in hand when I first joined the squadron has, after all, only the ordinary standard values. The fact that you have achieved a little advance makes no difference to me. I've always valued you as a man in favour or in disrepute – for what's in your mind.'

For the matter-of-fact McScotch this was quite a soul-searching speech and he felt slightly embarrassed at having spoken so frankly, but in the next moment all that disappeared. To his surprise Edward started arguing and trying to justify his new attitude.

'Do you remember what you said the first time we met?' McScotch interrupted, struggling to control his rising temper. 'You said something to the effect that what mattered was not education but what a man had in his head and his guts.' He paused before putting in the final thrust. 'Are your ideals really as steadfast as you consider them to be?' He tapped the ribbon of the Military Cross on Edward's tunic. 'Don't tell me *that* makes any difference to what you think of yourself!'

This onslaught against his esteem caught Edward off guard. He rapped back: 'Hell, none at all!' He tugged at his friend's sleeve, his voice softening, 'Come on, old son, you win every time. I suppose it's because you've been to university. I'm going to study!'

They drank a toast to his command and then Edward left McScotch to his own devices while he concentrated on Odette, ostensibly to improve his French. McScotch wryly reflected that this kind of study would not take him far.

He was still convinced that the combination of the Military Cross and being given command of 'A' Flight had debased Edward. As he sat there, nursing his drink, frowning over his thoughts, and wondering how it would all turn out, he was quite determined to remain on the middle path as far as Edward was concerned. Anything else would be wasted when you were dealing with such an odd personality.

They returned to the squadron in a fluctuating mood of semi – contentment, carefully guarding their remarks and letting the conversation rest on a neutral level.

Most of the pilots were sitting near the tennis court, listening to the gramophone, and as they passed by several caustic remarks were fired at Edward. He took no notice and was about to move on when one of the pilots said nastily: 'It's about time a *real* man went down to see that fair-haired bit of stuff in the estaminet.'

In the silence as the gramophone record finished, Edward swung round, going scarlet as he blurted out: 'Anyone who tries to muck about with that child will have his head knocked off!'

While they were all guffawing at him, one of them shouted over the catcalls: 'And who'll do the knocking?'

Before Edward could fund an answer McScotch chipped in, 'I will.'

This incident brought home to McScotch some of the true values of Edward. It was easy to be friend and foe at one and the same moment, due, perhaps, to the fact that both men were Celts with all the temperaments of the race. It was McScotch who made the final analysis.

'This drove home to me my very real perfidy in having left him that morning. His principal antagonist was also a friend of mine, and when he tackled me later about my change of front and tried to point out that Mick had frequently shown signs of timorousness and that as far as promotion was concerned I myself was more worthy, I told him of my high opinion of Mick. This pilot was a prince of good fellows, but, like most of us, he never stopped to inquire whether or not another pilot was showing signs of being merely cautious or cowardly; he had mistaken Mick's delay in joining the first dog-fights. Unless we knew a pilot very well all that worried us were the outward manifestations. I knew that both Mick and his antagonist were fine fellows in their ways, Mick's nature being the more sensitive of the two, and it was a great pleasure to me when I was able to bring them together to 'have it out'...'

So there was, after all, a true comradeship, not just the acid ribbing of the clique, and it was caused in part by the process of continual change which went on.

In 'A' Flight Redler had to be invalided home, where he became a fighting instructor. His place was taken by Lieutenant Tudhope, who had all the qualities of a good air fighter. Mannock was taken by his manner, although he knew that Tudhope had yet to endure everything which he himself had been through only a few months before, and it could easily change him. With McScotch and a young Canadian pilot called Kennedy, he made up his own patrol members, including Harrison, also Canadian. The five of them kept the sky clear between Douai and La Bassée.

Buoyed up by the triumph over von Bartrap, Edward took McScotch and Tudhope out to dinner at the Belfort Hotel at Amiens. Something was obviously on his mind, McScotch estimated while waiting for the champagne to start flowing. He was right. Edward's eyes shone with confidence as he leaned over and said quietly, 'Tell you what we'll do! Old Richthofen is supposed to be on Dorignies Aerodrome. Let's raid the blooming place tomorrow.'

McScotch joined Tudhope's enthusiasm but felt somewhat more cautious about taking on the famous Red Baron. The prowess of the German ace intrigued him, yet he was inclined to doubt his well publicized excellence as a pilot. 'You know Mick,' he said, draining his glass, 'although I've sat over Douai and Waziers several times, I've only seen two red Albatroses there. In fact, in my opinion, the Richthofen scare is just a myth and the cleverest piece of propaganda the Germans have put over on us.'

Simulating rage, much to Tudhope's quiet amusement, Edward half rose from the table. 'I *knew* you'd kick the guts out of the thing! You want to reduce it to an ordinary bit of flying, but you don't see the moral of it. We three are going over their aerodrome; they're our particular opponents, and if we fly round at a thousand feet we can take turns at doing them in as they try to take off. We'll larn 'em even their home aerodromes aren't safe!'

He quickly filled up the three glasses again and raised his own. They must join him in drinking damnation to Richthofen and his red Albatros.

Next morning a thick white mist covered the aerodrome. Edward rose early, waiting impatiently for the others to join him. When McScotch was late, he wasted no time but went and rooted out young Kennedy, who was only too glad to take part.

The three planes shot forward into the mist, engines at full throttle, and very soon there was silence again, broken soon by McScotch's arrival and his picturesque curses as he interrogated the mechanics and found that his place had been taken by Kennedy. Realizing that it was no good trying to follow on, because Edward would now have the mission well in hand, he went and sat down on a box and chatted with a sergeant fitter, who was working on a dismantled engine.

There was not very long to wait. As the last of the mist was dispersing, Edward's plane came bumping over the turf, its engine coughing to a stop. McScotch loped towards it, expecting to see his friend come out of the cockpit grinning from ear to ear. But there was no sign of him. Not until he reached the Nieuport did he see Edward with his head clasped between his hands, sitting motionless. Hearing McScotch, he wearily held up his hand. 'It's all right, old Mac. I'm damn sorry. I'll never do it again. I've had all the gruelling I want this morning. My God! Never had such wind up in my life.'

McScotch was about to demand the details when Tudhope and Kennedy landed, one after the other.

Raising himself in the cockpit, Edward watched them taxi towards the hangars, then jumped down and started off towards them followed by a puzzled McScotch. What the hell had gone wrong?

Tudhope's Nieuport was in a terrible mess. An explosive bullet had burnt its way through his main spar, dangerously close to the V-strut, and one of his top planes was cut to ribbons by bullets. Every one of his instruments had been smashed to bits. As he got down, looking white-faced, Edward pointed out the hole in his coat collar where a bullet had ripped its way through. Fingering the hole, Tudhope's face became a study in cynical amusement.

Kennedy's machine was only slightly better off; bullets had passed through the fuselage in several places.

Scratching his head, McScotch turned to Edward. 'Did you get any of *them*?' he asked, not bothering to restrain his humour.

'No!' Edward retorted. 'My only concern was to save my blooming skin! I thought they had all of us. Thank God we're back, anyway.'

As they went for breakfast he told McScotch the full story...

After crossing the lines they sighted nine German scouts flying in formation. Full of his idea of 'showing 'em' what was what, Edward went hell for leather for them. He anticipated that they would break up and scatter as they often did. It was different this time! They resisted vigorously and attacked with dogged determination. Nine against three made the odds too heavy, so he took defensive action and felt thankful to get away without any damage.

'Then,' Edward continued to McScotch, 'the Germans, finding they couldn't destroy our three Nieuports, evidently considered the 'victory' was not assured and scattered. As we reformed we had the satisfaction of seeing them going east with their noses well down and their tails properly between their legs.'

Although Edward was well on towards the jocular stage, and wanted to hide his feelings, McScotch was quick to realize that he was actually despondent over what had happened. It was true, the Germans were not as stupid or as cowardly as Edward liked to think. Some of their tactics did not match up to those of the Royal Flying Corps, but they nevertheless had some capital pilots who knew how to use their machines to advantage in a fight.

'Well, anyway, you have one consolation. Think of the moral effect on the troops of seeing three of you wading into nine of them, and chasing them, too. Besides there's the demoralizing effect on the Huns themselves. Teach them they can't damned well fly in *our* sky when we're around.'

Feeling cheered, Edward forced him to repeat it to the others. Nodding agreement, he cried: 'Come on, let's have a drink. We'll chase the Huns out of *our* sky. That's our motto now!'

A new age started that day for Edward. Realizing that two men might have lost their lives through his own foolhardiness, he began seriously to review his fighting technique. There were some drawbacks to maturity. He was troubled by 'feelings', and once admitted to McScotch that he had definite premonitions about others. He believed, for instance, that some of them would definitely meet their deaths. His uncannily correct foresight did not, unfortunately, extend to the exact time when they might be shot down.

A month after his frightening experience with the nine enemy planes, he realized that he might be on the right track to learning leadership. In that time he lost only one pilot.

The greater testing time was yet to come.

CHAPTER EIGHT

The portents of death were embodied in unusual shapes.

The out-of-tune Mess piano, for instance; its scratched and scarred wooden panels were as sinister as the ghosts which infantrymen swore they saw corning at them through the evening mists.

The pilots hated the piano, but could not bring themselves to chop it up or feed the wood and wire to a bonfire. If anybody dared sacrifice it, he would probably die. It had already accounted for a number of deaths. Those who played it seemed to fall out of the sky under a hail of German bullets and the men said that anybody who touched those yellowed keys would not survive more than a week.

Edward did not want to believe in the piano's spell. For two pins he would have attacked it with an axe to prove there was nothing in the story. But something stayed his hand. As a Celt, he did not want to flaunt the fates, even if they did not really exist. And there had been too many unpleasant coincidences to support the superstition…

But tonight he was determined to put the thing out of his mind. The weather had made flying too risky and he joined the Mess card school which went on interminably, more for something to do than out of any real interest in the game. The orderly brought him his usual lime juice and soda and he settled himself in a vacant chair.

'Four spades to us, partner.'

Edward was playing a very slow, ruminative game. In the end he revoked.

'Honours…'

Another contemplative moment, then somebody else offered – 'Queen and knaves.'

Leaning back during the pause while they collected the cards and shuffled them, he rammed tobacco into his pipe, wafting a match across the charred bowl and drawing hard on it until it caught. He could not endure the curiously dreamlike looks which came over the card addicts' faces. 'Come on, you crab wallahs!' he bawled suddenly,

A new pilot looked at him gratefully. He was still finding his feet in this atmosphere of men waiting for action in the air. In a slightly nervous tone he offered: 'If I get much more of that tea with condensed milk and bloody rum every morning, I'll just about conk out.'

Inhaling, Edward nodded. 'Wait until you've had a few more months of it. You'll never notice the taste.' He grinned at the tyro, then picked up the cards which landed in front of him, forcing himself to apply his thoughts to the hand and play it well, but his mind's eye drifted away down the hours to the morning of the same day when he had gone out early, noticing the slight tremor on the money spiders' webs thrown across the bushes. The wind had felt liquid and fresh on his newly shaven face. Getting into the cockpit of the Nieuport he felt very happy.

Feeling 'used to things' had become important. He still remembered the time when he was so damnably conscious of what everybody else was thinking and saying about him, but all that was finished now, thank God, and he could sit here with the best of them, his long legs stuck out under the table. He was accepted!

Accepted, too, was the sustained drumbeat of the war itself, making a mockery of all the political optimism which came like successive gusts of hot air into the theatre of real war. Only a fighting pilot could hope to gain an Olympian view of it...

As you flew across at night you could see the intermittent light patterns flickering between the trenches. You were scavenging for a Hun, but those poor bastards down there were only waiting or, at best, attacking and knowing the glutinous setbacks caused by the mud. In daylight you sometimes spotted the men, shadowy shapes which went from one ferro concrete topped pillbox to another, encumbered by helmets and gas masks. At such moments your own freedom was real and true.

'Your turn, Mick!' a voice sharply reminded him.

Taking a card at random he put it down and then, too late, saw the disgust on his partner's face.

The bar orderly straightened the calendar, tilted to the left by somebody's erratic shot with a rolled-up muffler. August 22nd, 1917. The three songsters who formed the Mess glee club were going through 'Where the Black-eyed Susans Grow' for the tenth time and getting on everybody's nerves, just as they always did.

One of the card players finished his hand and pleaded an early night, so McScotch, glass in hand, slipped into the empty chair.

Edward nodded at him cheerfully. 'We'll bash you...' He started playing hard to win against the handicap of not being very polished in his strategy, at the same time ignoring his partner's savagely resigned glances. They were about halfway through the bout when the door opened and a tall man clad in flying kit walked in. To an Edward almost exhausted by having to battle against the better-playing McScotch, it was a welcome diversion. 'Hullo! Come in, old man, and have a drink.'

'I want your CO' Nobody could possibly miss the stranger's chilly tone.

Edward made a wry face. 'Oh, never mind about that. Don't be a bloody fool! Come in and have a drink.' He turned back to the cards, confident that his invitation would be accepted.

Without answering, the stranger started peeling off his jacket. As he hung it up everybody with the one exception of Edward did not miss the badges of a major-general. Some of the quicker-witted ones rose to their feet, others were caught in an embarrassment of indecision. Conversation died. Awkwardness spread like an infectious disease.

Noticing the silence, Edward slowly inclined his head, wondering what on earth was happening. At that moment McScotch gave him a cautionary nudge in the ribs.

Unabashed, because he knew that it was too late to do anything about his *faux pas*, Edward had to take the initiative. Slamming his fist in his palm in assumed annoyance, he cried boldly: 'Bang goes my squadron!' He was referring to his chances of promotion.

The abyss of awed anticipation closed as soon as somebody let out a nervous titter. The major-general smiled frostily, doing his best to reciprocate and put them at ease.

It was a resourceful McScotch who quickly shot up. 'I'll – er – the CO's in his hut, I think, sir, I'll go and'

'I'll come with you.' Standing to one side, the senior officer allowed him to go out first, then followed without once looking back at the frozen group in the Mess.

Edward glared up at the circle of amused faces. 'If any of you chaps treat *me* like that when *I'm* a general, I'll have you court martialled!' But it was impossible to keep the high spirits out of his tone. He relaxed and asked: 'Who was he, by the way?'

They were hardly over discussing Edward's gaffe before somebody else walked in, Padre Keymer, looking worried and tired. 'It's terrible to see so many young fellows killed,' he said. He had obviously just returned from conducting a funeral service. It always had a strong effect on him.

Edward did not reply. He pretended to be studying his cards. Keymer's abrupt manner was often difficult to counter.

'The wing's lost some good men the last few days.' Keymer's voice rose. 'I feel I'd like to learn to fly myself and fight. When you see so many good friends go like this…'

Many men wanted to fly against the Germans. Turning in his seat, Edward argued vehemently: 'My dear Padre, there are enough of us here to do the fighting. We've got 'em so well under we have to go over to their side and dig 'em out – and we can keep them there! We need the influence of men like you, particularly on the younger fellows. Yours is really a greater work than fighting and – with all due respect to your courage and your spirit – how old are you? How do you think you would fare as a fighting pilot?'

These were cruel but true words. Keymer appeared to assimilate them. At his age he did not profess to have the co-ordination of eye and brain, the reflex which would enable him to make split-second decisions.

McScotch returned just in time to hear Edward's remarks. He playfully reached out to the piano and thumped a thunderous theatrical finale to the speech on the piano.

The sudden sound went straight through Edward, making him leap up to face his friend. 'God almighty, I'll – I'll…' Remembering Keymer's cloth, he paused. 'Excuse me, Padre, that wasn't blasphemy, it was a real prayer. Rook played that thing before he was killed. Kennedy played the confounded thing the other night. Why doesn't Tilney give it away… or blow it up?' Then, noticing McScotch's amused expression, he shouted: 'You needn't laugh. I don't want to lose the lot of you!'

'Did Ken really play it?' McScotch asked blandly.

'He accompanied Mick until we stopped him,' Keymer confirmed. 'I'm not superstitious, but there certainly seems to be something sinister about that piano. You knew about it, why did *you* touch it?'

McScotch gave a lopsided grin. 'Yes, I knew, but – you know, it's really very queer. Last night Ken and I were sleeping up at the advanced landing ground at Mazingarbe, and he told me he had a hunch he wouldn't last more than twenty – four hours.' He regarded the scratched wooden panels and seemed about to touch the keys once more.

'If you do it again, I'll knock –' Edward was taut, both fists clenched.

Keymer's voice cut sharply into the situation. 'Shut up, you two.' He was just in time to quell the storm which could have blown up before Kennedy and some of the younger pilots arrived.

Still smiling faintly to himself, McScotch went to the bar to mix some cocktails. He was shaking them up when Kennedy spoke to him. 'Thank God it's all over for today, Mac. I mean, patrols. I *still* can't get that feeling out of my mind.'

McScotch remembered with too much clarity the youngster's voice at Mazingarbe. 'I'm glad it's over for today, too,' he admitted. Lining up the glasses, he shared the contents out, then started putting them on two trays. 'Here, take this lot over with you, Ken. I'll bring the other one,' he said pointedly. Kennedy had to be shaken out of his mood.

But peace was a long time coming that night. The drinks were hardly circulating before Major Tilney, the Commanding Officer, clattered in. 'Blast them!' he cursed. 'Some fool of an observer has reported that Dorignies Aerodrome is deserted by the enemy. We've got to corroborate the report – tonight!' As he looked round at the interested pilots his anger fell away slightly. 'It's a dirty job. As if it matters whether we find out tonight or tomorrow morning. I've tried putting them off, but they say they must know before dark.' To McScotch, still preoccupied with the drinks, he said: 'This looks like a job for you, Mac. You know those aerodromes around Douai.'

Theatrically doleful, McScotch agreed. 'All right, sir. But let's have our drinks first.'

Edward, who had been listening to Tilney, interrupted 'But look here, Major, Dorignies is just behind Douai. We can't let Mac go over them all alone at this time. All the low-flying Huns will be after him. What about an escort?' Without waiting for Tilney's agreement, he waved at the pilots. 'Who'll come? It'll be a damned fine lark!'

In the end Tilney had to shout for silence. 'Look here, Mick, we'll leave it to Mac. Would you rather go alone or with an escort, Mac?'

'Alone,' came the inevitable reply.

'It's not fair to put the question to him like that,' Edward argued, nettled. 'He's bound to give that answer. All the Huns around here would have a chance to take off to intercept a low-flying plane and Mac would have little chance of getting back at all.'

The piano... Mac played a chord on that blasted piano!

He tried again, urging and emphasizing, but still managing to disguise an anxiety based, he knew, on a stupid omen. Could a pilot give way to such primitive feelings? The others might laugh. They were young enough to giggle over the small things, but the piano had too ghastly a record, and the list of those who had played it and died was still growing. Who could disprove its spell?

Putting on a flippant tone, Edward knocked his pipe out in an ashtray. 'Anyway, as Mac is going in any case, it doesn't matter or not if the rest of the squadron uses him as – bait.'

It was an ugly way of putting it. Edward was skilled in the use of words as a means of influencing people.

'How about it?' he asked softly.

McScotch was puzzled. Edward was up to something and he would not come out with it in front of Tilney and the others. After some thought he said: 'All right then, I'd certainly feel more comfortable with some of our fellows about.'

Amid the small cheers, Edward tried to press his temporary advantage and go the whole hog. 'Look here, Major, what about taking the whole squadron out and raiding the German aerodromes? That –'

It was too much for Tilney. He shook his head in final decision. 'No, Mick, the flight that's doing the early patrol had better stay back here. After all, many of the mechanics will probably be up all night anyway, getting the machines ready for tomorrow.'

Edward capitulated while there was still time. 'Yes – yes, I see that. Anyway, the other two flights can come out.'

Tilney selected a drink, swirled it round in the glass and finished it at a gulp. 'That'll be quite all right...'

'I'll lead the first flight, then the second one can follow a thousand feet above us. Then when Mac's got his information he can climb up underneath us.'

Edward was at his best now, planning how to use the operation to advantage. What had been a routine evening developed into optimistic activity. Out of the hangars the planes were pushed by the mechanics and one by one their engines started exploding into life.

Silver-painted and swift in their new purpose, the Nieuports moved through the late evening sky, flying fast because the diminishing daylight could mean a big difference to success or failure.

Beneath the noisy flock, McScotch was too engrossed in his important mission to spare more than a moment to dwell on the awkward atmosphere that had existed in the Mess only twenty minutes ago. Edward's almost savage concern, which went far beyond his usual emotions, must have a reason for it.

He half – turned in his seat now and then to catch sight of the flight high above him, keeping an even pace like faithful hounds.

From his own commanding perch Edward mentally ticked off the Nieuports. They were just aeroplanes rushing through the darkening sky now, but in each one sat a man who was known to him, perhaps an individual who cracked jokes and fooled about or else one who was thoughtful and wrote home every day. Over there was a new pilot, doing his best to keep in line because he was not yet quite used to a team operation.

He knew them all.

A black puff of Archie blossomed ahead as the German gunners tried to get the range. They were predictable with their shooting. They would send up several more in a moment, perhaps getting closer.

Changing course slightly to throw the enemy guns off, Edward glanced across to see the rest of the Nieuports carefully following him. Mac was all right down there. He was flying fast at a low level. Nothing short of well – aimed ground fire would bring him down. The Germans were more concerned with the unusually large number of Nieuports. Already the observation posts would be phoning, passing on the news. From now on the raiders would have an attentive audience.

More black puffs from exploding shells grew in the sky. It was bad marksmanship, the aimers put off by the uncertain light.

Then they were out of it, through a clear stretch of sky again. As they tackled the next sector of hazard Edward leant forward, his eyes taken by a spattering of two separate dark specks away in the distance. They were coming closer, getting bigger, and he knew exactly what they must presage.

Almost gracefully but filled with an evil purpose, the interceptors spread out into key positions, moving as though guided by a giant hand which reached out of the cloud ceiling.

Edward gave a quick signal, alerting the Nieuports. They knew what to do – follow a prearranged plan in which they must start attacking the attackers. It would be no use sitting waiting for the Germans to come raking down with killing fire and hope to wriggle out of it. You had to be prepared, and start shooting as soon as the range was good. It might also prevent them spotting McScotch.

They must not get at Mac!

Edward's Nieuport almost stood on end, trying to reach round and gain a position where his gun barrels would point straight at the first of the diving Germans. He had less than a second in hand. The Nieuport swerved steeply, levelled out and then seemed to grasp the measure of what he was demanding of her. He sent out a preliminary round to make sure his gun was working.

Mac must know what's going on. He'll go up to five thousand and stay there while this lot's on ... ha! here comes the bastard!

Coolly studying his quarry's flying, Edward pressed the trigger, then cursed as the enemy's speed seemed to increase so that the bullets went wide.

Next time you clever little Hun, next time.

With its engine running hot, his Nieuport spun round to provide a view of what the others were doing, and he discovered them spreading out in a series of arcs, pursued and pursuers firing spasmodically. Then they closed in again in a sharp-edged fight with no quarter given by either side, planes angrily charging at one another until they seemed to be less than an arm's length away.

There was no time for fancy flying now, only those given moments when a German appeared in the sights and you fired for all you were worth, puncturing his mainplane, trying to rake him from one end to the other, watching for any slumping movement of the pilot's leather helmeted head which might denote the end.

The Nieuports were all following Edward's lead now, trying to sever the Germans' handhold on the sky. It was difficult to tell which side was winning as the shapes cut through the darkening sky, chasing one another towards death.

Then, almost in resignation, an Albatros went down, smoking heavily as flames tore at the engine.

One up for the Royal Flying Corps!

The old satisfaction came to Edward's mind as he set about grappling to close in on a German, spraying him with bullets and refusing to level out as the enemy desperately attempted to turn on him with an engine thrashed to the limit.

A Nieuport with devil tongues of fire lashing the air began to fall. Long before it hit the ground it had crumpled into an unrecognizable piece of wreckage. At a thousand feet there was a small explosion and the engine parted from the airframe. Debris could be seen, tumbling about like oil-clogged feathers and intestine. Somewhere there was the pilot. He would know nothing about it.

Two more biting attacks and then the Germans decided to give up. It had been a clash of giants over acres of sky, yet the results, one German down and one Nieuport crashed, would not give the reality when put in the reports.

The Germans scattered, flying away into a distance where it would be hopeless to try and corner them. Edward watched them coming together as he waited for his Nieuports to gather once more from the quarters of the aerial battleground.

First one came, then another, and after a short period the Nieuports again assembled. Edward checked them over, anxious to discover who the unlucky one might be. One man out of two flights had hurtled to his death. It took time to find out. Holding back, so as to inspect them, he forced himself to accept the identity of the dead pilot.

The truth needed very little verification...

The rest of the operation went off very smoothly with McScotch joining up with them after his low-level inspection of the German aerodrome. They all flew back towards Bruay landing ground in small groups. Edward had already landed and stood waiting when he saw McScotch's plane come lumbering to a standstill. He set off at a run and, as the machine stopped, jumped forward to greet his friend. 'Thank God you're safe, old boy. I thought you'd gone, too!'

McScotch wiped his hands on his leather flying jacket, then pulled off helmet and goggles. It took a few moments to become accustomed to the stillness of the air on the ground after flying. 'Who's missing?' he inquired heavily.

Edward hesitated. He had carried this truth home with him, knowing that few of them would guess who had been killed in that fracas until they put their wheels down at Bruay.

'Ken. I saw him going down,' Edward said at last.

There was nothing more to be said about it. They could not blame that absurd piano. It would only sound childish or hysterical. For his part McScotch did not feel inclined to pinpoint the fact that Kennedy had been filled with premonitions when they were up at the advanced landing ground together.

They set out for the orderly room with the intention of completing their reports when two pilots, both young men, intercepted Edward and tried to argue that he ought to have given them a chance of closing in on the Huns before he started attacking. They were in the second flight and could have done better.

He appeared to be listening attentively while they chattered on excitedly.

'If you'd done it properly, instead of –'

'I mean to say, we *were* better placed.'

'If your flight had taken advantage of their height you could have got into the thick of it,' Edward said in a carefully controlled voice. Every man saw an air fight differently. Youngsters often blamed everybody else but themselves for their own ineptitude. He pointed towards the waiting McScotch. 'Anyway, it was only a matter of a few seconds before they would have seen Mac.' Then the scorn went through his tone. 'Seven of them! *I* hold back? Not Pygmalion likely!'

Still wearing their heavy flying boots, he and McScotch trudged on towards the orderly room, conscious of the critical animosity behind them. He wanted to feel some understanding for them, but at this moment it was almost impossible because he was still preoccupied with Kennedy's death. It welled up in his mind until he wished that he had not seen the boy's plane in its final disintegration. He could see two mental pictures at once, the burning, falling Nieuport and, superimposed against it, Mac's tall figure as he light-heartedly banged out that chord on the piano in the Mess. Kennedy had played the piano, too, and at the time Edward thought nothing about it as he stroked a tune out of his violin. Was the curse starting to move about now? Or did it lurk, waiting for a chance to kill those who wanted to defy it?'

Edward looked quite composed if rather silent when they split up. Later on, when McScotch searched for him in the Mess, glancing quickly from one face to another, he put down his glass and went outside.

As he neared Edward's hut, moving quietly under a sickle moon, he made out a series of low groaning sounds coming from inside. Turning the door handle, he stepped inside, not knowing what to expect.

Edward was hunched forward on the edge of his bed, hands on knees, swaying back and forth, a look of inexpressible grief written across his face.

The groans became words.

'Ah Ken, why did you die, why did you die?... Why did you?'

Tears streamed down his face as he went on 'keening' for the dead Kennedy, following an ancient Irish custom, trying to discover the reason for it by stripping away layer after layer of civilization. A grief of the soul wracked him to the core of his being.

Kennedy's death affected others as deeply but in different ways. The next day Sergeant Gilbert, the fitter, intercepted Edward as he made his way towards the waiting Nieuport. Gilbert was a little older than the others and tended to look upon men like Kennedy as 'his' pilots.

It was obvious what was on his mind as he stood there in his oil-stained overalls. He wanted to fly and avenge Kennedy. 'They needn't give me any stripes as long as they let me *fight*!' he said in a low urgent voice. 'Then I would go and pay them back...'

It was not unusual for mechanics to want to wreak a personal revenge when pilots were shot out of the sky. The difference lay in Gilbert's urgency and resolution.

Edward shook his head. Even if Gilbert *did* manage to become a pilot, what good was an angry man at a time when so much team work and individual effort were demanded? To fly against the Germans you had to be cool-headed, which was difficult enough for seasoned men.

'No, I'm afraid you're too old for this game, Gilbert,' he said. 'And besides, good fitters are scarce and we all need you here.'

When a friend was shot down others were often faced with the necessity of breaking the news. It was not always a question merely of writing a letter to the wife or parents.

Kennedy had been very fond of a French girl in a Bethune cafe where they often went to tea. Her comely looks invited a nickname, and the cafe itself came to be known among habitués as the 'Queen of Sheba'.

It was to this place that Edward and McScotch went, knowing that it was going to be difficult to explain to her what had happened three days ago. She was certain to wonder why Kennedy was not with them.

They sat down and told her what they would like. She did not smile but took their order with a quiet, *'Oui, monsieur.'*

'She hasn't said anything about Ken,' Edward remarked after she had gone to make the tea.

McScotch did not answer.

As she was putting the crockery on the table Edward took the plunge. 'Don't you wonder where our – your friend is, *mademoiselle*?'

He waited while McScotch expertly translated.

She nodded. *'Certainement, monsieur le Capitaine*, but I dare not ask. It is forbidden for us to ask any questions of the English officers. Where *is* the nice English boy?' She looked round anxiously, not wishing to be overheard.

Attempting to break the news gently was a hard job. '*Il est parti,*' he said hesitantly.

'*Parti?*' She was surprised and relieved at the same time. '*Parti – ou?*'

'Not that *parti,*' Edward answered quickly. '*Parti pour toq ours – il est mort.*'

She rushed away, her apron held to her mouth. As they started their tea in silence, they could hear her sobbing in the kitchen.

Before the month was finished Edward shot down two more Germans, a DFW two-seater and an Albatros.

His triumph over the DFW impressed many when they heard about it.

He was flying alone at 10,000-feet over Avion when he noticed another machine flying south-west while he himself was on a south-easterly course. Because of the light he could not be certain whether it was a Royal Flying Corps machine or a German while it remained about 500-feet above him. When it was 300 yards away, he suddenly decided on a plan. He turned south – west so that he was now flying the same course as the other, with his tail towards it. If it were British, he thought, it would take no notice of him because his markings would be clearly visible. If it turned out to be a German, the pilot would assume that he was unobserved. With luck he might come down to the attack.

Waiting, Edward kept the other under keen observation. Sure enough, the DFW put its nose down and came in to finish him off. He was ready for it. With a tensing of the muscles, he put his Nieuport round in a tight turn, dived and zoomed up behind it. Caught, the German realized his mistake and tried to turn, but he was much too slow for the Nieuport.

Firing in short bursts, Edward let fifty rounds go. It was enough. The DFW went down in flames, pieces of wing and tail dropping away from the wreck as it plunged in a blazing mass.

Feeling slightly sickened by the sight, Edward let the Nieuport drop after it and, when it had crashed behind the British lines, he touched his controls, lifted and made for home.

He always referred to this victory as 'my first flamerino', but the memory of those flames remained with him.

As he sat at the rough wooden table in the orderly room, putting all the cold phrases down on paper, he reflected that it had been an unusual fight. Not too easy, not too hard. It was one combat which he would always remember but exactly why he was not sure.

Some days later Lieutenant George C Pilgrim, a balloon observer, was aloft, taking routine observations, when he noticed a German Halberstadt coming over the trenches, flying with some purpose towards an unknown objective. Getting ready to take to his parachute, he waited, following it with his binoculars.

The Germans, particularly the Richthofen 'circus', were at constant war against allied observation balloons. It was rarely that they missed this sort of sitting duck. Pilgrim waited, incredulous as the Halberstadt flew on, ignoring the obvious temptation of the gasbag.

As the plane banked he saw a streamer fall from the cockpit Taking a bearing on it, he put down his binoculars and made a reckoning before reporting the incident to the chart-room. Two soldiers were sent out to retrieve the streamer. When they returned it was unpacked and an envelope fell out addressed *To The British Flying Corps.*

Not until January 1918 did the message reach No. 40 Squadron. By that time Edward was on leave, but it was forwarded to England for his inspection.

Smoothing out the creases, he read: *The 4th Sept I lost my friend Fritz Frech. He fell between Vimy and Lieven. His respectable and unlucky parents beg you to give any news of his fate. Is he dead? At what place found he his last rest? Please to throw several letters that we may found one. Thank before, His friend, K L PS. If it is possible, send a letter to the parents, Mr Frech, Konisberg, i, Pr. Vord Vordstadt 48/52.*

He clearly remembered the place where he had sent down the DFW. This note put the event into too human terms so that he could hardly lift a pen and write to the parents. It took a long time and when he read what he had written he knew that the words were totally inadequate. Would the Frech couple understand?

Special arrangements had to be made for delivery of the letter, but Edward managed to send it on its way. A new kind of maturity settled over him that day.

During his leave there was more time to think. He now saw how little known was the real position of the fighting pilot. The people at home wanted to be regaled with accounts of actions which he had no wish to discuss, and he often used his charm to wriggle out of it without offending them. What they were asking for was a re-living of the terrors and the dangers, not the satisfactions.

By the time he was back in France he had resolved many of his doubts, but the grisly solemnity of the war was thrust upon him whenever he read the newspapers.

When he was awarded another decoration he tried to keep the news quiet. The telegram, which was read over the phone to him, said 'Captain Mannock awarded Bar to MC'. That was all. The words contained no particular accolade. He replaced the receiver and went to his own hut.

He stayed in his hut, writing to the Eyleses in Wellingborough, then left for St Omer to pay a call on Sister Flanagan, a nurse with whom he was friendly. It was thought that he might marry her. He was nearing her hospital when he saw the familiar face of Captain Buchanan. It was a long way from Fenny Stratford and their long discussions.

Buchanan was very struck by Edward's mature appearance and quiet manner. 'You've done awfully well,' he said. 'I heard about your MC, by the way.'

Smiling shyly, Edward confided: 'I've just had a Bar to it.' Then he remembered Sister Flanagan. 'Well, must be off! Nice to have seen you!'

It never occurred to him that Buchanan might feel surprised at such an abrupt leavetaking. But then, Sister Flanagan was much more important than any medal.

CHAPTER NINE

New ambitions now began to burn in Edward. He was entering a fresh and often difficult phase in which he did not want to be bested in anything, and the thought of other pilots being able to pull off something which he considered to be his personal prerogative was enough to make him secretly irritable, although he always muffled any emotion with a quick outburst of humour. He was not finding it too easy, keeping up his growing reputation as a celebrity. Among his habits was one of 'dropping in' on the soldiers in the trenches and having a chat with them, to keep in touch. Throughout the ranks he was known as a 'good chap' and a 'fine fellow', while in the smaller world of his own squadron there was full agreement that he had guts, although some pilots still criticized his aerial leadership. He never could resist flying away on his own and having a crack at the toughest Hun. When he was able to claim successes like these it rattled lesser men.

Towards the younger pilots he tried to be kind and understanding, but in his own group the nerve ends did have a habit of protruding. McScotch, together with the younger Tudhope, represented a very real opposition, and Edward often remarked on it, though in a joking fashion. Yet they knew that he was genuinely worried lest he lose his supremacy. It came out in small ways...

One day, when the three of them were visiting an Advance Ordnance Depot, Edward turned to the storeman and said: 'I want a telescope!' It sounded like a typical leg-pull.

The NCO did not know whether to take him seriously or not. You never could tell when the famous Mick Mannock was joking.

'This ain't the Naval Stores, Sir. We've only got prismatic binoculars. I got a lovely pair 'ere.' He reached for them on the shelf and flourished the polished leather case.

With a gesture of mock despair, Edward turned to his friends. 'There you are, what did I tell you? I want a *telescope*. What's the use of having two eye-pieces when you can use only one? However, I must have them.'

Picking up the case and sliding them out for inspection, Tudhope queried: 'What on earth do you want them for?'

Edward lowered his tone, pointing at McScotch and making sure that McScotch could hear what he was saying. 'I can't have that fellow beating me at anything to do with fighting. He's not going to see anything *I* can't see things on the ground, I mean.'

There was probably a grain of truth in it.

However difficult he might sometimes appear, he was always generous when it came to risking his own life. As a ruthless hunter of Germans, imbued with the deliberately instilled killer-instinct demanded of all Royal Flying Corps pilots, he had heard the summons of death so many times that a new fatalism took hold of him. But when it came to flying for the sake of flying, risking everything on a flimsy promise of getting home in one piece, he insisted on being at the head of the queue.

Lieutenant S Collier, of No. 43 Squadron, was ordered out with two other Sopwiths on a dangerous photographic mission, No sooner was he over his objective than a swarm of enemy aircraft surrounded him, flying in all directions and giving him no chance with the camera. Startled, because the escort was nowhere to be seen, he was forced to fly home as fast as he could and report that the guardian planes had failed to provide the promised protection.

He half expected his superiors to call the mission off, but was told to go out and try again. It was useless trying to explain that it was certain death to go near that sector again. Senior officers did not acknowledge the word 'impossible'. The memory of those German hunters lying in wait was sufficient to deter the most experienced pilot. It was not as though he could fight back. His job was to take the pictures of that sector. Could any pilot be expected to surrender his life for the sake of a few photographs which could not be brought back?

In desperation Collier went to the phone and rang up No. 40 Squadron. When he got through he asked for Edward and then explained what had happened. 'Our escort fell down on us,' he admitted. 'Could *you* be our escort this time, Mick?'

Without hesitating, Edward shouted: 'Of course! When are you going out?'

'At once. Can you meet us over the lines at eleven?'

'Right, Collier, I'll be there!'

Promptly at eleven the three Sopwiths flew over the lines for the second time that day. Collier anxiously cast about. He had heard no more from Edward. He wondered what he would do if the request had been turned down by somebody higher up.

Edward's Nieuports appeared briefly, then moved up into the bright sunshine with a characteristically racy flourish. Relieved, Collier turned to his observer and grinned.

Even with an expert escort the experience was terrible, because the Sopwiths had to fly directly through showers of anti-aircraft fire before reaching the photographic target. The Nieuports circled watchfully, waiting for a chance to engage enemy interlopers. They, too, were in a precarious position, and Edward was able to keep them out of the danger margin only by utilizing the glare of the sun, which made them almost invisible to lower flying aircraft.

Full of admiration for the way Edward had managed the operation where the earlier escort failed, Collier flew back. After landing, his first action was to phone No. 40 Squadron and when Edward came on the line he exclaimed fervently: 'Thanks very much for the escort, Mick. We knew we were safe with you there!'

Edward was quietly amused. There had been several ticklish moments for his Nieuports. 'Oh, that's all right,' he said, dismissing the idea that it had been dangerous. 'We didn't do anything. But *you* ought to have a VC, flying through all that Archie. I couldn't have stuck it – it would have driven me mad!'

This was quite true. He preferred to be in the thick of things rather than witness the ordeals of others. It was all the more bearable when you were directly involved in a scrap.

His reputation did not grow in direct proportion to his successes. In Britain, mention of Mick Mannock appeared now and then in local newspaper reports of air action over France, but he hated these 'blurbs' and did everything he could to prevent more appearing. In letters to the Eyleses he asked them not to tell the reporters anything and in a postscript ordered, 'Keep it out of the papers'. But the fact remained that he was good 'copy' at a time when those at home were in need of news to boost their flagging morale.

Late in August he did come face to face with newspapermen, three American reporters who were on an official tour of the battlefields. They arrived prepared to meet a dashing knight of the air, having already heard a great deal about him, especially concerning his spectacular victory over von Bartrap. The two wings of the German ace's plane were now suspended in the hangar, a trophy of which everybody in the squadron felt proud.

Anxious to do the Americans a favour, Major Tilney dragged Edward out of semi-hiding and marched him across to the hangar where the Americans waited. Up till now they had not met any near legendary figures. This was going to be quite an experience.

What they saw was a tall figure of a man wearing a shabby tunic and slacks, dressed so casually that he might have been taken for a mechanic or an off duty orderly. His hair was thick and stood on end as though it had not seen a comb for a long time.

After making the introductions Tilney urged him to tell the von Bartrap story. He reluctantly complied, watching them scribbling in their little notebooks. At the end of his halting recital, they said thank you and examined the German's wings, pleading with Tilney for some small pieces which they could show to 'the folks back home'.

Syndicated reports of the interview, which appeared in many leading American papers, resulted in Edward becoming more famous in the United States than in his own country.

One raider had become a stinging gadfly. He had been across and shot down several observation balloons and destroyed five planes. He was both audacious and clever, obviously a bandit with strong nerves.

With Tudhope and McScotch, Edward stood staring up at the sky, the emptiness of Mazingarbe all about them. The arrangement was that one of them should always be in the air, patrolling, while the other two stood by on the ground. So far it had been completely fruitless and they were beginning to feel very restless, waiting for the engine hum which would be the signal for action. The sky remained silent.

The raider was clever enough to know exactly when to attack. He came out of nowhere and whipped off again as soon as the destructive job was done. His pet targets were balloons. This suggested an experienced pilot, because trying to shoot one down – and with luck get the observer at the same time – was really dangerous since one's whole attention had to be on that one particular job.

'Look here,' Edward exclaimed in disgust, 'that fellow's coming over this evening.' When the others protested he went on firmly: 'We aren't going to have dinner till *after* we've got him. We'll sit here till dark.'

From earlier discussions it was obvious that the rogue raider had an observer ally situated forward of the British lines, watching the balloon movements through binoculars and enabling him to leave the attack until the last minute.

'Just a minute, I'll ring up the Kite Balloon section to check on him.' Edward came back in a few minutes, grinning. 'I was right! Every one of the fellow's raids have been at the orthodox British meal times.'

'But he's taking a risk. How does he know –' Tudhope started.

McScotch, who saw that Edward was talking good sense, butted in: 'Don't you see, at those times low fliers are not likely to be in the air. The official patrols are at too great a height to be any danger to a low-flying raider. If I were that German, I'd have a concealed observer on the ground to report when all the patrols had landed, then I'd come over.'

'That clinches it,' Edward said. 'We've got to let them see us returning to Bruay, no humbug about it. Then we can come back when it's nearly dark and patrol above the balloons.' He trotted off towards the telephone again. 'In the meantime, I'll ring up the Kite Balloon section again and ask them to put up six balloons without any observers in the baskets.'

A short time later the jaws of the trap opened. Six balloons rose silently. They were the bait, as they swung gracefully on their cables.

After enjoying a smoke in the Mess, the three men returned to Mazingarbe feeling ready for anything. Each agreed to guard two balloons, flying well above them so as to remain unnoticed by the raider, who would be too busy looking at his targets to bother about the upper regions.

And then the unpredictable furies which lived in aircraft engines played a hand. While McScotch was patrolling above his bulky charges, a balloon to the south suddenly went up in flames. It was completely unexpected, and it came at entirely the wrong moment because Edward had just been forced to land with engine trouble, closely followed by Tudhope, whose engine was misfiring.

Cursing their bad luck, Edward leapt out of the Nieuport, saw the blazing balloon and yelled at Tudhope, who was just rolling to a standstill nearby: 'Look, Tud – go on, you'll get the blighter!'

Tudhope's machine wheeled round and, still stuttering, took off again. Flogging the engine to breaking point, he managed to intercept the raider and shoot him down.

McScotch, who had been watching developments and was about to give chase himself, came down in time to join an exuberant Edward. Together they thumped Tudhope on the back, yelling for the waiting tender to drive them to the scene of the crashed German.

When they reached the splintered wreck it was to find the pilot still alive, though badly injured and obviously dying. Then Edward noticed a group of Canadian soldiers advancing across the fields. The men on the ground had apparently seen more than the pilots. The Kite Balloon section *had* put an observer or two up with the balloons, and as it happened a man was in the basket which the German turned to after his first victory. When he jumped for it, the raider tried to follow him down, intent on finishing him off.

'We thought we'd come along and have a few words with that lousy bastard of a Hun,' growled the spokesman, waving an axe shaft. 'He's not going to live long.'

Edward knew too well that if they had their way they would thrust their bayonets into the dying German. The primitive desire for revenge nauseated and sickened him.

Reaching into his pocket, he pulled out a bulky Very pistol and levelled it at the gang. Shaken by his threat to put a Very light into them if they came any closer, they fell back and in the end tramped back the way they had come, swearing at him over their shoulders.

Ten years later, in peacetime, McScotch happened to meet a number of ex-servicemen in the foyer of an hotel, and began swopping experiences

'I had recounted the events that led up to the destroying of Tudhope's victim without giving the date or names when, to my surprise, one of them offered to complete the story. 'That happened at the end of September 1917, and it was Mannock, the VC, who brought it down at Souchez. I was there,' he said.

'I corrected him about Mannock and asked him where *he* was at the time. He laughed uproariously. 'I was the observer in the balloon just south of your landing ground. When the other one went down in flames the fellows on the ground telephoned me to jump, but as I had never done a drop before I was sitting on the edge of the basket, trying to pluck up courage to let go, when I heard your machine. I thought it was a Hun until I saw your markings. My relief was so great that I fell over backwards into the basket until they hauled the balloon down!'

Although Edward spent part of his flying career protecting observation balloons and attacking German ones he never actually made an ascent in a basket. Once, when invited to accompany an officer whose life he saved by shooting down von Bartrap, he retorted: 'What, sit up there on the end of a rope to be shot at without being able to hit back or dodge? Not Pygmalion likely!'

While he used his spare time lecturing younger pilots on tactics and the new techniques which were constantly being evolved, he still suffered periods of boredom when flying was impossible due to weather conditions. He would then sit and listen to his favourite records, playing music like Schubert's 'Ave Maria'.

Music exerted an almost supernatural effect over him. Kreisler's rendering of 'Caprice Viennois' gripped him so strongly that he was impelled to get out his own violin and try to emulate the master. When the more difficult passages almost defeated him he put the much-travelled instrument back in its case, slammed the lid down and exclaimed with earthy humour: 'Hell, I don't know how the bloody feller does it!'

Precisely the same remark was applied to Edward himself by his fellow officers, although they referred not to his violin playing but his flying skill and fighting spirit.

An Air Technical Diagram showing the 'sitter' strategy, borrowed from the German Air Force and improved upon by the Allies

While he despaired of ever becoming as good as Kreisler, he still went on practising, playing with such feeling that it attracted the attention of others. McScotch describes it:

'On watching Mick's expressive face as he successfully accomplished the difficult double-stopping passages in the 'Caprice' I was amazed at the emotional splendour of his playing. Technique was required, but there was something greater than that, something no other violinist had ever conveyed to me.

'Mick had the soul of an idealist, one that can endure agonies of mind and body for his ideals, can kill for his beliefs. He told us all this in his playing. Perhaps my appreciation was heightened by my knowledge of his emotions – but I noticed that many of the others were equally spellbound by the tall gaunt figure standing in the half-light at the far corner of the Mess. On my telling him of this he refused to play for several days and when we finally persuaded him to do so, he insisted on turning his face to the wall.'

A change of atmosphere resulted after the announcement that leave tickets were to be issued, and pilots would go home in pairs. Many who seemed to be prematurely old under the strain of war were suddenly transformed.

As soon as the forms were ready, Edward went to collect his. He gaily informed McScotch: 'I'm off tomorrow.'

Yawning, McScotch put his book down, trying to share the satisfaction although he was not due for leave for some time. 'Good show,' he said gravely. 'By the way, when is your flight doing patrol?'

'Oh, not till the afternoon, so I shall miss it. Just as well! Wouldn't want to do a patrol with a leave ticket in my pocket, old boy. It's suicide.'

McScotch quizzed him dryly: 'But *you're* not superstitious, are you?'

'No!' Edward's voice sounded firm and convincing, although he was still trying hard to forget the piano with the curse on it.

McScotch said: 'You know that Wolff's going on leave tomorrow, too? The new fellow.'

For a moment Edward did not reply. He was busy filling his pipe and hunting for a match. 'Good! Then we can do a few shows together in London. I've been wanting to go and see –'

'His flight's got the dawn patrol tomorrow,' McScotch added.

'That's rather rotten for him! Oh well, I think I'll just go up and have a chat with him. Cheer him up!'

Nodding, McScotch reached for his book again, holding back a smile of satisfaction. There were ways and means of doing things.

Finding Wolff alone in his hut, Edward walked straight in. 'I hear you're going on leave tomorrow,' he said. 'So am I. So I thought we might see one or two shows together.'

Surveying his half-packed kit, Wolff moved some things to one side, lit a cigarette and postponed the question of what to take and what to leave behind. 'I'd like that very much.' He felt secretly flattered that Edward was giving him some attention because he was still very much the new man.

'Have you seen 'The Bing Boys'?' Edward inquired.

'No, not yet.'

'Good! Neither have I. We'll go and see that.' He mentioned one or two other shows, then in exactly the same tone remarked: 'It's a bit unpleasant, having a dawn patrol just before Blighty.'

Wolff agreed wryly. 'It rather spoils the enjoyment, having to go out with a leave ticket in one's pocket. But anyway, you're lucky, Mick, you'll miss yours.'

Ruminating to himself, Edward made for the door. 'I think I'll try and snatch another Hun before I go.'

He affected not to notice the relief on Wolff's face. Flying with Mannock could be like flying with a protective god. It could also be exactly the reverse.

The flight assembled next morning at dawn. Strolling towards his Nieuport with his usual striding gait, Edward paused to give a cheerful wave to Wolff as he sat in his cockpit.

The flight commander held up his hand. One by one, satisfied with their engines, they signified readiness and started taking off singly as soon as the leader gave the signal. Each plane made a preliminary circuit, formed up with the rest and headed for the lines through the broadening light of day.

Edward, who had been waiting for them to get clear, opened his own throttle and took off. He flew behind and about 2,000-feet above the formation, keeping his position like a guard dog, ready to dash in at the slightest sign of trouble.

It was a familiar drill, the four 'beats' of the patrol, then the flight back home. Towards the end of it the lone Edward suddenly disappeared, flying fast in an easterly direction. Noticing his absence, Wolff was worried. It would be a tragedy if the great Mannock was brought down with a leave ticket in *his* pocket!

After landing he ignored the cheerful banter as his fellow pilots went for breakfast, and stood on the edge of the landing ground, straining his ears for the sound of an engine. Just when he was about to give up hope and start making inquiries, Edward's plane came winging in to a perfect landing.

The young pilot could hardly contain himself. Running to the side of the machine, he yelled: 'Well, Mick – did you –?'

The propellor swung to a stop and Edward jumped down to the ground. 'Yes, I found a nice fat one!'

Sharing his triumph, Wolff linked arms with him and they set off for the Mess, grinning with satisfaction.

But boredom was still the mind-rotting enemy. Confined to the Mess by heavy overcast skies and beating rain, some of the pilots grew so restless that the suggestion of a trip to Amiens was enough to send them running for their greatcoats. With them went the thirty-two-year-old Brigadier General Shepherd, who flew a great deal and with whom they felt they could share their different enthusiasms, despite his seniority. The party finished up in a room at the Hotel Beaufort where they released their pent-up spirits to such a wild extent that the dinner ended with a throwing match. Anything in the least portable was hurled through the air, including chunks of bread, showers of salt and sugar, cutlery and even the remains of the meal. In one salvo, a large vicious-looking lobster claw happened to hurtle out of the window.

McScotch glanced down into the street to see what had happened to it, then drew back, horror on his face. 'Look out, there's going to be a row!'

As if to underline his prediction, they heard irate voices on the staircase.

Quickly checking his own exuberance, Edward called for silence. 'Leave it to me – and remember, *we don't know what happened*.'

The door immediately flew open to admit the most bucolic of all majors, one hand holding his forage cap and the other, covered with blood, clasped to his injured bald head. Edward took one theatrical look at him. 'Good heavens, what's wrong, sir? Can I help you?'

'Wrong be damned! Which of you swine threw that bloody thing at me?' With reddened suspicious eyes, the wounded man glared at each in turn. 'I'll have the whole damned lot of you arrested!'

Edward let him rant on for a time, then, in a conciliatory way said: 'I'm sure no one here would throw anything at you, sir. If he did, he'd be up before the orderly room tomorrow! If that claw came from here, it was entirely an accident. Sit down and have a drink, sir. Oh, but first let me introduce you to *General Shepherd*.'

Realizing what a fool he must look before a senior officer whom he had not noticed until this moment, the major permitted Edward to help him into a chair. He huffily accepted a glass of wine which he gulped down while Edward personally attended to the wound, fighting to suppress a broad grin.

Edward was fated to come face to face with many awkward situations out of which he usually managed to charm his way. McScotch was the unwitting cause of another incident.

'On one of our trips,' he recalls, 'I found a bedraggled kitten mewing for help in the middle of the road on which the rain was beating down in torrents. Filled with sympathy because of its shivering misery, I put it in the pocket of my warm sheepskin – lined coat and took it back to the camp. On taking it out I saw that it had dried into a fluffy ball with beautiful grey and black markings.

'After inquiring where I had found it, Mick held it aloft for everyone to see. 'By jove, we've got a fine cat now – anyone got a name for it?'

'Several orthodox names were suggested and it appeared as if 'Sonia' was going to win, when the kitten (fortunately for me) took the opportunity of doing what all cats and dogs have to do on occasion.

'Look out, Mick,' someone called.'

'Mick placed the kitten gingerly on the floor and wrathfully shook his finger at it while it mewed up at him.

'That's what we're going to call you – Piddle!'

The name stuck and Piddle became an honorary member of the pilot's Mess.

Some time later, when the squadron was being visited by a party of nurses, one of them asked for the kitten's name. Tilney actually blushed and it looked as though Edward might have to shock or amuse her, depending on her temperament, when he airily said: 'Oh – it's *Fiddle* as a matter of fact.'

Changes were on the way. Early in October the GOC directed that certain RFC equipment must be classed as obsolete, amongst it the faithful Nieuport. It did seem high time something was done to show the Germans that the RFC was alert to new needs and the Staff recognized that the frustration of many pilots must stem directly from the fact the Nieuport was not as fast as it should be at a time when the Germans were steadily improving their planes. Innumerable combat reports told their own sad story. Unless the British acquired faster planes, the outcome looked dismal.

The successor to the Nieuport was the SE5a. Some said that it was infinitely superior to the Nieuport because it could reach a speed of 120-mph, climbing at 765-feet a minute and diving at 200-mph, a definite advantage over the Nieuport's diving speed of only 150-mph. But the SE5a had less endurance – only two and a quarter hours as against the Nieuport's two and a half hours.

In armament the SE5a sported a Vickers gun fixed forward and synchronized to fire through the propellor in addition to the Lewis gun mounted on the top plane.

Many of the so-called experts predicted that the new planes would skin the Germans alive, but this was after all only theory. When the SE5as were tested under fighting conditions several faults were apparent. It was not long before many of the more experienced pilots started calling them deathtraps. They said that the engine tended to cut out and the Vickers gun jammed. These faults alone were enough to put a damper on all previous optimism.

Among the disillusioned pilots, Edward was one of the most furious and the most vociferous. He lost no time claiming that he wanted his Nieuport back. At least it was dependable. Sending men out in the SE5as was tantamount to putting them up against a wall and shooting them.

The protests had unexpected effects. Noticing a growing file of negative reports from a squadron known to be among the most active, General Trenchard decided personally to investigate the cause during one of his visits. While he was standing on the edge of the aerodrome, discussing the position with Major Tilney, Edward landed. As he taxied in it was perfectly obvious from the way he handled the plane that he was in a rage.

Trenchard did not miss a thing. His eyes on the plane as it jerked to a stop, he asked for the identity of the pilot.

'It's Mannock, sir.' Tilney glanced towards the heavens for deliverance.

'Well, let's hear what *he* has to say.' Trenchard watched the leather-clad figure stamping towards them, apparently oblivious to the presence of a very senior officer.

'Look at this Vickers gun – *look at it* – fired two rounds – spop-pop – and then it stopped, jammed properly! If I had my good old Nieuport I could have had two nice juicy Huns.'

Trenchard's ADC interposed himself to try to take control of the situation. 'What do you think of the machines, though?' he asked.

'Pretty awful with these engines and guns.' Edward had now noticed General Trenchard's presence, but he did not intend losing any ground. 'The machines themselves are all right, I suppose, but give me the Nieuport any day.'

The group moved off towards the Mess, giving Major Tilney a chance of asking Edward to be more tactful in front of General Trenchard.

Shaking his tousled head, Edward said as loudly as possible so as to reach the General's ears: 'I'm sorry, sir, but if it results in my getting my good old Nieuport back, I don't care!'

McScotch, who had by now joined them, tried to calm his friend down into a more reasonable frame of mind. Edward was no worse off really, because the Vickers gun was a substantial addition to the usual Lewis gun. Surely that warranted a good mark for the SE5a?

'Yes,' Edward conceded, 'but what's the use of carrying a gun that's no use to you? All it does when it fires is just go pop-pop-pop, as slowly as one of Jerry's guns, and if the mechanism isn't right you shoot your own prop. These are all things that need consideration by the authorities, and if *we* don't say things outright, nothing will be done about it.'

The conversation petered out. It seemed that nothing *was* going to be done about the delinquent SE5a after all. But two days later the result came of Edward's outburst in Trenchard's presence.

They were having another spell of bad weather and most of the pilots were gathered together in the Mess anteroom, waiting for the rain to stop. Conversation died as a stranger entered, holding his cap. He was wearing a trenchcoat, so it was impossible to see his rank.

Looking up, Edward called out breezily: 'Good afternoon to you, stranger! Take off your coat and come into the warmth. Orderly!'

As the caller removed his trenchcoat, the blue tabs of a staff officer struck Edward in the eye. 'And may I ask who you are?' he asked acidly. Everybody knew how much he hated tabs, especially blue ones.

'I'm Gunnery Officer at headquarters. I've come over – '

'You mean *you* have something to do with those guns? Orderly! *Quick!*'

The man appeared. 'Yes, sir?'

'Fetch a hatchet,' Edward ordered.

'A – a hatchet, sir? What for?'

Edward spelt it out. 'H-a-t-c-h-e-t... now, do you understand? I want a hatchet.'

The orderly was about to obey blindly when Edward suddenly grinned at the visitor. 'Now you know my sentiments, what will you have to drink?'

When they reached a more convivial mood, the Gunnery Officer explained how impressed General Trenchard had been by Edward's firm opinion of the SE5a. He had ordered an immediate investigation and instruction in the gun synchronization would be given to all pilots without delay.

Even Major Tilney had to admit that Edward was right to speak out, although it had been a devilish moment. You never knew how Trenchard would take things. It was a clear victory for Edward.

CHAPTER TEN

The severity of that winter practically petrified them in their cockpits before they could even leave the ground to meet the Germans. In the air the bite of a constant flow of near-arctic air did everything to paralyse all but the toughest – and even they experienced frequent mental numbing when they came face to face with the enemy. One consolation was that the Germans must also be suffering. If anything the zero temperature put a new edge on the business of flying to kill, but once the calculated excitement of a patrol was over and the planes had landed, many pilots were in the awkward position of having to shout for help before they could move a limb. It was not unusual to see two mechanics carefully lifting a pilot out and waiting until his circulation started up again.

It was McElroy, a new Irish pilot naturally imbued with an imp of merriment, who invented a 'pocket warmer' consisting of a tin containing lumps of glowing charcoal. Wanting to prove that this was the answer to the weather, he took it along with him on one operation, but on landing was seen to be hopping about nimbly beside his machine, slapping his flying suit and cursing to high heaven because it was *too* hot. When he undressed he found a great blister on his pink thigh.

Just before Christmas, Edward, whose spirits kept swinging between an enormous self-confidence and a belief that everything was hopeless, had engine failure several miles away from the aerodrome. Without a smoke or food, he had no alternative but to remain where he was in one of the most desolate landscapes it is possible to imagine. Skeletons of Colonial troops, massacred by the Germans in some past infantry advance, stood out white against the grey frozen mud. Wherever he looked he could not avoid noticing the grisly reminders of war. Watching the grey snow-bulging sky for any sign of rescue, he stamped up and down near his grounded plane for six hours, trying to keep warm. When at last he reached camp he felt both dejected and angry. Such terrible sights made a man think when he wanted most to avoid all thought. That silent landscape peopled by ghosts to him meant the end of everything.

He ate his dinner in silence, ignoring everybody, then went to his quarters, misery sweeping over him, and permitted the anguish to possess him as one racking spasm after another echoed in the groans which forced themselves out from between his lips while he rocked to and fro.

So held was he by this mental pain that he did not notice McScotch standing there after entering silently.

'Here, stop it Mick!' McScotch could hardly stand seeing him in this condition.

His face wet with tears, he looked up. In a harsh broken voice he said: 'It's a miserable life, Mac. Do you know, there's only one bright spot in the whole of my existence out here?'

To McScotch the confession was dangerously close to maudlin sentiment, something he could not understand. He gesticulated and argued: 'Come on – into the Mess or to Bethune!'

Pulling himself together, Edward wiped his eyes. 'I mean it – only one bright spot, Mac. I'll give you three guesses and you won't find out.'

Puzzled, McScotch said: 'Well... ?'

Tapping his Military Cross ribbon over his pocket, Edward said: 'When you bought this bit of ribbon and had it sewn on my tunic.'

To McScotch, who had seen his friend in every kind of condition, it was unhealthy to look so far back into the past. He searched Edward's face. 'It's high time you had a rest Mick. Come on, let's go and have a drink.'

'All right, Mac... but –'

Giving him a gentle push, McScotch said with mock severity, 'Shut up and come on! I'm thirsty!'

It was not an especially cheerful harbinger for Christmas Day, now a few hours away. When it dawned only one flight carried out a patrol in drizzling rain before the hangar flaps were buckled down.

The determination of everybody else to enjoy themselves seemed to the materialistic and not particularly religious McScotch a piece of sentimental nonsense. Throughout lunch he took only a grudging part in the general conversation, then escaped to go and put on his flying boots. He was just thrusting his feet into them when Edward arrived.

'Will you come and make a fourth at bridge?' Seeing what was going on, he cocked his eyebrows. '*Hullo*, what on earth are you doing? You aren't going up?'

Scowling, McScotch stood up. 'Yes, I've got no belief in this – this *goodwill*,' he said roughly. 'We're still at war and I mean to do a bit extra as it's Christmas Day.'

He walked outside, squaring his shoulders, fully conscious of Edward's growing disapproval and trying to shake him off. He put on a spurt through the thick drizzle. Edward, without a greatcoat or any protection, kept up with him.

'But look here, Mac,' he started forcibly. 'I know that fighting is our job – but all work is supposed to stop on Christmas Day, therefore it's your duty to remain on the ground.'

Unconvinced and looking more truculent by the minute, McScotch headed for the hangars. 'Well anyway, I'm going up the line to make sure Fritz isn't up to any mischief,' he grunted.

Edward slowed down on purpose to delay him. 'But look here Mac, you're not *really* going up today. Don't tell me you're serious?' A Scotsman as brave as this one ignoring the best day of the whole year? It seemed incredible. But, of course, a true Scot placed more importance on Hogmanay, and this probably explained his intention of going out to fight.

'*Of course I am!*' It was almost a shout as he pushed the hangar flaps open, yelling out for Davidge and Biggs, the duty mechanics who must be there, Christmas or not. When they appeared, he said impatiently: 'Fit four Cooper bombs to my racks, will you?'

The result was a certain amount of jostling confusion. McScotch was happy to leave Edward watching them as they carted the bombs towards his plane. He paced up and down outside, curbing his desire to be off immediately.

When the machine was ready and he was in the cockpit, Edward shouted cheerfully: 'All right – good luck, old boy,' and then walked quickly away towards the Sergeant's Mess, whistling under his breath, his previous protests apparently forgotten.

Giving his attention to the contact drill, McScotch waited for the engine to fire. Nothing happened. Thinking it might be cold, he tried again and obtained the same result.

A few minutes later he was still urging the raincoated Davidge and Biggs to swing the propellor once more. They were about to obey when a sergeant came hurrying to the side of the machine. 'Captain Mannock's compliments, sir. Will you join him in a drink in our Mess.' As McScotch looked round, annoyed and uncertain of himself, the NCO advised him: 'It will give the mechanics a chance, sir.'

'Oh well...' He threw one leg over the side of the cockpit and levered himself out, then set off with the sergeant to the Mess, just across the road.

It was fortunate that he gave no more than a single glance back at Davidge and Biggs, both of whom suddenly had broad grins on their faces. When they met his stare their faces froze.

Edward was sitting at one of the tables, talking to the sergeants as McScotch's escort brought him inside. 'What will you drink? Captain Mannock refuses to have anything but a grenadine, but you'll have something decent, won't you, sir?'

Rattled by the engine failure and what sounded like the sergeant's unctuous tone, McScotch swallowed his gall. 'Well, a very small one, then. I'm just going up.' He took the glass of whisky and sank into a chair, his flying coat dripping rain on the floor.

Edward was engrossed with the NCOs. 'Did you see Mac land the other day when the Australian squadron was here for the night?' he asked in a peculiarly penetrating voice.

'No, sir – why?'

'Well, he forgot to switch his engine off and –

'I didn't!' McScotch butted in loudly. 'It was overheated and it wouldn't stop!'

As though he had not heard, Edward continued smoothly: 'Anyway, he landed sideways and smashed up two of their machines. Then he went to the Mess and wrote a letter to their CO, explaining how to crash three machines in one landing!'

Enraged, McScotch slammed down his glass. 'I was writing to apologize! *Really, Mick –*' His face went a bright pink. It was totally unlike Mick to humiliate people.

'Wouldn't you like to take off that wet coat of yours, sir?' one of the sergeants asked.

Shaking his head, McScotch automatically glanced through the open door in the direction of the hangar. Then it dawned on him that he must be the target of a gentle conspiracy. 'Look here, the hangar's shut!' he blurted out. 'Where's my machine? It's not there.'

In a roar of laughter which swamped his indignation, he looked suspiciously at Edward, who was studiously examining the pottery mark on the underside of a plate.

A flight sergeant explained: 'It's all right sir. You couldn't possibly have taken your machine up, anyway.'

'Oh? Why not?'

'Because the starting magneto had been disconnected.'

'What the hell –'

'On Captain Mannock's orders, sir.'

On December 27th, 'A' Flight took off for patrol with Wade, McElroy, Learoyd and Harrison, McScotch (leading) and Mannock sitting above them, playing the 'watchdog'.

They sighted about thirty Albatroses in the distance, and made a round-about approach, climbing steadily. The enemy split up into flights. One group went to the north and the other turned south. This latter consisted of two flights of six each and one flight of three above the others. They were 2,000-feet below the Nieuports. So McScotch made his attack on the upper flight of three machines and destroyed one of them. Then he saw McElroy charging on down into the lower flight of six, one of which he shot down. McScotch described what happened after the Nieuports landed safely as follows

'McElroy waited, expecting some praise from his fellowcountryman.

'There was a lively twinkle in Mick's eyes as he said 'What do you think our Pygmalion duty is, to risk our lives protecting you, you hot-headed Irish spalpeen? You might have lost Mac the whole blinking flight. Couldn't you wait to see what Mac was going to do?'

'Poor McElroy, he did not know now whether we were serious or not, and only after having filled in our reports did I congratulate him on his first 'blood'. There was no doubt that the Albatros had gone down to its destruction. Mick then gave him a severe lecture on tactics and flight policy – telling him that against fourteen of the enemy we should really have had little chance in a dog-fight. 'Remember, McIrish, none of us want to see you 'go', as you certainly will if you behave in that high-blooded Irish way of yours. You leave it to your leader. The flight might have had half-a-dozen of them if you hadn't split them up."

A few days later, Edward strode into McScotch's but at breakfast time, a sheet of yellow paper in his hand: a month's leave and two months' home service, 'Got my leave ticket, old boy. Home to good old Blighty, then back for the big fight. And *you're* coming with me. Your ticket's round there as well. They wouldn't give it to me. We've only got forty-eight hours to get out of France, and we'll still be together.'

'But that's damned unfair.' McScotch's quick temper flared up. He hated the idea of being stage managed by anybody, except when he was flying, and Edward seemed to take such a hell of a lot on himself at times. 'But that's unfair,' he protested. 'I've only been out here seven months. I'm going to have it out with the new Wing Commander.'

'Not the slightest use, old boy.' A knowing look came over Edward's smiling face. 'You're going home on medical grounds –'

'*What* –?'

'You're cracking up. I told the doctor so. If you come quietly now, we can stick together till the end. We'll be back for the big fight.'

It was exasperating. McScotch stared at the incredible Irishman and felt like punching him. At the same time a laugh bubbled in his throat. 'Well, of all the –'

The chance of a last-minute flight was too good to be missed. On January 1st they flew out together, and Edward managed to shoot down one German plane while McScotch usefully laid some bombs across an important railway line.

That evening at their farewell dinner, the Commanding Officer spoke about Edward's 'outstanding courage and initiative and leadership', dwelling on his abilities as a flight commander which would never be forgotten by those who had the good fortune to serve under him.

Such a very tame ending to this phase of Edward's war could not be tolerated. McScotch, who felt much the same about it, next morning barged into Edward's quarters and suggested that they fly one last mission together. Although he knew that it was against all the rules and regulations, Edward dashed straight out to the hangars. It was nearly eleven o'clock and the tender was due to pick them up at 2 p.m. There was just time!

Edward's plane was pushed out and quickly airborne, and McScotch was about to follow when a worried Major Tilney appeared to investigate these unauthorized take-offs. Leaning against the fuselage, he said half-heartedly: 'Look here, Mac, you can't go up. You're already struck off the strength.'

Half in and half out of the cockpit, McScotch grinned down at his senior. 'Hang it all, Mick's just gone up. I'm to meet him over the lines.'

Tilney wanted to argue it out. 'But neither of you has any right to have a machine.'

'I know, Major, but after all it is our sky!'

It sounded unanswerable. 'Oh hell!' Capitulating, Tilney stood back and wagged a school-masterly finger as McScotch gave the signal to the waiting mechanics. 'But I don't know anything about it,' he bellowed over the stuttering engine.

Waving cheerfully, McScotch signalled 'chocks away'. 'Shan't be long,' he yelled.

But it was an abortive mission for both of them. There was no sign of the German Air Force and, as a chagrined Edward said when they had landed again, 'They wouldn't wait to say goodbye!'

To Edward's surprise McCudden was waiting in the Mess, also posted home for a spell and calling now to say farewell to some of his old friends. With Edward, McScotch, Soltan and McIrish, also due for a short leave, he sat down for lunch.

As the two tenders drove away early that afternoon, Edward could not help but feel moved by the sight of the entire personnel, who turned out to wave and cheer him on his way. News of his departure had also reached the nurses at the nearby hospital and they were waiting to have a word with him. Among them was Sister Flanagan. The looks which they exchanged meant more than words.

After spending the night at the Hotel du Louvre at Boulogne, he came down next morning to find McScotch tucking in to a large plate of bacon and eggs.

'The porridge here is damn good, Mick.'

The sight of his friend's steadily champing jaws was a little too much. Edward made a wry face. 'Don't mention the word. The Channel is as rough as blazes and I must confess I'm the world's worst sailor.' He reached out for a *petit-pain* and slowly buttered it.

'Well, I'm damned!' McScotch stopped chewing for a moment, amazed. 'After seeing what you do in the air I can't see how you can possibly be seasick.'

Nibbling thoughtfully, Edward caught his eye. 'That crossChannel steamer hasn't got any joystick you can wiggle.'

Just as they were getting on with their food a total stranger wearing civilian clothes paused by their table. His voice had a dangerous heartiness which they did not relish. 'Morning! Mind if I join you?'

There were plenty of vacant tables nearby. McScotch gave it up as a bad job. 'Not at all,' he said politely.

'I've just returned from Switzerland – having treatment there.' Slightly put off by their coldness, the stranger ran on: 'The medicos said I had a groggy lung. I came to France in '16 with Number Two Squadron.'

In the terrible pause that ensued Edward and McScotch exchanged significant glances. This fellow was definitely a little too much at breakfast time.

'How many Germans have you brought down?' The question was asked in a genial tone and he probably meant well, but he was unaware that he was committing the cardinal sin. You simply did not ask such damn fool questions. It was something which was never inquired into and had it happened in the Mess the questioner would have been chucked out on his ear, regardless of rank or station.

By silent consent Edward and McScotch stood up and said in acid unison: 'The whole damned lot! Except the ones we're going to shoot down when we come back next time.' They then marched out of the dining – room, conscious that he was the colour of an embarrassed shrimp.

At Folkestone they had very little chance of conversation because of the crowd of soldiers and RFC men, who were rushing for the leave train and London.

'Well, have a good time, old boy. We'll be back for the big fight then –' Edward paused, 'Sizzle, sizzle, wonk!'

As they shook hands, McScotch shouted over the din, 'Goodbye, Mick. I'll probably see you at the club.' Heading for Canterbury to see his mother, Edward could not have guessed that he was about to be tested in something far more difficult than battle. His next fight was to be against red tape.

CHAPTER ELEVEN

Enthusiastic to throw himself back into the simmering cauldron of France, Edward was eager to escape his mother's uncertain moods and get up to London as soon as possible to discover what they intended doing with him.

When he arrived at the War Office he had one purpose in mind, to ask for an immediate posting to a fighting squadron. Hardly were the words out of his mouth before a General coolly informed him that he might find himself detained in England as an instructor.

Edward was flabbergasted, he could not believe it. The idea of being a 'desk pilot' was enough to make him speechless. When he did find his tongue again what had started off as an amicable and friendly routine interview developed into a shouting match in which his Irish rancour shattered the British way of running the war. Underneath his patriotism he was still very much the hot-blooded Celt and he now picked up the flaming Irish brand.

What was the good of holding a man back? After all his experience as a fighter pilot, should he be wasted in some home-based training job. In any case, he could *not* stomach that sort of life.

The General heard him out. He had no option, although much of what Edward said about armchair pilots went right over his head. He was not by nature a harsh or unreasonable officer, but Edward was carrying things a little too far, flaring up like this. The fellow was spiking his guns.

Although he argued himself practically blue in the face, Edward at last had to admit that 'they' would never change their minds. He would have to go to a reserve unit as a – a teacher!

Walking purposefully along the Strand, making no attempt to stifle his burning anger, he turned into the Savoy Hotel and immediately bumped into Lieutenant Collier of No. 43 Squadron, whose photo reconnaissance flight he had successfully escorted a few weeks before. Over a drink he poured out the story of the interview, recounting with scorn what the General had told him and lashing staff officers with all the venom he could muster. It was a most impressive piece of vituperative speaking, but as Collier was only a junior officer he could offer no useful advice.

Kicking his heels in London for several weeks, Edward found nothing interesting to do with himself. He generally frequented the RFC Club in Bruton Street, where the atmosphere was as close to the Mess as it was possible to get. Most of the time he kept himself to himself, unless he happened to meet somebody whom he especially liked.

One day an acquaintance introduced him to General Sir David Henderson, who commanded the RFC in the field.

'How long have you been home?'

'A month too long, sir,' Edward said, barely restraining himself. Titled gentlemen and generals were anathema to him at any time, but more so now.

Henderson, who knew his record, tried to be cheerful but it was difficult because the man's manner was so uncompromising. Also he happened to know what had happened during Edward's War Office interview. This might be just the time to try and placate him. 'Well, you'll have to be here for two months at least – if not more. You must have a rest –'

They were entirely the wrong words as far as Edward was concerned. General or no general, he felt that he must speak out and they could think what they like.

'If I can't get back to France soon *with* permission, I'll return without it, sir,' he ejaculated coldly. 'I'll take a machine out of the hangar one day and fly back to my old squadron.'

Several others heard him and conversation stopped while they waited for General Henderson's reply to *that* one.

'If you do that, Mannock, you'll be court-martialled and shot.'

'Death is better than dishonour,' Edward whipped back quickly.

Henderson could not hide a smile. 'You win, Mannock. I'll see what can be done.'

After that they were able to chat in a better atmosphere. Edward, it appeared, was anxious to fill in his waiting time usefully and said that he would like to get permission to hunt the German Gotha bombers which were night bombing London. All he wanted for the job was the loan of an SE.

Still slightly amused by the way the Irishman had put him into such an awkward situation, General Henderson drew the line at this proposal. 'No,' he said. 'No SEs have been flown at night and they'd be too difficult to land.'

And that seemed to be the end of it. Living on hope, Edward went back to the drawn – out purgatory of waiting and fuming.

It was almost impossible to get in touch with General Henderson to find out if he had been able to do anything for him. Another broken promise...

A few days later Major Dore, DSO, MC, formerly of No. 43 Squadron, happened to meet Lieutenant Collier in London, and after a preliminary greeting broke the news that he had just been given command of No. 74 Training Squadron at London Colney in Hertfordshire.

'That's damned good!' Collier enthused. 'Who have you got

Dore mentioned Captain W E Young and Captain Meredith Thomas as two of his flight commanders. The third man would be Mannock.

He finished his drink, obviously delighted by the prospect before him. 'Mannock's better than a whole squadron,' he exclaimed, 'so it ought to be a damned good outfit.'

When the information reached him, Edward took it sombrely, because it was a million miles away from what he had been hoping for and willing so hard to happen these past few weeks. He started packing his gear...

Training squadrons had changed since first he learned to fly. In those days pupils and pilot-instructors 'mucked in' together, but as soon as he arrived at London Colney he noticed that the barriers were up between the two groups. For one thing the instructors seemed to have very little time for the normally high – spirited fledglings or 'Huns' as they called the pupils, and on their side the pupils, some of whom had seen perhaps two years' active service in the Army, lacked confidence in the instructors. Edward was quick to see the need for comradeship.

As things stood they could have a very bad effect on the new generation of pilots, and it could even slow down the whole training programme if the two factions kept to their own camps and were unable to recognize the basic needs.

In February, when rain gusted down over the sodden Hertfordshire landscape and the 'No Flying' notice had been posted, Edward knew that he could not stand the stuffy monastic atmosphere of the instructors' Mess any longer.

Bursting in through the connecting door, he surveyed their drooping heads. This was as bad as the instructors' Mess 1. Next moment they all sat up with a jerk as he hollered: 'All tickets, please! Please pass right down the car!'

There was a stunned silence. They could not believe it! Nothing like this had ever happened before. The thought of an instructor even deigning to enter the pupils' Mess was alone overwhelming, but there he was, grinning delightedly at them as though waiting for a joke to be cracked.

Not many of them knew him except by sight, and what they now saw was a man about six feet in height wearing the faded uniform of a captain of the Royal Engineers with a pilot's badge over his left pocket and, below it and just as faded as the rest of the uniform, the ribbon of the Military Cross with the rosette sewn in the centre. Round his neck in lieu of a collar was the usual silk stocking, which he fingered from time to time. He was never without that stocking, nobody knew why.

'Beer – Waiter!' somebody yelled encouragingly.

Edward held up his hand, and gravely remonstrated: 'I want no waiter, but I can do with some beer.'

It marked the beginning of his acceptance, the start of a *rapport* between pupils and instructors.

His lectures soon came to be regarded as star pieces in the curriculum, and it was remarkable how he managed to project his personality during sessions which once had been considered deadly dull. His advice was lapped up because he spiced it with personal reminiscences, and this gave him an advantage over other more academically-minded instructors, many of whom had failed at the front and been sent home to teach. Edward was a man who had actually been up against the Germans, so he must know what he was talking about.

He introduced a slogan governing fights against single-seater scouts, which was painted up on the hangar walls:

Always above; seldom on the same level; never underneath.

These nine words contained the truth of successful air fighting in a nutshell.

Scanning their youthful faces, he said: 'You'll be flying SE5s when you get your squadrons. The Huns have produced a good triplane fighter – a Fokker triplane. It's easier to handle than the SE, but not as fast. It isn't strong and several have broken up in the air, diving. But you can dive an SE as fast as you like...'

When he was particularly engrossed in a subject he would stop and smile at them in a very human way. A pilot was not a machine, he was a man and he must have certain weaknesses. The idea was to keep the plane under control and not to let yourself down. A dead pilot was no good to anybody.

Almost despite himself, he was a natural teacher, and it took very little time for him to imbue his pupils with enthusiasm for what had once been considered classroom material.

Many memories came back to him as he went on talking, and he knew that what he said now could mean a world of difference to the war in the air once these youngsters started flying against the might of Germany...

'When we get to the war,' he said, 'don't ever attempt to dog-fight a triplane on anything like equal terms in altitude. He'll get on your tail and stay there till he shoots you down. Take my advice, if you ever get into such an unfortunate position, put your aircraft into a vertical bank, hold the stick tight into your belly, keep your engine full on – and pray hard!

'When the Hun has got tired of trying to shoot you down from one position, he'll try another. Here's your chance, and you'll have to snap into it with alacrity. As soon as your opponent starts to manœuvre for the next position, put on full bottom rudder, do one and a half turns of a spin and then run like hell for home, kicking your rudder hard from side to side, so as to make the shooting more difficult for the enemy. And keep praying!'

That piece of practical advice was to save many lives.

'Practising stunting is a waste of time. It is the quick turns that are needed more than anything else in a fight.'

He warned them to beware of the enemy pilot who fired in short bursts. 'On the other hand, if the Hun is firing long bursts at you, you can bet your bottom dollar that he's windy and probably a beginner. Fight him like hell – he should be easy meat.

'And finally, remember that even good flying never beat the enemy. You must learn to shoot straight. It's one failing of some of our finest pilots. By the way, I advise you to sight your own guns. It's no use just leaving it to the armourer – he hasn't got to do the fighting!'

He had to admit it, be was getting used to being a 'teacher', and beneath his often gay exterior nobody missed the steely intent and purpose. He was out to transform these lads into first-class pilots.

He did not make many really close friends at London Colney but seemed satisfied with long investigatory conversations, some of which did, in fact, lay the basis for future comradeship in France.

One day he wandered across the tarmac towards a solitary figure sitting on an oil drum, apparently waiting for a plane. This was Lieutenant Ira Jones, generally known as 'Taffy' due to his ancestry, and destined to become second best shot after Edward. In the Mess he often sang 'Burlington Bertie' with a monocle jammed in his eye.

Edward selected the next oil drum and perched on it. He was silent for some time while Jones felt increasingly conscious of his examination but said nothing. At last Edward pointed at Jones's tunic ribbons, the Military Medal and the medal of St George, a Russian decoration. Both had been awarded for the same incident when Jones rescued a comrade while under fire.

'What did you get those for, Taffy?' Edward asked, smiling, well aware of his own cheek.

Jones was distinctly hot under the collar, because such questions were not generally asked. 'I'm told it was for so-called bravery,' he answered hesitantly. 'It's – er – it's stamped on the Military Medal.'

'Good answer, Taffy.' Was Mannock ragging him or something? He looked serious enough, especially when he demanded: 'What makes you fight so hard?'

Jones almost took umbrage. Mannock had all the nerve in the world! Nevertheless, he gave a perfectly straight answer, staring straight ahead across the aerodrome. 'I fight for my King and country, of course, but – well, as I'm religious I also personally fight for Christian principles.'

'By Christian principles do you mean that you're fighting for freedom?' Edward shot back at him intently.

'Yes. I believe in liberty of thought, free speech and kindness to those who need it.'

The simple words stimulated Edward. 'Well done, Taffy! I also fight for liberty.' Then he added, with a deliberate brogue, 'Particularly for the liberty of the Emerald Isle! The world must never be held in bondage by the Kaiser and all he stands for. And *I* would readily die for such a cause, Taffy.'

It was the beginning of a very close association between them which, while it revealed many different aspects of Edward's character, never became quite as revealing as the one which he had enjoyed with McScotch.

If anybody believed that he was settling down completely in his new life with No. 74 Training Squadron they were badly mistaken, but for the time being he was forced to accept what he labelled the sedentary life, which had only one real consolation, the training of pilots to form a fighting unit.

There was so little to do apart from lecturing and flying! In the evenings he sometimes entertained the others on his violin. To his favourite 'Londonderry Air', a lament at best, he added the livelier 'Phil, the Fluter's Ball'. When he played he was a changed man.

During March, Major Dore revealed that he would be leaving the squadron. Edward was horrified. Dore was a fine commanding officer. Changes like this were bad for morale during a training course.

'Leaving the squadron?'

Dore tapped an official-looking letter he was carrying. 'Yes, I've been appointed to a staff job.'

'*What?*' It was too much for Edward, and he catapulted out of his chair, running his fingers through his untidy hair. 'But you don't really mean to say that you'd rather stay at home on a staff job than be in command of this fighting squadron in France?'

'But I'm going to be promoted.' Dore was filled with pride and protest. He had been expecting congratulations, not argument.

Jumping about in real agitation, Edward's voice rose a pitch. 'What? But that's worse than ever!'

'Yes, but I've been out there the whole time since 1915 and that's more than any of the others, so – '

It was, after all, reasonable. Edward calmed down. 'I didn't think of that at first,' he admitted. 'I'm sorry. And I'm damned sorry we're going to lose you, too!'

'Thanks. I'm sorry to go in a way – this is a rattling good squadron. But anyway, you've got the best man you could have in command.'

'Who's he?'

'Major Keith Caldwell.'

'What, 'Grid' Caldwell from No. 60 Squadron?' Dore nodded. 'Yes. You know him, of course.'

'Rather! I first met him when they came over with 'Zulu' Lloyd at No. 40

Squadron.'

'Jack Scott says he's the bravest man he's met. He says 'Grid' has been in more fights than any man he knows for the number of patrols he's done.'

Rubbing his hands together and looking more than satisfied, Edward muttered half to himself: 'I can see, we're going to have some fun!'

'Grid' Caldwell took over the squadron at a most crucial time. As he said in his introductory speech to the assembled pupils, only three weeks remained before they left for France.

'We must make the best of that time, gentlemen, and when we get there we shall seek out the Huns and fight them like hell...'

The final selection of pilots was not made until March 7th, and inevitably there were a few disappointments among those who had not made the grade.

The final list read:

'A' Flight
Commanded by Captain E Mannock
2nd Lieutenants Roxburgh-Smith (aged thirty-four and known as 'Dad'); Dolan, MC (a close friend of Edward); Howe (called 'Swazi' for his South African background); Atkinson (a Scot); Hamer and Clements (both Canadians).

'B' Flight
Commanded by Captain W E Young
Kiddie ('The Old Man'); Piggot; Richardson; Bright; Stewart-Smith; Savage (a South African).

'C' Flight
Commanded by Captain W C Cairns
W B Giles (formerly SLI and an observer in No. 43 Squadron); Begbie (who was supposed to be a very distant cousin of Richthofen, the German ace); Birch; Skeddon (a Canadian); Ira Jones, MM (later to become Wing Commander Jones, DSO, MC, DFC and Bar, MM).

The squadron gunnery officer was Lieutenant Harry Coverdale, the England and Blackheath rugby half-back.

As they gathered round the notice board to study their allocations, Edward entered, looking solemn but obviously with a mischevious idea in mind.

'Pilots of the Fighting Seventy-Fourth,' he intoned in a priestly voice, 'hearken unto me. I want you all to fall in outside the Mess.' When they were assembled, cracking ribald jokes, he gave the order: 'Odd numbers – one pace forward – MARCH!' An untidy mix – up resulted. 'Oh, I forgot! You're not numbered, are you? Well – NUMBER!' As soon as this was accomplished, he told the odd numbers to step forward one pace, then cried: 'Follow my movements!'

Heading his entourage of guffawing pilots, he marched off across the network of paths, stopping now and then to do a knees bend or an exaggerated arm stretch, the rest following suit. When he burst into a version of 'Keep the Home Fires Burning' and then 'Rule Britannia' the bellowed chorus kept time until the sound reverberated throughout the entire camp.

When they reached the instructors' and senior officers' Mess, Edward did not hesitate but marched straight past his Commanding Officer, who was just finishing lunch. Taken aback, 'Grid' Caldwell threw down his knife, but on seeing the hot faced exuberance of Edward at the head of the column he relaxed and watched the invasion with amused eyes. High spirits were a pretty good sign.

As soon as they had clattered rowdily out of the Mess, Edward put his sights on the adjutant's office. Just the thing! The home of all that terrible paperwork! And ripe for a shake-up, too!

The adjutant, a Guards officer, was a gentleman who took everything very seriously indeed. As the door flew open he sat bolt upright, one hand going to his clipped moustache. Everybody looked drunk! Mannock really was the end!

After creating total confusion in the administrative department, Edward finally guided them all back to the spot from which they had started and gave the word to dismiss, following it with the advice that there would be no more work that day.

Next day they went to Scotland for a one-week course at the Air Fighting School at Ayr, commanded by Colonel L W B Rees, VC. It was practically the finishing touch before France.

But before the final departure the now qualified pilots gave the customary display of formation flying. This went very well until Skeddon, a Canadian with an individualistic turn of mind, suddenly winged away at the top of a loop and went into a flamboyant stunting display.

Watching from the ground, Edward's face wrinkled, and after they landed he said only two words, 'Very pretty,' then walked away, leaving them in puzzled silence.

At the farewell dinner he came to the point.

'...and when I watched your flying display the other day – well, I was very gratified by your enthusiasm, and especially that half-roll at the top of a loop.'

Of course, he was directing his shafts at Skeddon. The Canadian misinterpreted the meaning and started to preen himself. This was certainly praise from the master!

'But,' Edward continued, his voice hardening, 'I wasn't particularly impressed by all those pretty evolutions. They'll be no damned use to you when you get a Hun on your tail... So the thing to remember is, gentlemen, always above; seldom on the same level; never underneath! Our CO is the bravest man in the Air Force and he'll frighten hell out of you when he leads the patrols.'

A few moments after sitting down and acknowledging the applause, he turned to Captain Cairns, whom he knew fairly well, and asked, 'Tell me, what do you imagine would be your first conscious thought in the event of your aeroplane catching fire in the air?'

Cairns had not been expecting anything like this. It took him some moments to find an answer while he slowly revolved his glass between his fingers. 'Good Lord! Well, I think my thoughts would be confused between whether I could put the fire out and what my fate would be.'

Edward swallowed a mouthful of wine. 'My reply would be – a bullet in my head.' But he did not admit to Cairns that he always flew with a Colt revolver for company.

On March 30th, after a three-day delay at Goldhanger, Essex, the only casualty on the cross-Channel flight to St Omer was Contact, the small black puppy mascot. Ira Jones, who had Contact as a passenger in his machine, tipped over on landing and the shock shook the little animal up so much that it was sick on the spot.

As for Edward, he tramped up and down, glad to feel the soil of France underfoot again. It would not be long before the gun-barrels turned hot.

Next day they flew to Tetengham, near Dunkirk, and started practising on targets floating in the sea. The gun-barrels were only warm as yet.

CHAPTER TWELVE

Although the squadron was kept moderately busy attached to a naval wing up north at Dixmude, flying regular patrols and often returning with nothing very important to report, the sense that something must happen soon maintained morale. News from the distant front was discouraging because the Germans were systematically pounding away at the allied defences, waging an aggressive war and never letting up. Rumours said that Haig must soon spring his surprise. What it would be, nobody guessed.

After April 12th, 1918, which marked No. 74 Squadron's first day in action, Edward realized that the war had changed. He had done his damnedest to hunt out a German Air Force which suffered from more than the usual excessive shyness. He thought that this almost embarrassing absence of Germans was caused by the first flush over the lines by other flights in the squadron, but after taking his brood out first one day he realized that the Germans were, in fact, timorous. Half-joking, he asked Cairns, who led the dawn patrol, not to disturb the enemy too much and leave something for 'A' Flight. It was not like the old days...

In the end, 'Grid' Caldwell got in touch with Colonel Pierre van Ryneveld, who agreed to have the squadron moved to his own wing on the Ypres front where the war might become hotter. The Royal Flying Corps, with little enough to do, prayed for one big chance to put the pressure on the enemy, especially in the Amiens sector where the Germans were now taking a bloody advantage of allied weaknesses.

In such a situation it was hard to keep spirits high.

What they needed was a morale-booster, something better than the after-dinner 'rugger' in the Mess when the Colonials challenged the United Kingdom. It came when Caldwell walked into the Mess at eight o'clock on April 12th just as they were finishing breakfaSt As the clatter of cups and cutlery died down, he sat on the corner of a table and smoothed a sheet of paper. His face told the twenty – two men nothing.

'Gentlemen, I've got something for you here. Listen to this. It's an order of the day from General Haig.'

He started reading out the words in a clear, clipped voice which grew more intense towards the end.

'To all ranks of the British Army in France and Flanders. Three weeks ago today the enemy began his terrific attacks against us on a fifty-mile front. His objects are to separate us from the French, to take the Channel ports, and destroy the British Army.

'In spite of throwing already 106 divisions into the battle and enduring the most reckless sacrifice of human life, he has as yet made little progress towards his goals. We owe this to the determined fighting and self-sacrifice of our troops.

'Words fail me to express the admiration which I feel for the splendid resistance offered by all ranks of our Army under the most trying circumstances. Many amongst us now are tired. To those I would say that victory will belong to the side which holds out the longest.

'The French Army is moving rapidly and in great force to our support. There is no other course open to us but to fight it out. Every position must be held to the last man; there must be no retirement. With our backs to the wall, and believing in the justice of our cause, each one of us must fight on to the end. The safety of our homes and the freedom of mankind depend alike upon the conduct of each one of us at this critical moment.'

On the last words of this desperate call for a renewed faith 'Grid' Caldwell slowly lifted his eyes, inviting a response. It came, almost inevitably, from Edward, who leapt to his feet, throwing one hand up in the air in a gesture of inspired defiance.

'They're going to get it now – and they won't have more than half an hour to wait for it!' He swivelled round to face the members of his flight. 'Come on, 'A' Flight, we take off at eight twenty-five!'

His actions were a mighty signal to an outburst of air activity all over the front. In a tumultuous climax to Haig's 'backs-to-the-wall' message, 'A' Flight returned from that first mission firing Very pistols and whooping with satisfaction to announce four enemy Albatroses out of a group of eight shot down by 10am, the first two by Edward, although he insisted on putting one to the credit of the flight as a whole. And all without any losses.

The new air war was on!

It was as though his action set off a reaction which went right through the RFC Pilots on both sides took to flying as low as 200-feet above the ground to seek out the movements of infantry and artillery. All over the sky dog-fights of incredible savagery went on. In one day alone thirty-five Germans were shot down against an overall British loss of only four machines.

The first casualty was Begbie of 'C' Flight. He went down on April 21st in flames, chased by a German who continued pumping bullets into the smoke and fire. Flying confidently, he failed to notice that Giles was on his tail. At the last moment Giles shot him to pieces.

When Edward heard about Begbie's end he said to Ira ones: 'I hope he blew his brains out first.'

News that Richthofen, the leading German fighter-pilot, had been shot down was greeted with shouts of triumph and regret. There were those who believed him to be the greatest ace of the war up to this time. History was to prove them wrong.

That night at dinner someone stood up, glass in hand, and proposed a joint toast to the departed Begbie and Richthofen. Edward refused to toast the latter; he had nothing but contempt for a man who usually chose novices or lame ducks as his targets.

Caldwell then said, 'The death of anyone among us must never be allowed to affect our morale, so come on! Let's liven up.' He waited for the rustle among them. 'Those Hunerinoes fought better today – probably because of Richthofen's death. The spirit of revenge was carrying them through. Good enough! The squadron will avenge Begbie a hundredfold. We shall have some good fighting tomorrow.'

And on that prophetic note they all burst into 'High-Cockalorum'.

Every time they suffered a loss the sting of death had to be assuaged by a boisterous party. One by one, well-known faces were there no more. Stuart-Smith, Bright, Skeddon on May 8th, and on May 12th Dolan, DFC, had all gone.

The loss of Dolan on a particularly successful day, when they downed six out of eight, created in Edward a feeling of sheer misery and unhappiness, and it was all he could do to sit through a Mess party. When he reached his hut later that night he practically broke down as sobs welled in his throat. What a waste it was! Dolan, who had been so promising, who had shot down eight enemy planes in a month.

From that day on discipline in his own flight was strict and a new regime was introduced the day after Dolan died. A new pilot, who had cut away at a most decisive moment, was faced by Edward in the Mess in front of everybody. 'You left the flight just now – when we were about to attack those Huns –'

The rest looked on, silent jurors in uniform.

The new man stammered: 'Yes, sir, but I –'

'Well, you can't do that,' Edward said coldly. 'I won't have it. It's cowardice and if you do it again – I'll shoot you down myself.'

As he strode out, slamming the door behind him, few of them doubted that he meant what he had said.

'Grid' Caldwell commented in these words on Edward's flying technique

'Mannock and Dolan were up together and, on seeing British 'Archie' bursting on our side of the lines, they chased along to see what could be done. They spotted a Hun two-seater beetling back towards the lines and got down just in time to prevent this.

'The Hun crashed, but not badly, and most people would have been content with this – but not Mick Mannock. He dived half-a-dozen times at the machine, spraying bullets at the pilot and the observer, who were still showing signs of life. I witnessed this business and flew alongside Mick, yelling at the top of my voice (which was rather useless), and warning him to stop.

'On being questioned as to his wild behaviour after we had landed, he heatedly replied, 'The swines are better dead – no prisoners for me!' '

Lieutenant Ira Jones was also flying in the vicinity on May 21st when Edward shot down three enemy scout planes and a Hannoverranner two-seater and describes the incident as follows:

'In his first fight, with commenced at 12,000-feet, there were six Pfalz scouts flying east from Kemmel Hill direction. One he shot to pieces after firing a long burst from directly behind and above; another he crashed; it spun into the ground after it had been hit by a deflection shot; the other, a silver bird, he had a fine set -to with, while his patrol watched the Master at work. It was a wonderful sight. First they waltzed around one another like a couple of turkey-cocks, Mick being tight on his adversary's tail. Then the Pfalz half-rolled and fell a few hundred feet behind him. Mick followed, firing as soon as he got in position. The Hun then looped – Mick looped, too, coming out behind and above his opponent and firing short bursts. The Pfalz then spun – Mick spun also, firing as he spun. This shooting appeared to me to be a waste of ammunition. The Hun eventually pulled out: Mick was fast on his tail – they were now down to 4,000-feet. The Pfalz now started twisting and turning, which was a sure sign of 'wind up'. After a sharp burst close up, Mick administered the *coup de grâce*, and the poor old fellow went down headlong and crashed.

'This was a really remarkable exhibition of cruel, cool, calculating Hun-strafing. A marvellous show. I felt sorry for the poor Hun, for he put up a marvellous show of defensive fighting. His effort reminded me of mine on April 12th. The only difference was that he was miles over his own lines and had a slower machine. Had he only kept spinning down to the ground, I think he would have got away with it.

'I asked Mick after he landed why he fired during the spin. He replied, 'Just to intensify his wind-up.' And a very good answer, too! This was the first occasion that I saw a machine loop during a fight. It was obvious to us, watching, that to loop under such circumstances is foolish. Mick managed, however, to keep behind him, though, and did not lose contact with him, although it was obvious by his manœuvres after he came out of the loop that the Pfalz pilot was all at sea, for he twisted and turned his machine in a series of erratic jerks, just as if he was a dog stung in his tail. Mick said he only looped as well for a bit of fun, as he felt his opponent was 'cold meat'. He said what he should have done instead of looping was to have made a zooming climbing turn as the Pfalz looped, then half-rolled and come back on his tail as he came out of the loop. By this means he would have been able to keep the Hun in sight all the time, while he would not have lost control of his machine as the Hun did while coming out of the loop.

'Mick's other Hun was a Hannoverranner two-seater, which lie shot down after a burst at right angles. The old boy crashed into a tree near La Couranne, south of Vieux.'

Like many others, Jones wanted to learn the secret of Edward's startling success, and he came to the conclusion that it could be summed up as 'the gift of accurate shooting, combined with the determination to get to close quarters before firing.'

'Grid' Caldwell, who studied Edward's technique and personality closely over a period, viewed him as a strategist rather than a brilliant pilot. 'His successes were largely due to his tactical approach to a fight and his extraordinarily fine deflection shooting once he was engaged. In an air fight most people try to get behind the other man to get an easier shot and where you cannot be shot at (in the case of fighter *versus* fighter), but Mannock was able to hit them at an angle.

'With two-seaters he usually came down from an angle in front where the pilot's vision was obscured by the top wing, and if he missed in his approach, he half-rolled to come up under the tail and attacked where the gunner had trouble getting at him. When he landed back after a successful show, he was always in tremendous form, shouting out to the other pilots about incidents in the fights.

'His main policy was to enter a fight with the advantage, and so shoot the other man down before he could you. To this end he usually led his men in behind the enemy lines at 19,000-feet or so, and attacked from above and towards the lines, and so often effected surprise. He did not take kindly to being shot at as he considered there was no future in it and preferred to get away and seize the advantage the next time.

'The enemy aircraft on our front were as follows and were treated by Mannock: Albatros and Halberstadt: an SE5 could outfight these unless the Hun pilot was a particularly good one, so you could take these on any way you liked; Fokker D7: as the Fokker could turn inside an SE, you did not mill round in circles, but attacked from above and zoomed up to your height again. The SE was very little faster than a Fokker, but it had an inferior climb; Fokker Triplane: it could turn inside and outclimb an SE, so you treated it with more respect and adopted up-and-down tactics, although the SE was faster.

'Mannock was not a stunt pilot; I never saw him looping or wasting energy or engine power in this manner, nor was he better than an average pilot. He really hated the Germans – there was absolutely no chivalry with him and the only good Hun was a dead one. I am afraid we rather fostered this bloodthirsty attitude in No. 74 Squadron, because it helped to keep a war-going atmosphere which is essential for the less tough types.'

Edward's continued concern for men who seemed to lack the guts to fight made him ask Caldwell what had happened to the man he had chided for leaving a fight before it had started.

'They sent him home to England,' Caldwell said.

Edward flared up without attempting to control himself. 'Good God! Why the blazes can't they send these useless swines to the trenches?' he demanded hotly. 'That's where they ought to be. Now I suppose he'll become a flying instructor and get a nice fat staff job.'

For men who really were doing their bit, he had nothing but praise and admiration, and when Ira Jones reported that he had just shot down a two-seater, Edward was lavish in his congratulations.

The war in the air might be as serious as death itself, but there had to be time for jokes of singular enormity, like the Orange Raid...

One day Caldwell said blandly: 'Look here, Mick, I think No. 1 Squadron need waking up, don't you?'

Puzzled, because he knew how busy they had been on operations, Edward asked: 'Why? I don't –'

'We've got a surplus of oranges, more than we need,' Caldwell said craftily. 'I think we should use some of them.'

They agreed that this was a fitting way of celebrating the recent promotion of Captain Young to the rank of major. And he was now commanding officer of No. 1 Squadron!

A hail of ripe oranges from the low-flying planes of No. 74 Squadron took No. 1 Squadron personnel completely by surprise. Showers of bright-coloured fruit rained down without warning, some of it 'exploding' on the roof of the pilots' Mess and one, at least, nearly knocking out a dumbfounded pilot who emerged to investigate.

Wearing highly superior expressions and smug grins to match, Caldwell and Edward signalled withdrawal and led their flock home.

They had not been back more than half an hour before No. 1 Squadron's planes zoomed over and dumped a shower of bananas.

War was not usually as lighthearted as this, but in the RFC every man must find a distinct role to play. For Edward it meant a partial return to teaching. Any newcomer was subjected to a lengthy scrutiny, and although he might not know it he was assessed by Edward, who always felt curious to discover what sort of fellow he was.

The day after the orange raid he was sitting in the Mess after dinner when he saw a fresh, incredibly young face. A new pilot was expected – this was a *child*! After a time, he rose and approached, smiling.

'Are you the new pilot?'

He sprang to his feet. 'Yes, sir.'

'It's pretty miserable, arriving in a strange place, among people you don't know, at night like this.'

'Yes, sir.'

'Have a drink.'

'Thank you, six.'

Edward shouted for an orderly to bring lemonade, then turned again to the tyro. 'How old are you?'

'Er – I'm – I'm eighteen, sir.' He was careful to avoid Edward's penetrating eye and missed the hint of humour.

'By which you mean you are seventeen – or is it sixteen?'

Confused and by now out of his depth, the youngster stumbled. 'Well – I – '

'Faked your age, didn't you?'

Taken off guard by so direct a question, he admitted: 'Yes, I did, sir. Actually, I'm seventeen, nearly eighteen.'

Edward thought it over. 'Well, I think you'd better come into 'A' Flight, but I won't let you go over the lines for at least a week. I'll fix it with the CO.'

The earlier tenseness left the new pilot. Talking to Edward, he thought, was like talking to an elder brother. Later, when he heard that the 'elder brother' was shooting down an average of one enemy plane a day – he once scored four victories in less than twenty-four hours! – the younger man marvelled that one of the RFC's most famous pilots found time even to talk to him, let alone arrange for him to enter his own flight.

In the next few days the novice had another opportunity of observing a man whom he recognized as a master.

When Edward returned from one of his patrols, he bounced into the Mess, shouting: 'All tickets, please! Please pass right down the car!', holding up four fingers and telling them: 'Flamerinoes – four Sizzle, sizzle, wonk!' He seized the arm of the young pilot with whom he had been flying. 'Come on! Toast the warrior. This bloodthirsty young devil's shot down a Hun!'

One young pilot later had a quiet talk with the 'bloodthirsty young devil'. 'How did you do it?' he asked wonderingly.

There was an embarrassed silence as though a confession must be made. 'Well, it was really Captain Mannock who did it all. He said to me this morning, 'Have you got a Hun yet?' and when I said I hadn't, he said, 'Well, come on out and we'll get one for you.'

'It was after his patrol and he took me with him – just the two of us – and I don't quite know where we got to, but I saw him waggle his wings and dive, and I followed him. Then suddenly he zoomed up and I found the Hun – a two-seater – right in my sights. He'd already given the Hun a burst.'

'That was damned decent of him.'

'Oh, he's like that. He's the most unselfish man I ever knew, and, of course, you are absolutely safe with him.' Edward often deliberately gave what was legitimately his own score away to younger men. Although his intention was to act as the master – huntsman, usually going out with two

SEs and a pupil-killer, cornering enemy planes and putting them in such a position that the waiting pupil could not miss, there were occasions when things did go wrong and he, Edward, had to play the executioner. A young pilot, new to the often terrifying emergencies which could materialize during combat, might not yet have had time to develop and attune the instantaneous reactions by which the more experienced pilot survived. To err on the wrong side of the half-second margin could mean death and Edward, his nerves taut and fighting instincts honed, had to see that this never happened. While he always gave precise instructions to the younger pilots who went out with him to get their 'first Hun', there still remained so many unknown quantities. If the new man seemed at all uncertain, Edward dashed in, firing for all he was worth and downing the prey. Anything short of the most blatant cowardice in action was enough for him to unhesitatingly file the victory in the younger man's name.

This happened during a period when the replacement of pilots was frequent, and few of them failed to receive the invitation to 'Come out and get your first Hun' from him. Even allowing a reasonable percentage of these as real victories, many men later admitted that they were Mannock's triumphs from beginning to end.

That the new aggressive action of 74 Squadron made a great impression on the Germans about this time was evident from a conversation between Caldwell and Colonel Pierre van Ryneveld (now knighted), the officer commanding the wing to which No. 74 Squadron belonged.

'We had a captured German airman at HQ today and he said they knew that this squadron – he knew the markings on your SEs – is at Clairmarais – and this is the part that will amuse you; they think you are a hand – picked squadron commanded by McCudden,' Ryneveld said.

Caldwell replied: 'They're obviously referring to Mannock. He's already got about forty Huns. In fact he got his fortieth today.'

The subject of their conversation was sitting in the corner, a moody expression on his face, which he supported with a clenched fist. He did not want to join in the laughter. He was beyond it. Ira Jones, who had been watching him for some time, broke the silence between them. 'What are you thinking about?'

Sure enough, it had been Edward's fortieth victory, but he could not somehow rid his mind of the ghastly picture it evoked. 'That damned Hun in flames,' he said. After a long pause he glared round the Mess and demanded: 'Why the hell haven't we got parachutes?'

This question had been asked before, but there was no answer to it, apart from the widely-shared idea that the high-ups assumed that if a pilot had an escape open to him he might not bother to fight very hard. The truth, whatever it is, has never come out, but if current supposition was correct, then it does represent a grave slur on the courage of men like Mannock and his contemporaries in the RFC.

On May 24th, when 'A' Flight was landing, Caldwell advanced over the field with General Plumer, commander of the Second Army. Plumer was described by Ira Jones as being 'a quaint little man to look at but very charming to speak to. He is about five feet eight in height, corpulent, has a podgy red face, white hair and a moustache, a twinkle in his eye, wears a monocle, and stands like the grand soldier he is, very stiff and erect.'

Plumer was naturally a stickler where dress and behaviour were concerned and he had the greatest difficulty in accepting the apparently casual ways of the men of the Royal Flying Corps, who were under his command. There was, however, nothing he could do about it, and he had to admit that in recent weeks they had demonstrated an ability in action which was on a performance par with the best of the crack regiments.

Watching with interest the planes landing, he now turned his attention to the pilots as they jumped to the ground and started walking away, some of them passing close to him. Among them was Edward, looking as Ira Jones recounted, 'the most disreputable of all … he was hatless, without a collar, his tunic open, his hair ruffled; in fact, he looked a typical bush-ranger!'

General Plumer asked: 'Which is Mannock?' When the man himself was pointed out, it seemed as though Plumer would faint, but he pulled himself together and practically staggered up to an oil-begrimed Edward, shot out his hand and proceeded to confirm a rumour which had been going the rounds for several days.

'Mannock,' he stammered, 'let me congratulate you on your DSO – and on your first day's work.'

It was badly put and Edward misinterpreted what the great man was getting at, because he replied: 'We expected *that*, sir,' and grasped Plumer's pink hand in his own dirty paw.

The General turned away, mixed feelings going round and round in his brain. He probably thought that Edward was referring to the award of the DSO, whereas the reference made was to the first day's work – the successful flying operations.

The DSO which came to Edward was the signal for one of the rowdiest parties ever. Many later famous names were there that night, including 'Nigger' Horn, Loughton, MacGregor (a New Zealander killed in an air accident after the war) and the 'Three Musketeers' – Elliott Springs, Callaghan and Grider (all Americans) and Daniels. They came from No. 85 Squadron at St Omer and all started drinking a venomous cocktail called '74 Viper'. And all had hangovers as a result.

Edward's official score was now forty-seven. In actual fact, it was fifty-one. He was having the luck of the devil.

On May 28th Ira Jones and Clements, the Canadian, were talking together.

'Mick's an absolute marvel,' Jones said with enthusiasm. 'I believe he's got about fifty-two Huns now –'

Clements broke in. 'He sure is. He saved my life today, too. We were out looking for trouble, and hell, we found it! We ran into a bunch of about ten Pfalz. I tried to catch up with Mick, but the Huns were diving towards me. So what does Mick do but go right under them to draw them off on to him! Gee, it was a hell of a rotten sight to see all those Huns after one SE. And if it had been anybody but Mick I would have been scared stiff for his safety. But Mick knew what he was doing... One of the Huns got on his tail, so he went down – you know, like he was out of control. He was on his back, spinning, doing everything except bring up his breakfast. He started at eight thousand feet and at five thousand the Hun flattened out to watch him crash. Then at four thousand feet Mick flattens out, too, and dives for home. The Hun started after him, but I was right on top of him and I cracked him. He was quite a stout guy – he turned on me and as his pals were coming to join the fun I reckoned it was time for supper. No Hun will ever shoot Mick down.'

Jones, who had been listening intently, nodded. 'Mick *saved* my life two days ago. My Vickers gun had a stoppage, and at that moment an Albatros sat on my tail. I thought my number was up when suddenly Mick appeared from nowhere and in about five seconds that Albatros was finished.'

On top of his form, it did seem that Edward just could not miss, nor could he get enough fights to satiate his loathing of the Germans.

He had just shot down an enemy plane on May 29th when he saw six SEs in another part of the sky. Signalling Clements and Jones to follow, he flew across to discover that they were from No. 85 Squadron, led by 'Nigger' Horn. Waggling his wings, Edward invited them to join his formation. Together they took on twelve of the enemy.

Flying strongly and using all his skill, Edward singled out the German leader and charged head on at him until he was only 300 yards away. They fired simultaneously. Edward was the victor by less than a second.

In the same engagement Clements bagged one and the pilots of No. 85 Squadron also reported sending one enemy down. It had been an excellent concerted effort.

That same evening, when 'Nigger' Horn phoned, Edward took the call, a copy of Tennyson's poems under his arm.

'Hullo, Mick!' Horn sounded festive. 'I've got my patrol here. We're drinking double brandies! What a day it's been. We all want to come out with you again tomorrow.'

Laying the book down on a ledge, Edward laughed. 'Right! Join us on the dawn patrol. We'll find some more Huns for you.'

And then he went back to the calm of Tennyson.

CHAPTER THIRTEEN

War for Edward had become the ephemeral victory and the flight home, the unrestrained and often momentary joy of being able to announce success. And for him war was also the sinking into a chair without any attempt at controlling the nervous reactions, the shaking hands and bunched muscles which somehow refused to relax.

He had no means of dissolving the pictures and phantasmagoria which formed unwanted in his mind's eye, he found no escape from the connection between the furnace of an enemy plane after he set it alight and the horror which he himself might have to suffer some day.

'Flamerinoes... God, what a death! God spare me from that. Bloody awful!'

He rammed his face down into his spread hands, mumbling to himself and taking no notice of the curious stares of the younger men. The acute perception lacking in most of the others spread over him until he had to make a visible effort to get rid of the picture of the burning aircraft as it broke up in wreaths of smoke and fell to the waiting ground. Hour after hour he went on feeling the beating heat, imagining what it would be like frantically to jerk at the dead controls and feel their looseness. Without so much as a parachute – *why, why, why wouldn't they authorise them?* – a man had to endure those flames, screaming unheard as they reached his face, sucking the air out of his lungs in a vacuum. In those last moments he might still be sufficiently alive to know what was happening to him.

Without having some confidantes Edward could never have carried on. He often talked to the VAD nurse, Sister Flanagan, and from her drew part of his strength to carry on, because she belonged to that sharply different world of materialistic efficiency and the silence of the wards.

Whenever he tried to rationalize the horror of being roasted alive in the cockpit of his plane, he knew that she would understand because she was a nurse and appreciated what the fear of being burnt meant. Behind these talks was a growing fondness for her.

No matter how much he talked, every incident held a heightened intensity and significance and the death in combat of a friend was still a personal bereavement.

It was also a warning and a threat. As the thunder of war grew louder even brave men turned to their own innermost thoughts in search of strength to carry on.

When Ira Jones returned from leave in the middle of June he was quick to notice that Edward was definitely in need of rest. One special symptom stood out, Edward's unusual talkativeness during their first meeting.

'Are you ready to die for your country, Taffy? Will you have it in flames or in pieces?'

Few of them missed the fact that fire somehow dominated Edward's conversation.

Jones soberly replied: 'It's a good thing you're going on leave today, Mick. It's just about time you had a rest.'

Edward vehemently denied it. He could not even see his own worn-out self and worked hard to persuade the Welshman that he was still as fresh as the day when first he arrived in France, and flying better than ever. However, in the end he meekly collected his leave ticket and travelled to London with the knowledge that Colonel van Ryneveld wanted to post him to No. 85 Squadron. When the bar to his DSO had come through with a hint of future promotion, 'Grid' Caldwell spoke to the wing commander to try to delay the posting. No promises had been given.

Carrying his bags, he walked into the RFC Club in Bruton Street and automatically inspected the board where letters awaited collection. One yellow envelope stood out among the rest with his name on it. Frowning, he plucked it out and slit the flap with his thumbnail.

What he saw gave him no elation. He was beyond feeling.

He was promoted to major and appointed to command of No. 85 Squadron in place of Major W Bishop, VC, the Canadian, who had been selected to organize air training in Canada by his own Government. His squadron, formed at Hounslow early in 1918, went overseas in the spring of that year, first to an aerodrome near Dunkirk, then to St Omer.

This really was the peak for Edward if only he could have appreciated the fact. From nothing, he had quickly risen to a point where confidence existed to entrust him with a fighting unit. He was filled with a peculiar negation at the thought. What made it worse was the thought of having to leave No. 74 Squadron.

He went to his room, noticing that spells of shivering and nausea which had started before leaving France were getting worse. He could not think straight, only sit on the bed, holding the crumpled telegram in his hand, wondering why he felt so spent. Over everything spread a growing premonition of death. The law of averages, proven so many times in No. 74 Squadron, suggested that he would not come through alive, he was sure of it. The Germans would be beaten, yes, but he would not be there to see it.

Alone, he wrestled with the muscular pains as they settled in his arms and legs until it dawned on him that what he was suffering from must be influenza. The bout laid him very low. Huddled on the bed, sweating freely, he had to force away the almost supernatural horrors which came oozing out through his battle memories. Memories came unbidden of all the times when he had joked with a man before a patrol and then, less than an hour later, seen him going down with flames eating away at the cockpit. If you were flying close enough every little detail was clear and painful. For a moment you might even see him feebly beating his arms about, trying to push back the encroaching raggedness of the fire. The fire always won.

If he were to command No. 85 Squadron, it could mean only one thing, an intensification of the horror... unless he managed to control his feelings and become what he had been and was no longer. What he must find, what he most needed, was a public face, a public self. In private he might wrestle with fear, but if he had to lead and command he would summon up strength.

Perhaps he learned something from McCudden, who arrived at the RFC Club a little later. Here was a man who had a great permanency about him which never failed to attract Edward. They shared many talks and thoughts. McCudden sensed without being told that Edward was having a hard time holding on to his senses. Not that he was the only one.

When Edward, by now thoroughly depressed, went off to Wellingborough to stay with Mr and Mrs. Eyles, they quickly noticed that he was far from being his usual self. Some days prior he had written to them: '...Just heard that I've been promoted (major) and am taking command of Bishop's squadron in France. I'm not sure that I'm glad of the transfer, as I don't like the idea of leaving the old squadron, but it can't be helped now...'

This letter was so alien to an Edward who accepted challenges; it was full of apathy and resignation, and soon after his arrival the Eyleses noted that he was looking very much older, his face lined with worry. It was the war, they agreed, but this was only half the story. Edward was suffering deeply. In the next few days they remembered many other things, laughing over the time when he made an unauthorized landing on the playing field of a local school, creating a wave of enthusiasm for aviation among the boys...

The same man – or was it? – sat talking to them in a low voice, discussing what he knew must come. Sometimes gripped by gloomy foreboding, his eyes filled with tears while saliva poured from his mouth.

They did their best to cheer him up, but it was no good because he grew more and more morose until by the time he said goodbye – a final goodbye, he thought – it was obvious to Jim Eyles that he was in no condition to return to duty. But Eyles could do nothing about it, he was completely powerless as he stood and watched Edward walking slowly away to catch his train and the leave boat on July 3rd. Feeling very troubled and apprehensive, he went back into the house – to wait.

During the long hours of that journey Edward struggled to achieve a metamorphosis, building up his public self and at the same time realizing how greatly he must have shocked the Eyleses. The man who had discussed his own death with them must not be allowed to reach France. What an effect it might have on others! During the long miles through the night, he turned once more to his basic beliefs. He wanted to find a younger, better Edward.

It was almost unfortunate that he had to visit No. 74 Squadron at Clarmarais north aerodrome before going on to take up his command. Once in the familiar environment, among the faces he knew so well, he insisted on prolonging the agony by staying there overnight, and this proved too much for him. He broke down and wept. News of a second bar to his DSO meant nothing compared with the core of living sorrow and resignation which had by now hardened in his brain. Glory, new chances, even the challenge of taking command of Billy Bishop's squadron, none of these factors seemed to have much effect on him.

Next day he had a last breakfast with his old squadron and was then driven over to St Omer, where No. 85 Squadron was stationed. *En route* he did manage by a miracle to pull himself together, and find something of that long-sought-after new confidence.

By the time the tender halted at St Omer he was ready for anything.

The pilots of No. 85 Squadron had been used to their commanding officer playing a lone hand. A brilliant airman who shot down seventy-two Germans, Bishop seldom led a squadron patrol because he was at his best alone. Edward made up his mind to change all that. He knew how badly the pilots here needed morale and leadership. 'Grid' Caldwell later said, 'He brightened up 85 considerably.'

Before the first patrol he gathered them all together. What he was about to say would probably shake them up.

'When you go out tomorrow I shall take three with me to act as decoy. The rest of the flights will follow in two layers above. I shall give the signal to attack – but they must *not* attack before I give that signal.' He looked round in search of 'Nigger' Horn. 'You, with McGregor and Callaghan and Inglis, will form the top layer. You, Randall, will have the remaining three with you in the middle...'

Mannock the strategist was a new one on them. It would be interesting to see the results.

As it happened the plan worked out. The enemy, represented by ten Fokkers, divided and five of them thundered down the bleak blue corridor of the sky to stage a murderous assault on Edward and his three companions while the other five Fokkers stood back to await Randall, who, having seen Edward's Very signal, went in to attack the first five Germans. Just as the other five aircraft were going to ambush Randall, 'Nigger' Horn's flight screamed in, all guns firing.

When he introduced the idea of concentrating a whole flight, or even a squadron, on one target it failed because some pilots opened fire too early for fear of colliding.

That day four Fokkers were destroyed, and Edward lost none of his men or machines. It was due only to clever planning. It also set the pattern for the future.

Lieutenant C B R MacDonald, a Canadian pilot with the squadron, noted his commander's methods to draw out the enemy: 'Mick would select one of the young pilots to fly with him in order to give him instruction, and together they would hunt about the sky at about fifteen thousand feet, while the rest of the squadron would be about three-quarters of a mile away flying at a high altitude, awaiting their leader's signal, a red Very light, that he was about to attack. Then the war would commence in earnest, and Huns would be seen tumbling in flames or diving helter-skelter for the ground.'

Because of his new rank Edward's life changed as he now took overall responsibility for the squadron as a whole. He also had much more time on his hands and went over to Bruay to see Odette, the girl at the estaminet. He took tea with Sister Flanagan at the Duchess of Westminster's hospital. He even allowed his batman to spruce up his uniform and sew a clean set of medal ribbons on his tunic!

Where the Mess had been a second home to him, he was not now found there quite as frequently. It seemed that most of his jokes and pranks were behind him, although he still found time to have a drink and talk to the younger pilots who needed guidance.

He worked hard to conceal how he really felt from the founder members of the squadron, many of whom had specifically asked for him as their commanding officer when news of Bishop's posting came through, and they soon noticed that he was getting very tired through living most of the time on his nerves, although his judgement of character was still as sharp as ever. This was graphically illustrated when he decided to adopt Caldwell's methods and post a number of pilots who did not seem to be shaping up very well. They were packed off at short notice to other duties in reconnaissance and bombing.

Patrols continued. Successes mounted. Several more enemy planes were shot down, still without loss.

'To fight is not enough,' he drummed into his pilots. 'You must *kill*!'

On July 10th Edward was once more attacked by the sadness which came with bad news. McCudden, his old friend, was dead, killed while taking off to assume command of No. 60 Squadron. His plane stalled and crashed during a climbing turn, the flying gambit which had become his trademark. He had forgotten that he was carrying a heavier load than usual.

A few days later Edward phoned Ira Jones, now in command of 'A' Flight at No. 74 Squadron, to announce that he had just shot down another Hun in flames. They must avenge McCudden, no matter what the odds.

Next day he phoned again to say that he had scored two more victories. In a bantering voice he told Jones that he must be losing his clever Welsh touch, because he had not shot down one since McCudden went west. He would have to pull his socks up!

Four days later, on July 14th, it was Jones's turn in the telephone duel. He had shot down two.

Laughing, Edward said: 'Come over and have lunch and tea with me tomorrow, and you can explain your methods.'

Jones gruffly retaliated to the friendly sarcasm: 'Silly ass!'

'A couple of days ago I shot a Tripe's tail off over Lille. I've caught up with Bishop's score now – seventy-two,' Edward said.

'They'll have the red carpet out for you when you get back to England after the war!'

There was a short silence, then Edward answered slowly: 'There won't be any 'after the war' for me.' He had said the same thing to others, including Cushing, the recording officer. Did he *really* know? Was he being 'fey' and typically Irish?

An exasperated Jones ordered, 'Now just stop that!'

There was no reply.

Next day Jones and Clements, the Canadian, arrived at No. 85 Squadron in good time for lunch, and it did not take either of them long to notice that Edward was in a very curious sort of mood. One moment he larked about in the highest spirits, the next he seemed utterly depressed. Jones was inclined to put it all down to nervous strain, but in his heart of hearts knew it was more serious than that. Edward looked fated. He had a certain fixed expression on his face most of the time, and to Jones it boded nothing but uneasiness for the future.

After lunch Edward sat with them outside the Mess in the brilliant sunshine, and soon they were joined by Lieutenant Donald Inglis, the young New Zealander who had been with the squadron about two months. Edward was deep in conversation with him while Jones and Clements looked through a snapshot album.

Towards tea-time a car arrived with Sister Flanagan and another pretty VAD nurse. As soon as he saw the vehicle bumping along the track, Edward dashed into his quarters to get his tunic. He could hardly welcome them in his shirt sleeves! Jones, who knew how fond he was of Sister Flanagan, grinned to himself but did not say anything. Strange what a woman could do to a man!

It developed into a gay party, marred by one incident destined to hold a strong memory for Ira Jones. He happened to mention that he had brought down a two-seater that same morning. Ordinarily there would have been congratulations from Edward, but this time he wryly asked: 'Did you hear the blighter screaming at you?' As Jones looked at him searchingly, he added lightly: 'One day they'll get *you* like that if you don't watch yourself. You're getting careless, my lad! Anyway, when it comes, don't forget to blow your brains out – you won't notice the difference, Taffy.'

Their laughter at his sally stopped as he described what he thought it would be like to go down in flames. Nobody enjoyed his grisly recital. Only Jones knew that he always carried the loaded pistol in his plane during operations.

Sister Flanagan, who had been very silent, suddenly turned to him. 'You're very casual about this dangerous game of yours, Mick. Aren't you ever afraid?'

Sounding jocular, but with a depth of meaning, he nodded.

'We've got a *job* to do, my dear, and the cooler you are the more successful you'll be. And as to being frightened – I'm just like any other pilot, I'm scared stiff when I see my Hun floating down in flames. Ugh!' He raised his hands as though to shut out the picture, grimacing and shouting in what he wanted them to believe was mock horror. But it was real.

Then, in a moment, his mood changed and he revealed the source of his strength. 'God will thank us in His own way for fighting – and if necessary dying – for Christianity and freedom.' With a small laugh, he quickly apologized. 'I'm getting morbid.'

Sister Flanagan was watching him steadily across the table, noticing that the slight breeze disturbed his hair and how his eyes were, by turn, like a furnace and then resembled the surface of a pool on a summer day.

He turned to the silent Inglis. 'Have you got a Hun yet, Kiwi?'

'No, sir,' the New Zealander had to admit.

Edward rose to his feet at once. 'Well, come on out and we'll get you one.' Turning to his guests, he asked: 'Will you excuse us for a few minutes?'

CHAPTER FOURTEEN

It was a strange prelude to an operation against the German Air Force.

The two nurses, attractive in their walking-out uniforms, strolled casually towards the silent hangars with Ira Jones and Clements, while up in front Edward moved impatiently with Inglis. They were two entirely different men, the one apparently sure of himself in his maturity and the other still very much a learner, not quite knowing how to say thank you for the chance of bagging his first German.

All of them were at that moment living in a sun-warmed world where war was totally out of place. It was only the bursting roar as Edward tested his engine that shattered the idyll.

But when Edward gave the signal to taxi out to the take-off point, Inglis groaned aloud with disappointment. His elevator mechanism was jammed. He could not move it an inch.

Without waiting, Edward took off, circled the aerodrome to see whether Inglis was airborne or not then set off, flying fast on an open throttle towards the east. This was the first time since joining the squadron that he had gone off alone.

Inglis refused to return to the Mess with the others and, cursing his bad luck, said that he would wait until Edward returned. They left him to it, a lonely figure pacing up and down in front of the hangar, waiting for the chance to apologize for his plane's failure.

Time dragged by. It was two hours before Edward's SE came winging back and landed. Before Inglis could stammer out an explanation, he was out of the cockpit, angry and frustrated. 'I tried my damnedest to get my seventy-third, but there wasn't a Hun in sight!' As he pulled off his helmet he noticed Inglis's contrite expression. 'What was the trouble?' On being told he inspected the elevator wheel and called the mechanic over for a severe reprimand. There was no excuse for this sort of thing, he expostulated. A plane should *always* be ready for take-off.

Softening, he turned to Inglis. 'Never mind, Kiwi, I'll show you how it's done in the morning. Now, see to your machine *and your guns* so that we can be off the ground just before dawn.'

'Thank you, sir.' Feeling rather more comforted, Inglis went off to find his usual mechanic, a tingling excitement stirring in his veins when he realized that he would be flying at dawn.

Going to the Mess, Edward picked up Ira Jones and together they walked towards his hut.

'How are you feeling, Mick – really?' Jones asked anxiously.

Edward smiled a little wearily. 'I don't feel I shall last much longer.' He put both hands on his friend's shoulders, and in a voice charged with emotion, admitted: 'Taffy, old lad, if I'm killed I shall be in good company.'

They walked on, Jones searching for an adequate reply, but knowing that what Edward had said was quite unanswerable, a plain statement of fact against which no man could argue.

'You watch yourself, Taffy. Don't go following any Huns too low or you'll join the sizzle-brigade with me.'

It was too much for the more earthy and matter-of-fact ones. 'Now you're getting morbid, Mick!'

'No, not morbid, just a premonition.' Edward's eye narrowed. 'Don't forget, Taffy, when you see that tiny spark come out of my SE, it will kindle a torch to guide the future air defenders of the Empire along the path of duty.'

Then he burst into 'Rule Britannia' and linked arms with Ira Jones as they swung back towards the Mess for dinner.

Later he took Jones's arm and drew him towards his quarters. There was, Jones sensed, something else he wanted to discuss. As soon as the door was shut, he came straight out with it. 'Taffy, this is a secret between us.' He looked at the Welshman as though weighing him up. 'I'm thinking of marrying one of those nurses. What do you think?'

Jones was immediately enthusiastic, with all the Welshman's warmth for anything savouring of romance. 'The 'Irish Colleen', I suppose?'

'You should marry an Irish girl, too.' he advised patriotically, squeezing his friend's arm.

It was by now almost time to collect Clements from the Mess and make tracks for home. As Jones reached the door, he turned, 'The best of luck, Mick! Beware of those flamerinoes!'

As he looked more closely he detected a most curious, almost faraway look in Edward's eyes. They shook hands in silence. There was nothing more to be said.

At five o'clock next morning, July 26th, Edward entered the cold emptiness of the Mess, groped his way to the nearest candle and put a match to the wick, then turned to look round, as though taking some kind of mental inventory... The furniture... Pictures... The table with its scattered illustrated magazines and the photographs of Society which he had scorned so often... but he had stopped scoffing lately.

He looked for a long time at everything, then walked slowly to the Decca gramophone and its pile of well-played records, his face becoming grim and drawn. Searching through them, he began to smile when he found the one he wanted. After winding up the machine, he gently lowered the needle and sat, quite motionless, listening to the 'Londonderry Air'.

The door opened very quietly and Inglis, clad in flying clothes, slipped in. Sensing that his commanding officer was lost in the music, he stayed where he was until it ended.

He stepped forward. 'I'm not late, sir?'

Edward glanced up from his thoughts. 'No, that's all right. I saw you leave your hut.' He turned off the gramophone, put the record back and turned cheerfully.

'I hope we'll be able to find an early – flying two-seater coming over.' He blew out the candle and led the way, explaining what he had in mind.

'Now follow me closely and you'll get into a good position before we attack. Then, when you get him into your sights, take careful aim and get as close as you can before you fire.' He was like a man planning a pheasant shoot.

As they tramped across the dewy field on their way to the hangar, a pre-dawn chorus of birds led by a sonorous blackbird sweetened the blank silence of the night. Hearing it, Edward stopped and, taking Inglis's arm, said brightly, 'Do you hear that blackbird? He's like me, full of the joy of life. He's wishing us luck!' He looked first at his watch and then at the first insinuation of pale light in the sky. 'Nearly ten past five. Just the right time.'

There was no cloud. It was perfect.

The two SEs were being pushed out by the mechanics. Seeing their CO and his companion, they said a cheery good morning.

Standing near the machines, he delivered his last instructions in a low voice. 'Now don't forget, keep close on my tail and follow my movements. If you're too far behind, I'll waggle my wings.'

Inglis climbed into his SE and waited, noticing what seemed to him to be an unusual little ceremony. Edward was doing something he had never done before, going from one mechanic to another, shaking hands as they wished him the best of luck.

'Hope you get your seventy-third, sir,' said one.

The choir of birds was hushed by the more throaty roar of aero engines.

Edward glanced across to check Inglis's readiness, then briskly signalled 'away chocks' to the mechanics, enabling his SE to move out to the take-off point, Inglis following. Edward's right hand flashed up, then down, and they were away. After one circuit of the aerodrome they flew eastward at between thirty and fifty feet, starting gradually upwards into the spread of the sky – during which Edward waved to the mechanics – something else he had never done before.

They were soon across the trenches. Edward did not fly straight for more than a few seconds at a time. His SE was up first on one wingtip, then on the other, as he searched the lightening area for the enemy.

Inglis had a double task, to keep his leader in view and also maintain the usual surveillance. Every now and then he saw Edward's wings waggling sharply, urging him to catch up and maintain speed.

The two machines had been flying east when suddenly Edward turned right-handed for home, climbing full out. Inglis realized that he must have sighted an enemy, although he could not see anything. Edward levelled off, made a quick turn and went into a dive, guns firing. As he pulled up, Inglis, coming in below him, found the LVG right in his gunsights. *What a chance!*

The quarry had been well-prepared. It showed the Mannock touch with the observer obviously dead and the machine wobbling slightly as though the pilot was injured.

A sitting duck, but still lethal.

Closing in with all speed, Inglis put a quick burst through the LVG's tank and, as he was by this time moving so fast, he had to lift his SE's nose to avoid crashing into the German's tail.

It was a complete triumph.

And then Edward did something against which he had continually warned his pilots. He chose to follow the vanquished plane down. Inglis naturally tagged along, excited by such sudden success.

Diving after the smoking, falling wreckage, the SEs waited until it went into the ground, belching out a plume of flame, levelled out at 200-feet to make two circuits, after which Edward signalled for home. He flew ahead again, kicking his rudder from side to side to put off the considerable ground fire which had developed. The Germans wanted their revenge and the SEs were ripe targets.

Still elated over his first victory, Inglis was sure they would be safe in a few minutes at the speed they were moving.

Suddenly Edward's rudder stopped moving and his plane went into a slow, right -hand turn, a small flame spurting out of the right-hand side of the fuselage and the left wing dropping until, without any warning, the SE ploughed straight into the earth. The wreck was at once enveloped in flames.

Unable to believe it, because it had all happened so suddenly, Inglis went into rapid circles at about fifty feet, staring anxiously over the edge of his cockpit, waiting for the man who must come running out of that inferno.

For several minutes he disregarded the stream of tracer bullets hissing through the air and barely missing him. When they got the range a thick concentration, almost a fusillade, started tearing the plane to shreds. If he stayed another few seconds they would slaughter him.

Just as he was trying to gain height he heard a loud bang and a spray of petrol blew back, soaking him. He still went on helplessly jiggling the controls until the engine finally stopped, its fuel tank holed, and faced the job of attempting a landing on the allied side of the lines.

His heart thumping, he switched off the ignition to guard against fire and concentrated on trying to make some sort of a landing.

His SE came down just beyond the British standpoint, and it was the signal for infantrymen to pour out and help him to the safety of their trench. Only when he was down there did the real reaction set in. Crouching in the dirt, he clapped his open hands to his face, weeping and shuddering in a paroxysm of mental pain.

'Poor old Mick. The bloody bastards have shot my Major down in flames ...'

While he was breaking his heart, some miles away many of the pilots of No. 85 Squadron were standing round in small groups near the Mess, some still wearing their pyjamas with flying jackets round their shoulders against the morning wind. Their uneasiness was like a collective ache, the only panacea for which would be the sight of the two SEs returning in time for breakfast.

The sky was empty. It remained empty.

One man glanced at his watch. It was 7.35am. 'He's been gone over two hours now.'

Callaghan tried to shrug it off, but he did not sound too sure of himself as he said: 'Oh, I guess he's okay. Mick's probably landed at No. 74 Squadron for breakfast. I'll bet he's celebrating his seventy-third.'

Nobody really accepted the idea, yet none of them felt like arguing. It was obvious that he would have flown straight back with Inglis.

Somebody suggested that they go back to the huts and get dressed. It was nearly breakfast-time.

At about eight o'clock they were sitting at the tables, going through the motions of eating, many mechanically chewing the same mouthful over and over again. There was generally a fair amount of chatter at this time of day but now everybody was silent.

Somebody put the gramophone on. Violet Lorraine started singing 'College Days' in that light, gay voice of hers, but nobody could enjoy it.

The telephone bell shrilled. 'Nigger' Horn sprang across, dragging the receiver off its rest. At the same time Violet Lorraine was silenced.

'Hullo –'Nigger' Horn speaking... Yes, this is No. 85 Squadron.'

'This is the Archie battery near Hazebrouche,' a voice crackled. 'Has Major Mannock returned yet?'

'No! Why?'

'Well, a couple of SEs, one with a red streamer on its tail and flown just like Mannock usually flies, attacked a Hun at about 5.30am, and shot it down in flames. We haven't seen them return, so it looks as if they may have got shot down themselves. We're quite sure it was Mannock because we know his tactics in the air.'

All Horn could say was: 'I see. Thanks.'

He put the receiver back, summoning up the will to turn round and meet the cluster of faces. There was no need to use words. The very atmosphere told them all they needed to know.

'It's – it's quite all right. There isn't a Hun pilot living who could shoot Mick down...' The man who stammered out the words was trying to sound optimistic. It fell flat. Only a few agreed with him, the rest did not want to commit themselves.

The silence moved in.

At 8.30 the telephone rang again. This time it was Lieutenant W E W Cushing, the Recording Officer, calling from the nearby commanding officer's office. 'Nigger' Horn took the call.

'Cushing here,' said the voice. From that moment Horn knew what must be inevitable.

'The following message has just come through from the Twenty-fourth Welch Regiment... 'Major Mannock down by machine-gun fire from ground between Calonne and Lestreme. Lieutenant Inglis shot through petrol tank landed on front line at St Floris. Machine OK. Pilot OK. Machine likely to be shelled, salvage tonight if possible. More later...'

Mannock gone.

'Grid' Caldwell and Ira Jones immediately flew over the Calonne – Lestreme area on receiving a phone call from No. 85 Squadron.

'It was really rather hopeless and useless; we couldn't see anything resembling a burnt out aeroplane and we couldn't hang about long as the firing was intense,' said Caldwell.

Only one man knew for sure that Edward was dead, and ironically he was many hundreds of miles away from the scene. Jim Eyles was sitting in his Wellingborough home, close to a bookcase at the precise time when Inglis anxiously circled the blazing wreckage. It was early morning and for some unknown reason Eyles felt restless. Sitting in a chair, thinking about the war, he was suddenly startled by a volume falling out of the bookcase and landing on the floor with a heavy thud. As he bent to pick it up, he knew with a depressing finality that Edward, his 'son', had just been killed. He was not a psychic man, he was a materialist, yet the omen taken in conjunction with the uncalled thought could not be ignored. Later, when he inquired what time Edward's plane crashed, he knew for certain that the falling book must have signified death.

But in France there was still uncertainty.

The news, worse than any huge strategic setback, reached the hangars shortly after the pilots quietly filed out of the Mess and went back to their quarters, and many of those who had flown with Mannock wept in private. Mechanics and riggers to whom he had been such a familiar figure went about their work, looking dazed, some with tears streaming down their faces.

When Inglis returned to give his report direct to Cushing, at the squadron office, Wing HQ was informed.

The report itself left very little room for hope, it was a confirmation of the worst:

COMBATS IN THE AIR

Squadron No. 85
Dated 26th July 1918
Type and No. of Aeroplane: SE5aE 1294
Time: 5.30 am.
Armament: 1 Vickers, 1 Lewis
Locality: Lestreme – Calonne
Pilot: Lieut. D C Inglis
Duty: Special mission
Remarks on hostile aircraft – Type, armament, speed etc.:
Two-seater: Type unknown.

While following Major Mannock in search of two-seater EAs, we observed an EA coming towards the lines and turned away to gain height, diving to get east of EA which saw us just too soon and turned east; Major Mannock turned and got in a good burst when he pulled away. I got in a good burst at very close range, after which EA went into a slow left-hand spiral with flames coming out of his right side. I watched him go straight into the ground and go up in a large cloud of black smoke and flame.

I then turned and followed Major Mannock back at about 200-feet. About half-way back I saw a flame come out of the right-hand side of his machine, after which he apparently went down out of control. I went into a spiral down to 50-feet and saw machine go straight into ground and burn. I saw no one leave the machine and then started for the line, climbing slightly; at about 150-feet there was a bang, and I was smothered with petrol; my machine cut out so I switched off and made a landing 5 yards behind our front line.

(Sd.) Donald C Inglis, Lieut
(Sd.) A C Randall, Captain.

Forty years later Cushing said, 'I can never forget the grief and consternation on every face.'

At first it seemed absolutely impossible to hold the usual 'party' that same evening. The curiously irreverent custom had grown into a *de rigeur* part of life because it helped men to forget the worst, and there had been times when Edward himself had to be forced into joining the 'celebration'.

Only when representatives from No. 74 Squadron, including Caldwell, Ira Jones, Young and Roxburgh-Smith, poured in along with others from nearby aerodromes did they realize the need to go on... and on...

Breaking through what was only a forced cheerfulness, Caldwell insisted on making a short speech. 'Mick would never wish us to mope,' he urged. 'We never do in Seventy-four so come on! Let's liven up. Put the bloody gramophone on.'

So far news of the death of 'Mick' Mannock had been contained within the newly-formed Royal Air Force, but sooner or later others would have to be informed. As the tidings spread many hundreds of men expressed genuine sorrow. A few officers travelled over to Bruay to the estaminet, where Odette met them with joy on her face. They could not keep up their false pleasure for long, and she was swift to understand that something was wrong.

'*Ou est mon brave aviateur?*'

'*Il est – il est mort.*'

Horror grew in her eyes, spreading across her pretty face, and as the tears started she cried out in agony: '*Mais non! Ce n'est pas possible...*'

And Sister Flanagan was told, too.

Padre Keymer wrote to 'Paddy' Mannock, Edward's brother:

> I feel I must write and tell you how grieved I am to hear of your brother's death.
>
> There are few men out here whom I have known better and was more fond of than Edward, or 'Mick' as we called him.
>
> I was padre with 40 Squadron when he joined it last year and have known him intimately during the whole of his wonderful career in France. We were very close friends and I shall miss him more than words can say.
>
> I knew him not only for the most dashing, brave and clever pilot that the RFC has ever produced, but also for 'one of the very best', and that is saying a good deal where the RFC is concerned.
>
> Only a week ago last night I sat next to him at dinner at 40 Squadron and we talked of the old days of '40' and of the future. And now he has gone, and I can scarcely believe it possible.
>
> He was always so keenly interested in my work and used to attend my services very regularly. How we shall miss his kindly way and irrepressible humour, but I trust we shall meet him again, and at least he has gone into wonderfully good company.
>
> With most sincere sympathy,
> Bernard W Keymer, CF

Cushing's letter to 'Paddy' Mannock recounted what had happened according to Inglis's report, and added:

> Please accept the deepest sympathy from a whole Squadron mourning a brave man and the best of comrades. There was no man or officer in the Squadron but loved him for his bravery, for his cheerfulness, for his skill, for his patience in teaching others, and for his personality, which made him at once the most efficient and the most popular Commanding Officer in France.
>
> He was a friend to us all and had a great affection for the personnel of the Squadron, which had he lived he would have made the most famous flying Squadron in the world, for he was endowed with the spirit of leadership, and any of his Pilots would cheerfully follow him, no matter where he led.
>
> I speak as if there was no spark of hope that he is alive; that is hardly true, but I am sorry to say the chance is one in a thousand. I will, however, inform you immediately we have any further news.
>
> Again let me assure you of the real sympathy of all the officers and men of this Squadron, and of other Squadrons with whom he came in contact, for he was beloved by all.
>
> Yours faithfully,
> W E W Cushing, Lieut.

A few days later Lieutenant Callaghan of No. 85 Squadron sat down to inscribe in his personal diary: 'Mannock is dead. The greatest pilot of the war. And his death was worthy of him...'

After a time he laid down his pen and blew his nose, remembering with terrible clarity the party the day the news came through when they had all linked arms and sung at the: tops of their voices 'Auld Lang Syne'.

CHAPTER FIFTEEN

Edward – 'Mick' – Mannock, the fey Irishman, was undefeated right up to the end. He was not shot down from the air by a German pilot, but almost accidentally snared by ground fire. Had he been flying slightly higher he might have seen the end of the First World War. But, as he had prophesied to Ira Jones and others, there would never be any 'after the war' for him. His assumption that he would die in a burning plane was correct.

Lieutenant Callaghan's words, which claimed that Mannock was 'the greatest pilot of the war' can, in the light of history, be carried over to embrace the 1939–1945 conflict. Not only did he introduce the special tactics of aggressive formation flying which was a considerable factor in the Battle of Britain, but also made the highest score of two wars. No other pilot of any nationality ever reached even the nominal number of victories officially placed against his name. Even 'Sailor' Malan, the top-scoring fighter-pilot of the Second World War, brought down only twenty-nine.

Mannock passed through many evolutionary phases until he reached the stage where he was able to command a squadron in the most desperate and hazardous kind of warfare ever devised. He was always circumspect and acted in a responsible manner. For ninety victories the men under his leadership suffered only two casualties, a record unequalled by any other commanding officer since that time. It is impossible to believe that his own death was due to careless flying.

Ever since 1918, when the qualities of the first men to use the air as a battlefield became due for assessment, the name of Manfred von Richthofen has been granted pride of place, and his victories appear to have set the precedent, yet even the most superficial examination of his official claims, when compared with what is known to have happened in the relevant sectors, discloses discrepancies. The myth of the superman, which grew in Richthofen's own native soil, has attracted many air historians to the idea that he was *the* premier combat pilot of the First World War. This is not true. Richthofen's claims were filed and accepted in many cases regardless of whether the conquered were totally destroyed or merely damaged.

Mannock, on the other hand, erred on the side of caution. In his early days he frequently refrained from making a claim unless it could be thoroughly verified and confirmed, either by those flying with him at the time or by ground troops in the area. During the latter part of his career, when he adopted the habit of teaching younger pilots the technique of aerial warfare and 'blooding' them by carrying out most of the preliminary attack, he sometimes found it necessary personally to administer the *coup de grâce*. But he would always insist through friendly bullying or by tacit agreement that the victory be placed against the younger man's credit. In this way it would be eminently feasible to bring his score up from seventy-three to something like one hundred.

Some conception of the tempo of his operational life may be gained by studying the following excerpt from 'Grid' Caldwell's diary of sixty-seven days in Mannock's flying life.

1918

12 April	Destroyed enemy scout. With Flight was mainly responsible for shooting down three more. Captain Young and I each got one, making five on our first day in action.
21 April	Helped Dolan in good scrap – very hot stuff triplanes, but no decision.
22 April	Got scout out of control.
23 April	Crashed enemy scout.
12–23 April	Late getting off the ground with his flight.
29 April	Shot observer in two-seater but Hun got away.
30 April	Led Glynn and Dolan against nine Huns and crashed one – excellent show.
3 May	Led patrol from 14,000-feet to 2,000-feet one mile east of Merville and crashed Hun two-seater (I saw this and it was very neat work).
6 May	With Dolan had running fight with triplanes and crashed one.
11 May	Got scout in flames in fight with Dolan versus eight enemy aircraft.
12 May	With his flight attacked larger formation from the sun. Mannock got three of them (two in pieces and one crashed). Excellent show again.
13 May	Several indecisive scraps and some gun trouble through double feeds.
14 May	With Roxburgh-Smith and Clements shot down a two-seater.
15 May	Got scout in flames.
17 May	Attacked four Pfalz alone and crashed one. Stout show. Recommended for DSO a few days ago.
18 May	Got two two-seaters, one in flames.
19 May	Awarded DSO
20 May	Shot up petrol tank of a two-seater but could not confirm crash.
21 May	Got two-seater and later in day got three scouts in big scrap. Four in one day – a great effort. Needs a rest, but won't take it yet.
26 May	Scout crashed. Recommended for bar to DSO
29 May	One scout out of control and one crashed.
30 May	Very fed up with gun trouble with easy Huns about.
31 May	Pfalz out of control.

1 June	Awarded bar to DSO Got Hun in flames and one in pieces – damn good show.
2 June	Got one of four scouts out of control.
7 June	Shared two-seater with Young.
16 June	Crashed Pfalz scout.
17 June	Got two-seater.

Caldwell's diary notes on Mannock's thirty-four victories in sixty-seven days end with: 'Took over 85 (Squadron) and killed a month later, shot down from the ground after getting sixty-eight Huns.'

On November 11th, 1918 – Armistice Day – after dinner in the Officers' Mess at No. 74 Squadron, the toasts were being drunk when Ira Jones, now promoted to captain, rose to his feet, glass in hand.

'Gentlemen, I propose we now drink a toast to all those friends, members of the squadron, who are no longer with us to celebrate this great occasion – and especially to the greatest air fighter of all – gentlemen, Mick Mannock, the king of air fighters!'

Eight months later, in July 1919, the RFC Club in London was crowded with pilots and observers, many of them in civilian clothes, having been demobilized into a bewildering peace, others still wearing uniform, but all enjoying a sense of being together for what might be the last time, apart from the many promised reunions.

Ira Jones was pushing through, when somebody asked, 'Have you seen the announcement in the '*London Gazette*'?'

'No – what's that?' Jones steadied himself. He half-guessed what it might be.

'Dear old Mick Mannock's got it at last! Posthumous VC Here it is. And just listen to this – 'For bravery of the highest order' – then it gives a list of victories and ends up, 'This highly distinguished officer, during the whole of his career in the Royal Air Force, was an outstanding example of fearless courage, remarkable skill, devotion to duty and self-sacrifice, which has never been surpassed.''

So the banding together of old comrades and the petition to ask that Mick Mannock should be so justly honoured had borne fruit at last, Jones reflected. He had been one of the leaders of the campaign and it was worth every minute of it. In Canterbury, others had urged the bestowal of the VC, including Dean Bell of the Cathedral, Mr Wright Hunt, the mayor, and Mr C A Gardner, the solicitor who had known him since his youth.

'Good old Mick!' he exclaimed at last. 'He should have got it long ago, and he might not have got it if we hadn't all signed that letter and brought it to the notice of the Air Minister.'

The name of the Air Minister was Winston Churchill.

A minor mystery still exists to this day concerning the disposal of Mannock's body after death. Although 'Grid' Caldwell and Ira Jones flew together over the Lestreme – alonne area less than an hour after Inglis's report was received, they failed to locate anything resembling a burnt-out aircraft. But that was only the beginning of it.

On July 24th, 1919, Mr and Mrs Jim Eyles received the following letter from the Secretary of State for Air:

'The information which we have has been received through the Central Prisoners of War Committee, who apparently obtained their information from German sources. Major Mannock, according to this report, died on July 26th, 1918. It is regretted that no information is available as regards his place of burial.'

However, if this temporarily satisfied the Eyleses, it did not suit others. Just under two years later a letter dated June 2nd, 1921, was sent to the Rev E Rogers, OBE, MA, of the Church Lads' Brigade by the Imperial War Graves Commission:

'I am directed to inform you that Major E Mannock, VC, DSO, MC, is reported to have been buried at a point 300-metres north-west of La Pierre-au-Beure in the vicinity of Pacaut, east of Lillers. I regret, however, to say that the officers of the Graves Registration Units have not yet been able to find the grave.'

Jim Eyles now pursued the subject. Edward had been like his own son, and he felt impelled to go on writing until the truth came to light. He finally received his reply from the Imperial War Graves Commission:

'With reference to previous correspondence, I am directed to inform you that the inquiries which were being made regarding the burial-place of Major Edward Mannock, VC, DSO, MC, have now been completed. I regret to say, however, that it has not been possible to identify his grave.

'As you are aware, Major Mannock was reported to have been buried at a spot 300-metres north-west of La Pierre-au-Beure on the road to Pacaut. Although all this neighbourhood has been searched, and the remains of all those soldiers buried in isolated and scattered graves reverently reburied in cemeteries in order that the graves might be permanently and suitably maintained, the grave of this officer has not been identified.

'A special search has been made for the grave, and the Representative of this Commission in France reports that the locality is now reconstructed and all the fields cultivated, and there is no surface evidence of graves anywhere in the vicinity. It is added that the remnants of an aeroplane were found, but unfortunately the condition of this aeroplane is so bad that no markings could be traced, all woodwork being burnt away and the metal rusted. The statements of local inhabitants differ as to whether this aeroplane is British or German.

'A further inquiry was sent to the Representative of this Commission in Berlin, to obtain more definite information as to the position of Major Mannock's grave. The reply, however, states that only the original report is available, and no sketch showing the position of the grave can be obtained; further that the report emanated from a German Intelligence Officer whose records were entirely lost during the retreat.

'The records of the exhumation work in this area have been carefully searched, but there is no trace of a report of the finding of any grave which can be thought likely to be Major Mannock's grave. There was the grave of an unknown British airman found in this neighbourhood and identified by wreckage of an aeroplane. The date of this unknown British airman's death, however, cannot be ascertained. Although this grave was found some distance from where Major Mannock was reported to have been buried, endeavours have been made to identify the grave as that of Major Mannock, but without success.

'As the records held by the Air Ministry contain no references as to the locality of the crashes in a large number of cases, it is not possible to compile a complete list of casualties for the area in the vicinity of La Pierre-au-Beure and Pacaut. It has not, therefore, been possible to identify this unknown British officer, and I fear that it is not possible to say that the grave is Major Mannock's.

'I need hardly say that any definite information which may be obtained will be communicated to you without delay, but I fear that there is now very little hope of this.

'It is the intention of the Commission to erect memorials to those officers and men whose graves cannot be found. You may rest assured that the dead who have found no known resting-place will be honoured equally with the others, and that each case will be dealt with upon full consideration of its merits as regards the site and the place of the memorial.'

That was the last the Eyleses ever heard of the matter.

But *somebody* went to the crashed plane when the flames died down, and they extracted from Mannock's body a number of personal papers and money, because soon afterwards a package arrived for his brother, 'Paddy' Mannock, in England. To him it was too saddening to examine at all closely, being charred round the edges as though the flames had attempted to devour all that remained of his younger brother. Shuddering and saying that it was 'gruesome', he destroyed it without ever attempting to discover who the sender might be.

Did the person who sent that package also bury what was left of Mannock? It is very likely – just as likely that he also did what he considered to be his humane duty but in the flurry of war omitted to notify the authorities or even mark the hastily-made grave.

As history has noted, when the time came for the investiture at Buckingham Palace of Britain's most honourable military decoration, the claimant was the father of the hero, who, many years before, deserted the family. He took it and then vanished again.

Each year a small and unpretentious service is held in Canterbury Cathedral in memory of Edward Mannock, called by McScotch 'the supreme fighter of all the air forces... that indomitable and lovable patriot...' Relatives and friends stand before a plaque placed there to his memory by those who knew him during his life.

As the years pass by the number of attenders grows less. Jim Eyles, who befriended the young Mannock and loaned him the money to go to Turkey in 1914, died suddenly in 1959. Ira Jones, who himself shot down forty Germans in the First World War, died in 1961 in Swansea, while 'Paddy' Mannock, Edward's only brother, entered an Edinburgh hospital at about the same time and died in August 1962.

Nora Mannock, one of Edward's sisters, is the last direct link, and she is living in London, although a number of his pre-1914 friends are still alive, including Mr C A Gardner, the Canterbury solicitor who administered his Service Will in which he left approximately £600 his brother for distribution to members of the family, excluding his father for whom the old hatred still remained.

But Mannock is not forgotten...

A wing of Canterbury Hospital is named after him and a block of dwellings, erected on the site of the cottage where he lived with his mother, brother and sisters, also bears his name.

His name also remains in perpetuity as an example to modern air-minded youth. When the Wellingborough Air Training Corps squadron was formed, Mr E Murray Witham, MA, now a master at Wellingborough School and, during World War I an officer-observer in France with No 107 Squadron and the first Commanding Officer of the ATC squadron, was instrumental in having it officially christened 'The Mannock Squadron'.

A small aluminium model of a Nieuport Scout, made by Mannock from part of a German plane which he had shot down, was given to the squadron as a competitive trophy by Jim Eyles. Unfortunately, it was never awarded. One week -end the ATC headquarters was broken into and the valuable relic stolen. The police never traced the culprit.

> *'Major Mannock was a very great airman and deserves worthy commemoration.'*
> Sir Thomas Pike, GCB, CBE, DFC,
> Marshal of the Royal Air Force and Head of the Air Council.

Index